Journey to the Heart

Daily Meditations
on the Path to Freeing Your Soul

Melody Beattie

HarperOne
An Imprint of HarperCollins*Publishers*

HarperOne

HarperCollins books may be purchased for educational, business, or sales promotional use. For information, please e-mail the Special Markets Department at SPsales@harpercollins.com.

HarperCollins Web site: http://www.harpercollins.com

HarperCollins®, ®, and HarperOne™ are trademarks of HarperCollins Publishers.

Library of Congress Cataloging-in-Publication Data

Beattie, Melody.
Journey to the heart : daily meditations on the path to freeing your soul / Melody Beattie.
p. cm.
Includes bibliographical references.
ISBN 978–0–06–251121–8
1. Spiritual life—Meditations. 2. Devotional calendars. I. Title.
BL624.B38 1996
291.4'3—dc20 95–42012

19 20 LSC(H) 70 69

This book is dedicated to life, the creative force in this universe, and the Creator. I wrote it for people on the path of discovering and trusting their soul. I hope that people interested in spiritual growth and those involved in creative endeavors, including artists, writers, and healers, will find it useful.

Acknowledgments

My heartfelt thanks to Nichole Marie and Shane Anthony for their continual love and support.

My thanks to Dr. Steve Sherwin.

I also want to acknowledge and thank Ann Poe. She was again more than an editor. For the third time in my writing career, she was a midwife.

The meditations and stories in this book were written on a journey across the western part of the United States. I don't know the names of many of the people who shared their stories with me. Some were strangers I talked to for just a short while. But I thank them for opening their hearts to me.

I also want to acknowledge the places I visited that inspired and breathed life into me and the book. The meditations were actually written in the places I visited. I did it so the energy of the magical, mysterious places I found could find its way into the pages of this book. Because of the influence of these places on the pages of this book, I wish to thank them too.

Here they are, listed in the order I visited them:

Desert Hot Springs, California
Sedona, Arizona
Petrified Forest National Park, Arizona

Chaco Canyon, New Mexico
Ojo Caliente, New Mexico
Chimayo, New Mexico
Pike's Peak, Colorado
Cottonwood, Colorado
Mesa Verde National Park, Colorado
Tempe, Arizona
Grand Canyon, Arizona
Bryce Canyon National Park, Utah
Lava Hot Springs, Idaho
Yellowstone National Park, Wyoming
Hot Springs, Montana
Olympic National Park, Washington
Hoh Rain Forest, Washington
Willamette National Forest, Oregon
Mount Shasta, California
Redwood National Park, California
Cleone, California
Kings Canyon National Park, California
Sequoia National Park, California
Colony Beach, California

Melody Beattie
July 17, 1995

Introduction

Meditations take us to a different place . . .

After weeks of wrestling with trying to write this book, I finally got the message. The idea, the vision, for how to write this book came suddenly, spontaneously, clearly, the way ideas come lately. I would drive to sacred, healing, spiritual places around the country, absorb the energy from these Meccas, and let it infuse me, and this book. I would begin this pilgrimage with no set plan, no itinerary—just a map, my intuition, some vague notions of where I was going, and faith that the universe would take care of the rest. That the journey would unfold.

The trip would test my beliefs, remind me of old lessons, and teach me some new ones. It would breathe life into this book. I would take the journey of a lifetime and transform it into the adventure of a year.

Two days later, I loaded some boxes into my Jeep, bought a portable computer, said my good-byes, and headed out for parts unknown, at least to me. As I traveled down the 10 East past the clamor of LA, wondering if I had brought enough supplies but fairly certain I had brought too many, a friend's prophetic words from years ago worked their way back into my consciousness. "You're not going to be *finding* your stories anymore, Melody," she had said. "You're going to be *living* them."

Soon, I became aware of another idea. In my sixteen years of professional writing, this is the eighth book I've worked or collaborated on and the second meditation book I've written. Yet it is a first. It is the *only* one that has not been based on, rooted in, *grounded in*, the concept of overcoming devastating pain. Instead, the book, like my journey, reflects a spirit of excitement, adventure, freedom, and joy. Yes, sometimes pain is still part of it, but suffering no longer plays the role it once did.

Meditations open the heart, free the soul. . .

That's what I've attempted to do in the pages of this book, in the pages of my life. This is not a travelogue, nor a book about recovery. It is a book about discovery. Use it as a map or guide for your soul's journey through the year. Read each day according to the date. Or meditate on your need, then read where you open the book. Or just open the book and read consecutively, obsessively, until you find what you need.

Meditations take us to places of power, healing, peace . . .

Come with me now, as we travel to the mystical, healing vortexes of Sedona, the ancient ruins of Chaco Canyon, the enchanted forests of the Pacific Northwest. Let the healing mineral waters of Desert Hot Springs wash away your aches and pains. Touch the sacred earth at the sanctuary in Chimayo. Breathe in the magic and the mystery of the universe around us, then return to your life renewed, refreshed.

Meditations take us to a different place . . .

Come with me now as we travel to places of peace, healing, and power; then know that you can find those places, each day, in yourself.

Begin your journey to the heart.

January

JANUARY 1

Honor the Beginning

Beginnings can be delicate or explosive. They can start almost invisibly or arrive with a big bang. Beginnings hold the promise of new lessons to be learned, new territory to be explored, and old lessons to be recalled, practiced, and appreciated. Beginnings hold ambiguity, promise, fear, and hope.

Don't let the lessons, the experiences of the past, dampen your enthusiasm for beginnings. Just because it's been hard doesn't mean it will always be that difficult. Don't let the heartbreaks of the past cause you to become cynical, close you off to life's magic and promise. Open yourself wide to all that the universe has to say.

Let yourself begin anew. Pack your bags. Choose carefully what you bring, because packing is an important ritual. Take along some humility and the lessons of the past. Toss in some curiosity and excitement about what you haven't yet learned. Say your good-byes to those you're leaving behind. Don't worry who you will meet or where you will go. The way has been prepared. The people you are to meet will be expecting you. A new journey has begun. Let it be magical. Let it unfold.

All parts of the journey are sacred and holy.
Take time now to honor the beginning.

JANUARY 2

Map Your Own Journey

Go on your own journey. Don't let others hold you back; don't hold them back. Don't judge their journey, and don't let them judge yours.

All persons are free to have the experiences their souls lead them to. Many of us started our journey by having the experiences others thought we should. Some of us tried to dictate the lessons and adventures of others, too. This caused pain and confusion for all. Learning those lessons, the lessons of setting each other free, became an important part of our journey. But now we're on to a new part.

Pack your bags. Get out your map. Don't worry about where you'll go and what you'll see. Go where your heart leads. Your soul knows the way. It will speak quietly through the voice of your heart, your wisdom, your intuition. Listen to the voice, the quiet voice within, that assures you you're safe. You will meet and learn from everyone you need to along the way. Don't limit your own experiences. Don't limit the experiences of those you love, or those you meet along the way.

Start today to follow your heart.
Map out your own journey. Have
the adventure of a lifetime.

JANUARY 3

Trust Your Heart

For so long, you relied on your head. Now it's time to make the shift—the great leap into your heart.

Are you beginning to see how your head gets in the way? How it creates so much noise? The chatter, the limited vision, the fear? Are you beginning to see how what you've relied on—your intellect, your assessments, and sometimes your logic—has complicated your life?

It isn't the head that sees clearly, nor does the head always see with love. Often, it sees with eyes of fear. The heart sees clearly. It balances the mind and emotions. It takes what's real and processes it into truth, then into action. It takes into account all that needs to be done, then draws a map, an itinerary, for how to accomplish that. *Yes,* you say, *but my head does that too. And then I don't need to feel . . .*

Your heart can do it better because it maps the way in love.

Learn to listen to your inner voice. Listen
to your heart. It's your connection to God,
to people, to the universe, and to yourself.

JANUARY 4

Go with What You Know

The commercial on the radio sang to me as I drove across the Southern California desert: "Don't just go with the flow. Go with what you know."

Sometimes answers come from outside us. The universe is abundant in its supply of guidance for us. It can't wait to share its signals, teachings, lessons, and words of wisdom. It is eager to give us guidance if we just watch, wait, and listen. Sometimes this guidance comes from people we know, other times from people we barely know. But even when this help comes from those we are closest to and love most, the answer must resonate with that place deep inside us. It must resonate with our core. It must ring true for us.

Listen to those around you. Listen to the guidance of the universe and all the voices it uses to speak to you. But always trust yourself. Trust your inner voice. Trust what you know, because ultimately your path will bring you back to that place. No matter what you do, if it's not right for you, you will need to return to your center, your place of peace, and figure out the action that is right.

It's good to go with the flow. But it's better to go with what you know—what you know to be true for you. Trusting yourself is the ultimate lesson. It's where all the guidance leads.

JANUARY 5

Let Life Reveal Itself to You

You don't have to strain so, trying to get your revelations. The guidance, the inspiration, the awareness you need will come to you.

The way we're living now—from the heart—is much easier than the way we lived before. Sometimes it is so natural we might not understand what's happening. We may even be uncomfortable at first with how easy it is. We find ourselves straining to lift a heavy bowling ball, when what we have to pick up is only a Ping-Pong ball. Then we wonder why it feels so light. We may question whether there's something wrong because it feels so different.

Just because your life feels lighter doesn't mean you're doing something wrong.

Your next step, the answer to the question you've been mulling about—the direction for the next stage of your growth, where you will live next, what you need to do next about work, money, or that problem you've been struggling with—will come. If you're fussing and straining, you may not hear it. Don't worry about getting all your answers or your agenda for the years ahead. That is not how this process works. In order to participate in this more magical way of life, trust that all you need to know will be revealed to you when it is time.

Relax. You're on a journey of discovery.
Let life reveal itself to you.

JANUARY 6

Embrace the Unknown

How boring it would be if we knew everything that was going to happen. Yet we are always trying to peek around the corner and see ahead.

If we knew everything that was going to happen, we wouldn't need to experience it. There would be nothing to learn, explore, or gain. We'd stay in our heads instead of our hearts. So often, it's the surprises of the moments and hours, the unexpected twists and turns that give meaning to our journey and make our lessons come alive.

You are connected to truth. You are connected to Divine guidance. You can trust and embrace your guidance from God. That means you will get all the visions, all the guidance, all the advance knowledge and wisdom you need. Not too much to spoil the surprise. Not too much to neutralize the lesson.

Just enough guidance to let you know you are never alone.

JANUARY 7

Remember to Be Happy

The sign hangs on the wall of a bagel shop: "Don't forget to be happy."

Sometimes we get so bogged down in dealing with feelings, issues, problems—the realities and details of our lives—we forget to be happy. Often happiness can be ours if we just *remember* to be happy.

Joy is a choice—a deliberate, conscious choice. That choice is available to us each day. Our joy isn't controlled by others or by outward circumstances. Joy comes from a deeper place, a place of security within ourselves. It's an attitude, not a transitory emotion.

Remember to be kind. Remember to be loving. Remember to feel all your feelings and to take care of yourself. But most of all, remember to be happy.

JANUARY 8

Love Yourself Until It's Real

What does it mean to love yourself? To do nice nurturing things for and to yourself? Yes, sometimes. But self-love runs deeper than that.

Self-love means loving and accepting yourself, your thoughts, beauty, emotions, your faults, imperfections, and flaws, your strengths, wit, wisdom, as well as your peculiar and unique way of seeing the world . . .

Loving yourself means accepting and loving each and every part of you, and knowing—*knowing*—that you're worthy, valuable, and lovable. It means loving and accepting yourself when you're surrounded by people who love you, and during those times when you think everyone's gone away, when you wonder if God's gone away, too.

During one of the darkest parts of my life, Al Franken, a comedian and producer, asked me to write an introduction to the book he was writing—Stewart Smalley's daily meditation book, *I'm Good Enough, I'm Smart Enough, and Doggone It, People Like Me.* I wasn't able to do much during that time in my life, except walk to my fax machine and tear off the curled-up pages. I'd take the pages back to my bed, lie down (because I felt too shattered to stand), and read them. I'd laugh a little at Stewart's outrageous behavior. But the pages made me smile about something else, too. Despite our search for sophisticated, sage advice and advanced learning, sometimes it helps to remember the simple wisdom of bumbling Stewart Smalley.

Sometimes, loving ourselves means accepting ourselves enough to tell ourselves other people like and approve of us. Sometimes, loving ourselves means approving of ourselves, even when they don't. It takes courage to stop cowering and openly love, accept, and approve of ourselves.

Don't just say the words.
Love yourself until you
experience that love.

JANUARY 9

You're Going Someplace New

You are opening up more and more. You are becoming clearer each day. Embrace the changes taking place. They are good. They will last. They will take you and your life to someplace new, someplace you can't fully imagine now because it's so different from where you have been.

All will be changed. Your love, your life, your friends, your work. Your quiet moments and your times of sharing. Your playtime, your rest time. Your attitude will change. Your ability to fully and joyfully experience your life will change.

Things that used to bother you, hold you down, hold you back will roll easily off you. Problems that used to plague and pester you, making you feel weighted down, will be lifted easily. You will know and trust that the answers you need will come to you.

Your powers will increase. You will find yourself doing, knowing, and feeling things that you thought only certain others could do. You will find yourself gliding through life in a way that brings you joy, and touches and heals others.

You will laugh a lot. And yes, you will cry a lot, too, because an open heart feels all it needs to feel. But you will not think twice about your emotions. You will feel them with the purity of a child and the wisdom of a sage. You will see, touch, taste, and feel life's magic in a way you never imagined. You will love, and you will be loved. And you will learn that it is all the same.

You are open now, more open than you've ever been. Trust the process and trust your heart. The journey is not in vain. Its purpose is to lead you to love.

JANUARY 10

Value Your Passion

For too long, we have wrongly judged our passion—our passion for living, our vitality and zest for places, people, things, and ideas. *I shouldn't have what I want. I shouldn't say what I like. I shouldn't get too excited.* What helps us come to life? What takes us out of the motions and into our emotions? What connects us to the energy of life, the energy of love, the energy of the life force that permeates us all?

All your growth, all your work, has not been to lead you away from your passions, to turn you into a robot. It has been to bring you back to life, to put you in touch with the vital energy of the universe, an energy that permeates all that is. An energy that permeates you.

Honor your passion by honoring your emotions. Feeling your emotions releases passion into life. Feel them. Feel them all. Then you will know what you like, what instills passion in you. Once you know and can recognize that, you'll know which direction to go.

Expressing passion and gratitude will guide your life. Say it again and again. Say it until you believe it. Say it until you live it.

JANUARY 11

Let Go of the Blocks

I wandered into the bookstore in a small Southern California town, browsed for a while, then began chatting with the clerk. "Times are different now," I said. "Changing fast. Turning into something so new, so different many of us can't imagine."

"Yes," she replied quietly and prophetically. "Things are going to be easier. Unless there's something you're still hanging on to."

Is there something you're still hanging on to? A remnant from the past that's blocking you from stepping into the future? From stepping into today?

Look into your heart. The answer is there. Perhaps it's a behavior, a person, a belief. Is there an issue from the past that's blocking your ability to love yourself, to connect with God, life, others? Ask yourself if there's something you're hanging on to that has outworn its purpose. Old chains can tie us to the past, to past pain, to a path we've already trodden, a place we've already been.

Now is the time to let go. Gently, quietly, let go. Allow yourself a few looks back and as many tears as needed. Where you've been has been important. It has helped shape who you are. But have faith that where you're going is important and wonderful, too.

Gently let go. Be free to step
into your future of joy.

JANUARY 12

Let the Universe Help You

Let the universe help you. You are not in this world alone. You never have been, although your belief may have created that illusion.

Tell the universe what you want. Tell a friend. Tell God, too. Tell yourself. Write it down on a list. Be clear and forthright about what you need and want. Talk as if you were talking to a friend. That is not control. That is learning to own your creative power—your power to help create your life. Then let go. Do not stand tapping your foot, impatiently waiting. Simply let go, the way you would if you trusted your friend to respond positively, in a way that was best for you.

Go naturally about the course of your life. Listen to your heart. Listen to your inner voice. What you are guided to do, where you are guided to go, where your attention is directed, the people you meet, the phone calls you receive, the experiences you have—even the problems that arise—these are some ways the universe can respond to you.

Open your eyes. Look around. See how the universe responds. Watch how it dances for you, with you. You are connected to a magical loving universe, one that will come alive for you, dance for you, in ways you cannot imagine—but in ways you will come to know as true.

Look within, too. Sometimes the most gentle, quiet, flickering thought—that glimmer of an idea, that awareness of a need or desire, or that small bit of inspiration or intuition—is how the universe prepares us for what it wants us to do or receive. Our inner voice, the one in our heart, is an important part of the way we're guided and led down our path.

You stand at a gateway now.
It's the door to universal love.

JANUARY 13

Honor Winter's Lesson

"See the pine trees and learn their lesson," a friend once said. "Pine trees are nature's reminder that growth continues even in the winter."

Winter is an important season in our lives. It is more than a time of coldness and snow. It's a time of going within. A time to rest from the work that's been done, a time to prepare for the lessons ahead. Long for the sun on your shoulders, but let the frost and cold come. The ground has been left fallow in preparation for nourishing the seeds of new life.

Honor winter's lesson. Despite this time of lifelessness and inactivity, this is still a season of growth. Trust what's being worked out in your soul. The snow will melt. The sun will shine again. The time will come to remove your heavy garb and return to the activity of life.

Cherish the winter. Cherish its quietness, the time
of going within to rest and heal. Cherish this time
of preparation that must come before new life.
Cherish the hope that lies beneath the snow.

JANUARY 14

Release Your Fears

The Royal Gorge Bridge in Colorado is the world's highest suspension bridge. Visiting it was a significant part of my journey, an important turning point.

Spanning a section of the Grand Canyon of the Arkansas River, the bridge is constructed of small wooden slats. You can drive across or you can walk it, peering down through the slats to see the river 1,050 feet below.

When I reached the park surrounding the bridge, I parked my car, grabbed my backpack, and got out to walk across the bridge. I neared the bridge, then turned around. I was too afraid to walk across, certain I'd blow off. I decided to drive.

I returned to the Jeep, drove to the bridge, but stopped again. I backed up, drove back to the toll booth, and hailed the man working inside. "Will I be fine?" I said. He looked at me strangely. "Will I be fine?" I repeated.

He finally got it. "You'll be fine," he said with a smile.

I drove back to the bridge. Inch by inch, I drove the car across the wooden slats. I was afraid to look to the right or left. Afraid to look down. Afraid to look. Afraid not to look . . . I never knew how much fear was in me until I drove across that bridge. And to get back, I had to turn the Jeep around and drive across the bridge once more.

Sometimes, we're so afraid we don't know how afraid we are. Sometimes, we carry so much fear that it interferes with our ability to enjoy life.

Feel and release your fears. See how needless they are? See how they keep you from enjoying life? Unclench your hands. Don't always look straight ahead. Experience. Adventure. Let yourself live.

As the man said, "You'll be fine."

JANUARY 15

You're Free to Follow Your Heart

No one has taken your freedom away. You may have relinquished it for reasons known and unknown. But you've always been free—free to choose.

And you have been choosing, whether or not you have been conscious of your choices. For many years, you chose not to be free. Then you felt stifled, so you groused and rebelled. That was an important part of your journey. It helped you break out of your prison, loosened the chains around you. Now you see the truth. You have always been free.

Celebrate the breaking of the chains. Celebrate your freedom. And share it joyfully with others. Tell yourself, tell others, too, that you're free to trust and follow your own heart.

JANUARY 16

See How Happy You Are

Most of us have very active imaginations. We have the power to visualize, to create in our minds what we cannot yet see with our eyes. The problem is that many of us use this power to visualize events we'd really rather not see. We conjure up all sorts of images about the bad, painful things that *could* happen. Maybe it's time to use the potent, creative power of visualization to create pictures of all the good we *would* like to see in our lives.

What would you like to see happen in your life? Create a picture you can see. The more real you make it, the better it will be. See yourself in the picture. Try to involve all your senses. Visualize yourself touching, hearing, speaking, smelling, feeling. Charge your picture with as much emotional energy as you can. Use any spare moments—stretched out on the sofa, in bed before you fall asleep, driving in your car, soaking in the tub—to create positive pictures for your life.

Make a project out of it. Make a list, and keep it nearby. If you don't know what to put on your list, ask yourself, ask God, ask the universe to help you, show you.

See yourself doing all the things you'd like to do. Take the time to use your creative power of visualization to create the life you'd like. But above all, take the time to see yourself being happy.

JANUARY 17

Awaken to the World Around You

There is a universe outside your door, waiting to touch you, soothe you, heal you. There is an entire world out there waiting to help you open your heart and nurture your soul. The universe wants to teach you things, show you things, help you come more alive than you've ever been before.

Open your eyes, open your senses, open your heart. Walk out your door, look around. You'll be shown. You'll be guided. Your heart will lead you to what you need. Listen, look, feel. You are connected to the universe.

Let the universe bring you all the healing you need. Let the universe bring you alive. Awaken to the world around you, and you'll awaken to yourself.

JANUARY 18

Set Yourself Free from Control

You don't have to let people control or manipulate you. You don't have to scream and beat upon your breast, telling them they're wrong, they cannot do that. That's letting them control you.

People are energy. Thoughts are energy. When someone tries to control, that energy limits love and growth. Any attempt to control other people, what they think or what they do, puts little strings, cords, tentacles that smother, hold back, and impact in ways that don't heal. Control is not the way of the heart. It's not the way of love.

As you proceed along this journey, you will become increasingly sensitive to attempts to control. You will see and feel when its tentacles reach out to you. You will see and feel how control affects you, how it makes you feel, how it pulls at you, bothers you, annoys you. You don't have to scream and yell. You can quietly recognize it as control.

Whether the person is someone you love, an acquaintance, a business associate, a friend, or a family member, you can recognize control for what it is—a block to the heart, a hindrance to love.

Set yourself free from control and
manipulation. Love can't be controlled.
Open your heart and let love be.

JANUARY 19

Honor the Process of Spiritual Growth

Don't wait for things to change. The change you're waiting for will come from within you. Start to nurture yourself through each stage of your evolution, your spiritual growth.

Waiting for things to change is a tiresome, irritating process.

But embracing our own emotions and growth is exciting. It can become a positive challenge that turns life into a vital, interactive process. The moment we surrender to this process, *something* happens. If we feel an emotion—an old, stuck, hardened chunk of emotion or a new one that has arisen along the path, we can release it and the belief attached to it: *I am unlovable. Life has to be hard. I deserve to be punished.*

When we release the emotion and the belief, our body shifts. It detoxifies. Changes. A new lesson then emerges. We discover we can choose joy, freedom, forgiveness. The lessons that can emerge are as unique as our old beliefs. We wrestle with each new lesson as it grows and appears in many different forms—on the job, in love relationships, in all the arenas of our lives.

Soon we come to a new conclusion about ourselves, about life. *I am lovable. I am creatively feeling what God and the universe have to offer me. I am free. I can bring my full essence and energy before the world.* Then when we change, when our beliefs change, our lives change. The change we've been waiting for happens, but it happens as a result of our own evolutionary process—not because we waited for something or someone in our lives outside ourselves to change.

Trust this process of change. Honor it,
respect it, revere it. You no longer
have to wait for something to happen.
Something is happening right now,
within you. Welcome the changes
that can be yours. Let life help you,
as you take an active part in creating
these changes. Let the process become
living, interactive, and magical.

Learn When It's Time to Adapt

Life is constantly changing. So are we. With change comes the need to learn to adapt.

Some adaptation comes naturally. On my trip, I watched even the subtle changes in my body as I traveled from climate to climate. In the warm, dry climate of Arizona, I needed more water. My body needed lotion, my hair different shampoo and conditioner. In the higher mountain climates, I found myself breathing differently, needing to give myself more time to rest. People who live in different places and different cultures adapt to the climate and ways of the world around them.

We can learn to adapt to the situations in our life, too—to the constant evolution of the world around us. At home, at work, within our social groups, change is constantly taking place. Most of us are constantly on the move—meeting new people, being exposed to new situations, or needing to deal with situations that have themselves changed.

There are times when we can't adapt to the changes around us. When no matter how hard we try, we cannot force ourselves into the new circumstance. Our body won't allow it because this change isn't right for us. We need to learn to adapt to change but we also need to learn to tell when a situation is wrong for us and not force ourselves to fit.

Be sensitive to the changes both subtle and dramatic around you—and in you. Give yourself time and freedom to adapt to these changes and figure out what they mean to you.

Give yourself time to catch up. Be gentle with yourself. Listen to your needs. Let yourself adapt to the changes that are right for you.

JANUARY 21

Discover Your Own Truth

No truth is ours until we make it our own.

All the truths in the world don't matter unless and until we discover them to be true for ourselves. That's what the journey is about. An insight, a lesson, a new belief is at the end of each adventure—whether that adventure happens in a moment, an hour, a day, or a year. This lesson doesn't come from books, although books might help along the way. It doesn't come from classes or lectures or well-meaning friends. The lesson we're seeking comes from inside us, from our hearts, from our deep abiding connection to consciousness and the truth.

It springs quietly from within as we notice one day that we believe something new, something different, something more free, more fun, and more life-enhancing than what we believed before. For a moment we may turn back and say, *Why didn't I know that? Why didn't I see that before?* Then we step back on our path, laugh, and go on our way understanding that is why we are really here. Not to know everything in advance. But to allow ourselves to go freely through all the lessons that teach us all we came here to learn.

You are on a journey of discovery. Find out what's true for you. Remember: A truth isn't yours until it rings true for you.

JANUARY 22

Open to the Power of Comfort

Packed in the back of my Jeep I stored my favorite red woolen blanket. I didn't need it for warmth because I didn't sleep in the cold. I needed it to remind me of the importance of comfort.

Open yourself to receive comfort, the comfort that touches the heart and nurtures the soul. Many of us grew up and lived our lives without experiencing true comfort, true nurturing. Many of us didn't know it existed. But at some level, that's what we've been looking for.

Comfort is the loving arms of a mother who sees only the beauty of her child. A mother who attends to the needs, who nurtures the heart and soul of her child. This kind of comfort is acceptance and love at its finest.

Open your heart to receive comfort. Learn to give it, too. Comfort touches and heals our souls. Take it with you like a favorite blanket wherever you go.

JANUARY 23

Honor the Needs of Your Body

Take time to rest and regroup as often as you need. At the beginning of the journey and along the way, take time to honor your body. When you honor your body, you honor your soul.

You have been working hard on yourself, on your spiritual growth. You are moving forward, evolving at a rapid pace. Give your body time to catch up. Your body isn't a bother; it's an ally. Your body knows what it needs, and what your soul needs, too.

Tune in to your body. Listen. On those days when your body is adjusting, regrouping, shifting because you're growing and healing emotionally and spiritually, let it do that. Don't ignore it. Don't force it. Be gentle. Recognize its nuances. Ask it what it needs. Juice? Vitamins? Rest? Exercise? Let it tell you. Then go easy. Do tasks that are easier, that seem to fit what you can handle that day.

After a spiritual growth spurt, our body works diligently to flush the toxins released when emotions are cleansed and healed. After a day, week, or month of intense spiritual growth, our body is tired from flushing through so many emotions, going through so many changes. To deny the body's connection to our growth, to push it when it needs to rest, is denying the importance and impact of the spiritual work we're doing.

By taking time to honor the body, to honor its shifts and needs, it will be there for you in a way that it has never been before. Rest and care will help it come back to center quickly. You will have the benefit of a healed spirit and a body that was allowed to adjust and adapt to that healing process. You will be honoring the oneness of body, mind, and soul. You will be honoring your newfound connection.

Taking time to honor the needs of your body
is taking time to respect the needs of your soul.

JANUARY 24

Stay in the Present Moment

Stay in the present moment. That's where you find life's magic.

How overwhelmed we feel when we anticipate the future, all that needs doing, all the tasks, the work, the potential problems, the responsibilities. How tired we become when we dwell on what we've done already, the energy we've expended, and the imperfect results.

Yes, sometimes to stay in the present we need to visit the past, to clear out an old feeling, to heal an old, limiting belief. But that visit can be brief. And sometimes we need to think about the future—to make commitments, to plan, to envision where we want to go. But to linger there can cause unrest. It can spoil the moment we're in now. Stay in the present moment, and the past and the future will fall naturally and easily into place.

Stay in the present moment,
and the magic will return.

JANUARY 25

Cherish Your Favorite Spaces

Our world abounds with quiet, free sources of revitalization.

"I love going into fabric stores," one woman told me recently. "I love touching, handling, fondling all the colorful bolts of material. It makes me feel good. It makes me feel happy."

"My favorite activity is spending an afternoon at the library," one man told me. "If I could only do one thing in life, go one place, that's what I'd choose. I lose myself in the pages of the books. They take me to faraway places, places I've never been. And when I leave the library, I feel like I've been touched and changed."

What are the places you like to visit in your town or city? Do you enjoy browsing through a bookstore? Is there a favorite shopping center in your neighborhood where the shopkeepers smile a little more and the window displays please your heart? Do you have a favorite restaurant where drinking a cup of tea changes your mood? Cherish old favorite spaces, and open yourself to discovering new places.

Healing doesn't have to be extravagant, expensive, or traditional. Sometimes it just means going to the places that make us feel good.

JANUARY 26

See Life Through the Eyes of Your Soul

Once many, many years ago, I woke up in the middle of the night. Only I wasn't in bed sleeping. I was on the ceiling looking down at my body lying on the bed. I studied myself, a little surprised at how unusual I looked from the outside. The next thing I knew, I was back in bed. My soul reconnected with my body. That experience was the beginning of a journey that led me to understand I was more than a body; I had a soul. I was about to embark on a path that would consciously connect me to that soul—experiences on the path to freeing my soul.

Throughout my life, I have had many conscious desires and expectations about my life. I wanted this. I wanted that. I wanted my life to be arranged just so. What I've understood over time is that the journey I'm taking is not one based on arranging my life in a particular way, then keeping it just so. The journey I've been on and what I've been seeking has been the journey of my soul.

Much in life can cause us distress and discomfort when we look with our conscious mind. But if we look beyond what we can see on the surface, we'll begin to see with the eyes of the soul. The lessons run deep. Often they take time to learn. We learn about power. We learn about love. Courage. Faith. Saying good-bye. Embracing deep love for ourselves.

> *Learn to see life with the eyes of your soul. Experience all the emotions that are there. Discover your truths. Seek conscious peace as much as you can, and seek peace in your soul as well. Let your soul lead you through meadows and take you down deep into the valleys, for all your experiences are just that—experiences—on this mysterious journey of the soul.*

JANUARY 27

Open Your Heart As Often As You Need

Opening our hearts is not something we do once or twice. It is a way of life. How quickly life does things that make us want to close off, wall off, shut down, go away. But our commitment to staying open has little to do with what life does to us. It has to do with how we decide we want to live. Open. Loving. Safe. We're safe because we know our ability and our willingness to love comes from within us. It is the ultimate form of learning to embrace our power.

A long time ago when you were young, you may have told yourself it was risky to love, to trust, to feel. You told yourself that everyone you trusted would in the end betray your trust. Your belief has many times been proven true. But it's time now to believe something else. It's time to believe that the opposite is true. It is risky to *not* love, *not* trust, *not* feel.

Your security doesn't come from trusting others. Your security comes from trusting and cherishing your own heart. Don't let life shut you down. Open your heart as often as you need.

JANUARY 28

What Interests You?

It's easy to talk ourselves out of trying something new, then sit home whining that we're bored. It's just as easy, and a lot more fun, to find something interesting to do.

Learn to make a basket out of pine needles. Try spelunking, or take a tap dancing class. Learn to fly an airplane or carve a walking stick. Take lessons on that musical instrument you've always wanted to play. You can learn to braid your hair, write a poem, or even act in a play.

Have you talked yourself out of doing activities you used to like to do? Is there something new you'd like to learn or explore, something you've always thought you might like to do?

Begin a journey of discovery. Find out what interests you. Don't limit your interests to activities connected just to work or spiritual growth. Opening up to the world and all it has to offer expands your creativity. Discovering what your interests are, then letting yourself pursue them will become part of your spiritual path.

There are many magical things in the world, and people happy to teach you how to do them. See all there is to do. Get out of your house and out of your rut and discover what interests you.

JANUARY 29

Seek Peace

I drove down the winding road into King's Canyon, California, not knowing what to expect. The road took me past lavender hills and ended alongside a rushing, roaring river spilling over with white-water froth. "Beware of Turbulent Waters," the sign warned. I parked the car and stepped outside, taking in the scenery. Soon, I knew—I felt—where this road had led.

It led to peace.

Cultivate peace. Commit to peace. Insist on it. Don't settle for peace based on outward circumstances or a particular arrangement in your life. Drive down the winding road and find the peace that prevails amidst the mountains, now purple in the setting sun. Find the peace that prevails even when the turbulent waters of the river roar through your life.

This is the peace the universe offers.
Settle for nothing less.

JANUARY 30

Warm Up

Sit in the sun and warm up.

Sit in the sun. Soak up the love and warmth from the world around you. Take that warmth into your everyday life. Open your heart more to the people you see, the people you meet, the people you greet, and the people you love. Practice being warm, loving, and open. Do more than just think a kind loving thought. Say it. Do more than just think of something nice you'd like to do for someone. Do it.

Fear is cold. Sometimes, we become so afraid of life, people, ourselves—so afraid—that we become cold. Cold toward people, toward life, toward God. We may not be aware of how cold we have become. We may have been cold for so long, we just don't see it. Being cold and afraid has become our everyday posture. It's the way we interact with the world around us. Now it's time to put warmth back in our lives.

Don't let your fears turn you cold. Sit in the sun and warm up. Then radiate that warmth to the people around you. Warm up to people. Warm up to life. Warm up to yourself.

JANUARY 31

Value Your Connection to Truth

Trust what you know. Not what you *think* you know, but what you know in your heart.

We often know the truth long before we let ourselves see and believe it, long before we're ready to acknowledge it. For many reasons—fear, timing, and a myriad of issues too long to list—we ignore and discount what we know in our heart. But the truth doesn't go away. What's true, what we know to be true, will nag at us and haunt us. And even if we try to run from that truth, our experiences will ultimately lead us back to it.

Life may bring us many issues we want to run from, issues that are a challenge. But the real challenge we face is learning to trust ourselves and trust what we know to be true. Maybe someone once told us we couldn't be trusted. That's too bad. But what's worse is that we began to believe it and started to tell ourselves that, too.

Your heart can be trusted. Don't doubt it.
It will inevitably connect you to what's true.
Love yourself enough to trust what you
know. Then stay connected to truth.

February

FEBRUARY 1

Transcend Your Limitations

You're free now, free to take the journey of a lifetime. Free to experience life, in its newness, its freshness, its magic—in a way you never have before.

The only limitations on you are the ones you've placed on yourself. Your prison has been of your own making. Don't blame or chastise yourself. Life has created certain challenges for you. But the purpose hasn't been to imprison you. The purpose has been to set you free, to provide you with lessons, experiences, circumstances that would trigger growth and healing. Life has been provoking, promoting, urging you to grow, stretch, learn, heal. Life has been trying to break you out of your prison.

Set yourself free. Let yourself go on a journey of love. Take notes. Be present. Experience. Learn. Love and laugh, and cry when you need to. Rest when you're tired. Take a flashlight to help you see in the dark. But most of all, take yourself and go.

Go on your journey of joy.

FEBRUARY 2

Cherish Today's Lessons

"I'm brokenhearted about my divorce," the man said. "I've spent four years searching for a new wife, trying to recreate my family, trying to jam the pieces of the picture back in place. All I've gotten from my desperate search is more pain and anguish. It's hurt other people. It's hurt me. I'm tired of trying to manipulate other people to meet my own needs, to postpone my own grief."

Some of us may be desperately trying to recreate the life we once had. But fear, pain, and desperation won't attract the answer we're seeking. Desperation attracts desperation. Pain attracts pain. And so the downward spiral goes. Yes, loss hurts. Sometimes life hurts, too. But loss can't be negotiated. Becoming obsessed with putting the pieces back in place is an understandable reaction, but it won't work. Yesterday cannot be superimposed on today. We need to go one step further.

Feel the obsession, and let it go. Feel the desperation, then release that. Come back to the lessons of today. They're different from the lessons of yesterday, but just as valuable.

We face many losses along the way. People we love disappear from our lives; we may lose a career, money, or something else we valued. We can lose our dreams, too. But looking for quick replacements as a way to avoid feeling pain about the loss won't work. And we'll miss the lessons. Before we can go on, we must feel our sadness about what we lost. Losses demand acceptance.

Eventually life will send you new people and new dreams. Cherish this time to grow and learn. Cherish what the universe is teaching you now.

FEBRUARY 3

Break Through Your Resistance

We sometimes resist new lessons. And what we resist the most is likely to be what we most need to learn.

Our lessons usually come with inner conflict. The action we should be taking, the idea we should be learning is sometimes hidden behind a wall of resistance. There's a border, a barrier we need to cross to get into the heart of the lesson. Most times, that barrier is within us. Lessons require us to let go of old feelings, old beliefs. If they didn't, they wouldn't be lessons. We'd already know them. Sometimes, the very thing we feel guiltiest about doing, the place we're most resistant to visiting, the person we're most convinced we shouldn't contact, or the behavior we're tormenting ourselves most about is exactly what we need to be doing.

And more often than not, the lesson we're learning is not what we think it is. We need to embrace the surprise element of life—embrace the mystery of life as it unfolds, as the lessons appear, as we grow and change.

Do what you need to do to break through your resistance. Often that means simply seeing your resistance for what it is. Remember that the point of greatest resistance is often the place of greatest learning.

FEBRUARY 4

See How Powerful You Are

People who believe they're victims get to be right. Each experience they have convinces them of that. They don't open themselves to the lessons, the growth, and the beauty of each situation they encounter. All they can see is their victimization.

Many of us have done the hard work to shift our belief system about being a victim. As we did that, we noticed that the scenery in our lives changed. When we believe something different, we get to see something different.

People who believe they have powers get to be right, too. Although we know there is much in life we can't control, we also know we have the power to think, to feel, to choose, and to take responsibility for ourselves and our lives. We're discovering our creative powers, and our power to love, including our power to love ourselves. We've embraced our power to grow, to change, to move forward. We know we have the power to claim our lives and take responsibility for ourselves in any situation life brings. Although life may deal us certain hard blows, we've learned to see beyond that. We see life's beauty, gifts, and lessons, and its mysterious and sometimes magical nature.

On the road to freedom we may have made a stopover. We believed we were victims and we got to be right. Now, our journey has led us someplace else. We know we have powers; we know we have choices. And we no longer need to be right. Just free.

See how powerful you are!

FEBRUARY 5

Learn to Live with Unfinished Projects

Whether your project is sewing a dress, reading a book, writing a book, building a home, or learning a lesson on your journey, learn to live comfortably with unfinished work. Whatever you're working on, whatever you're in the midst of doesn't need to be finished, in perfect order, with all the loose ends in place for you to be happy.

For too many years, we worried and fretted, denying ourselves happiness until we could see the whole picture, learn the entire lesson, cross every *t* and dot each *i*. That meant we spent a lot of stressful time waiting for that one moment when the project was complete.

Enjoy all the stages of the process you're in. The first moments when the germ of the idea finds you. The time before you begin, when the seed lies dormant in the ground, getting ready to grow. The beginning, and all the days throughout the middle. Those bleak days, when it looks like you're stuck and won't break through. Those exciting days, when the project, the lesson, the life you're building takes shape and form.

Be happy now. Enjoy the creative process—the process of creating your life, yourself, and the project you're working on—today. Don't wait for those finishing moments to take pleasure in your work and your life. Find joy all along the way.

FEBRUARY 6

Look at What's Right

Take time to notice what's right in ourselves, in others, and in the world around us. We may become so concerned with correcting ourselves we become habituated to seeing what's wrong. Not just seeing it—constantly looking for it. The question itself—*What's wrong?* —is enough to keep us on edge.

There are times to take stock, do an inventory. Times to learn and grow. But spirituality and joy do not stem from trudging around in the muck of what's wrong with others, ourselves, and life. We do not have to seek out mistakes and errors, poking and picking at ourselves to continue our growth. Poking and picking hurts. Our lessons will be revealed to us, and they will present themselves naturally. Growth will occur.

Give yourself a break. Ask yourself
what's right, what's good, what's true,
what's beautiful. Sometimes the lesson
isn't in discovering what's wrong.
Sometimes the lesson is discovering that
the world is all right—and so are you.

FEBRUARY 7

Experience Love for Yourself

To find love, you must first find it in yourself. Then the whole universe will mirror it back. See how people smile at you? Feel their tenderness, their affection, their respect. See how the whole world responds lovingly to you when you love yourself.

The world around you reflects how you feel about yourself. The beliefs of many years have kept you trapped in the illusion of separateness, apartness. Your hesitancy to love yourself was mirrored in the eyes of others. But you are not alone, you are not estranged. You are not a disconnected part. You are part of the whole, intricately connected to all of life.

Go out, and embrace your connection. Embrace life. Watch the sunrise. Smell the cypress trees, a field of garlic, the gentle scent of an apple orchard. Feel the breeze on your cheek, the rain on your hair, the earth beneath your feet.

Stay open. Keep loving yourself. Know you are a vital part of a living universe. Watch how much better, how much kinder life is, as you grow in peace and harmony with yourself. See how much more love is mirrored in the universe since you committed to loving yourself.

FEBRUARY 8

Listen to Your Inner Voice

Our inner voice, that quiet guide within, will lead us along our path, will help us create our destiny, will keep us in harmony.

So much stress comes from not listening, not trusting our inner voice. So much confusion comes from trying to act before we have heard, before we are guided. So much pain comes when we deny what that voice is saying, when we try to run from it or make it go away. We wonder how we can trust ourselves. The better question is, How can we *not* trust ourselves?

Our rage, anger, and most bitter resentments occur when we trust others rather than ourselves. Yes, sometimes promptings come from outside ourselves. The universe is alive, magical, responsive, and will guide us on our way. But the answer must always resonate, must always ultimately come from that place within: our heart, our soul, our inner voice. Sometimes, we need to listen to others until we become impassioned enough to hear and trust ourselves.

It takes practice, the quiet practice of listening, until we learn how to hear ourselves, then interpret what we hear. It is neither wasted time nor incidental to our lives to learn to hear ourselves, to learn to tune into our hearts and souls. That's part of the reason we're here—part of our destiny, our mission, our purpose.

Our best work, our finest moments, our joy
happen when we're centered, listening to and
trusting ourselves, allowing our hearts and souls
to guide us. They happen when we allow ourselves
to fully, completely, and in love, be who we are.

FEBRUARY 9

Keep Your Heart Open

Keep your heart open, even when you can't have what you want.

It's easy to keep our heart open to life's magic and all its possibilities when we have what we want. It's more of a challenge, and more necessary than ever, to keep our hearts open when we can't have what we want.

Even on the best journey, things happen. Plans change. Things shift and move around. This shifting and moving causes doors to close, relationships to end, blocks and frustrations to appear on our path. For now, that is what we see. For now, what we know is disappointment. We can't have what we want, and it hurts. When that happens, our tendency may be to shut down, close our hearts, forget all we've learned.

Keep your heart open anyway. Consciously choose to do that. Yes, you can go away, you can leave, you can shut down, but you don't need to. Now is a turning point. If you choose to open your heart, even when you can't have what you want, miracles will unfold.

For now, remember this. Even though you don't have what you want right now, keep your heart open anyway. Later, you'll see more. You'll see how it worked out. How it needed to be just so.

FEBRUARY 10

Free Yourself from Manipulation

Learn to recognize passive-aggressive hits. Learn to recognize when other people have hidden agendas, when they're trying to control or manipulate you. When we're being controlled, we may feel guilty, obligated, indebted. In our muddled state, we agree to another's wishes but we're not sure why. Then we wander around feeling uncertain, unbalanced, confused.

The lesson still isn't about them. The lesson is about how we respond. If their behavior, their energy, is affecting us that strongly, it's because something in us needs to be healed. A part of us isn't clear, is still mucked up by something old and outworn, such as guilt or fear. Once we heal ourselves, we will know how to deal with their energy, how to handle their passive-aggressive behavior and their attempts to control us. Then we can thank them for helping trigger our healing process, for helping us grow.

Everything that happens along the way is part of the journey. Everything can be incorporated into our healing process. All roads lead to growth.

FEBRUARY 11

The Universe Is Abundant

Watch out for greed—greed for money, for resources, for love. Greed can slowly corrupt the heart. Greed can slowly take over our lives. Greed and fear can block our connection with the universe, and with universal love.

Let go of the fears of deprivation, of doing without, that haunt you from the past. Having more and more won't solve your problem if what you need is to heal your fears. Look around with love at your life and the people in it. If you open your heart and look without fear, you may see that you have enough now.

Go back to your heart. Let love, not fear and greed, lead the way. Be led by your desire to joyfully serve, by the desire to bring your gifts, your healing, your comforts and talents to others. Go back to your heart as often as you need. And remember what is honorable and true. Say to those you love, *This is what I shall give. And I'll give it because my heart leads me to do so.*

The universe is abundant. Take your part,
take your place, in universal love. Go
back to your heart. Give from the heart.
And the universe will respond in kind.

FEBRUARY 12

Fill Your World with Color and Beauty

Fill your life and your world with the colors, textures, scents, and objects that are beautiful to you, that have meaning to you. Remember that we are connected to our environment. The objects and the colors in our world have energy and meaning. They have an impact on us.

The more we see how connected we are, the more carefully and thoughtfully we may want to choose the items we place in our home, or our space at work, if we have a special area, because these objects and colors can reflect how we feel about ourselves and what is important to us.

Objects have energy. They have energy already in them when we obtain them, and they have the energy and meaning we attribute to them. Choose carefully the possessions you want around you, for they tell a story all day long.

Fill your world, your life, with objects that are beautiful and have special meaning to you. What articles and hues have you surrounded yourself with at home, at work? Is there a special article you want close to you, on your desk, in your locker, in your pocket?

What story do these things tell about you, about what you're going through, about your place in your journey?

Choose objects and colors that make your heart smile.

FEBRUARY 13

Don't Let People Put Thoughts in Your Head

Respect the power of words and thoughts, both your own and others'.

Our ideas and inspirations sometimes come from other people, come from outside us. But if we're not careful, it's easy for others to put their ideas and intentions into our minds, to cast their spells on us. *You aren't very creative. Your heart isn't open. You're really not that healthy. You need me to succeed. You don't deserve success. In fact, you don't deserve . . .* How easy it is to be unaware of the process, to walk around with other people's words in our head, taking them as truth, taking them as our own, letting their ideas about us control our lives and our beliefs.

We don't have to let others put their spells on us. We don't have to believe what they say.

What are the words others have spoken to you, the spells they've cast on you and your life? What phrases are echoing in your mind, and who do they belong to? Listen to what you hear, and if they are not yours, get them out.

Words are powerful. Don't let other people put them in your head. And choose carefully the words you speak to them.

FEBRUARY 14

Send Love Letters

Sending love letters to people we care about is a rewarding experience, both for us and for them. Making the time to take pen in hand and express our thoughts is valuable. But there's another way to send love letters, too. This way takes as much time and attention as writing a loving note does, but it doesn't require a pen and paper. It requires concentrated thought.

There's an invisible thread of energy winding through the universe, one that connects us all. Have you ever noticed that sometimes you can tell if someone's angry or upset with you, even if you haven't talked to or seen this person? You can feel his or her anger, even if you haven't been physically present to experience it. Thoughts have power, particularly those charged with intense emotional energy. When we think mean, bitter thoughts, it can be like sending hate mail along our connecting wires. It can almost be a sensory attack.

Why not send loving thoughts charged with positive emotional energy? We can consciously choose to use our connections to others to send love. Send positive thoughts. Blessings. Peace. Assistance in time of crisis. We can send our thoughts in the form of a prayer; or we can simply think a blessing or positive thought, charge it with energy, and send it along the wires with love.

When someone you know or love comes to mind, or even someone you don't—perhaps someone in another part of the country or the world, perhaps someone going through a particular crisis—and you're not certain what to do, send a love letter. Your loving thoughts will touch them and your blessings will all come back to you.

FEBRUARY 15

Ask the Universe for Help

You have come so far. You have learned to ask for help from people when you need it. You have learned to ask God, God as you understand God, for help, too. Now you're entering into a relationship with the universe, an active, vital, living relationship. Now you can learn to ask the universe for help as well.

Talk to the universe. Talk aloud if you can. Say: *Show me, guide me, lead me, help me. This is what I want, this is what I need.* Say: *Show me which road to follow, where to go, and what to do.* Yes, talk to people. Talk to God. They are part of the universe and world we live in. But talk aloud to the universe, too.

Then listen to your inner voice. Hear what it says and trust what you hear. Answers come in many ways, from many sources, many places. But if the answer is right for you, your heart will know, and it will feel true.

Talk to the universe. Ask it for help.
Then listen to your heart. Because that
quiet voice, the one in your heart, is
how the universe talks to you.

FEBRUARY 16

The Answer May Be Right in Front of You

It was late at night. I had just pulled into Chimayo, New Mexico. The streets were poorly lit; addresses and signs were difficult to see.

I had been driving around for what seemed like hours, looking for an address. Finally, in desperation, I stopped the car, got out, and flagged someone down. A man stopped, but said he couldn't help me. I was at my wit's end. I turned around, staring frantically at the mailbox in front of me. To my surprise, I was right where I wanted to go.

How often we wave our hands in panic and despair, certain the answer, the insight, the piece of information we need will never come. Yet often the answer we're seeking is right in front of us.

There's a part of us, our heart, that knows where we're going, knows what we need, knows what the next step is. Our heart will lead us on. Our soul will move us forward. Our instincts will take us home like a radar signal beaming us to safety.

Feel your panic. Feel your frustration. But keep your eyes and your heart open. The answer may be closer than you think—maybe it's right in front of you.

FEBRUARY 17

Who Empowers You?

Most of us need people around us who empower and help us feel able, on track, in balance, hopeful. We need people who tell us we can. Even if they don't use words, they believe in us and that belief comes shining through. We look at them and what we see reflected back is our own power.

But sometimes we run into those who, instead, try to convince us of *their* power, convince us that *they* have our answers, that we need *them* to be able to see clearly, that without *them,* we won't be able to find the way. They don't believe in us; they only believe in themselves. That's not empowerment. That's an approach destined to create dependency, often unhealthy dependency.

Cultivate relationships with people who make you feel like you can, who help you know that you're on track, right where you need to be. Spend time with people who help you know that you can trust yourself.

Seek out people who empower you.
Learn to empower those you love. And
during those times when no one's around,
know that you can empower yourself.

FEBRUARY 18

Your Body, Mind, and Soul Are One

The body, mind, spirit, and emotions are more than just connected. They are one. To nurture the body is to nurture the mind, spirit, and emotions. To nurture the spirit is to nurture the body, mind, and emotions. And so it goes, a continuous connection. A continuing whole.

Do you feel fragmented? Have you disowned a part of yourself? Invite it back. Maybe you've focused too heavily on one part and neglected the others. You can be a world-class athlete and still not be in touch with your soul. You can be skilled at dealing with any emotion that comes along, and yet not see the delicate connection between that emotion and your conscious thoughts and beliefs. Or you may be so focused on tending to the needs of your spirit and mind that you neglect your body—resent it and think of it as a limitation.

Tend to each aspect of the whole. Do things that nurture your spirit, perhaps spend time in prayer and meditation or time with nature. Work on what you believe; clarify the thoughts that run through your head. Nurture yourself emotionally. Let yourself heal from the feelings of the past, and do what you need to stay current and clear. Listen to your body and give it what it needs—it's not separate and apart, it's not a nuisance. It's the form your spirit has created to experience the gift of life.

Find that place of balance in nurturing all parts of you. Then life will begin to be magical and you'll see what you believe. Your feelings won't be a bother. They'll fuel your life; they'll be the passion that adds color and zest to your life. Your body will lead you instinctively into what you want and away from what you dislike. And the longer you travel the journey to the heart, the more you'll discover and trust your soul.

Start by becoming connected. If you love
yourself and keep walking your path,
soon you'll see how connected you are.

FEBRUARY 19

Be Gentle with Your Heart

On this road, this journey to the heart, you will see more, feel more, and be more than you've ever been before.

Your heart is open, your spirit is alive. You're open to all that the universe, life, and God hold for you. Because you're that open, you are more sensitive than ever to people, energies, places, things. You are more sensitive to any unresolved issues in yourself and in those around you. You are open, more open than you've ever been.

Comfort yourself. Wrap yourself up in a blanket of love and hope. Know that you will be feeling, seeing, and taking in a great deal. Know that you will be healing at a deeper level than ever before. Most of the time, this will bring joy. But an open heart is not one-dimensional; joy is not the only emotion it will embrace. Make room in your heart, room in your life, and time in your days to feel other feelings, too—anger, grief, fear, exuberance, tenderness, betrayal, and exhilaration—all the emotions an open heart feels.

You're more open than you've ever been. Take gentle, loving care of yourself. Be tender with your heart.

FEBRUARY 20

Spread Your Wings and Fly

I sat on the ground on a dirt road that wandered off a main highway in Idaho. I leaned against a tree and watched a mother eagle and her babies in a nest overhead. She fussed as she protected them, watching me closely, responding with her call to any noise she heard. She was very protective now, but someday it would be time to push them out of the nest. It would be time to teach them to fly.

Many of us have been pushed out of the nest. Something unexpected happened, and our world changed. We may have fought valiantly to get back in the nest, to return to the safety of life as we knew it. But life had pushed us out. We had no choice but to flap our wings and learn to fly the best we could.

See how magical this time has been? See how much you've learned? With all your fears and resistance, it has still been a grand

and powerful time. You flailed around a bit, wondering who to trust. You tried to trust others, then found that didn't work. Finally you understood. The very lesson you were learning was that of trusting yourself.

You were learning to listen to and trust your inner voice. You were learning to open your heart. Despite all your fears, you have done a grand job. Look how much you've changed!

See all the powers you've gained? You've opened up to your healing powers, your creative powers, too. You know and sense things in a way that used to seem beyond reach and now seems both magical and commonplace. Your instincts and intuition are finely tuned. Your inner voice is clear. And despite all your fears about being abandoned, you now see how much you are loved.

When life pokes and prods you, it's not punishment or abuse. You're being pushed out of the nest. Spread your wings and take flight. See how well you can fly!

FEBRUARY 21

Let Love Be

You can't control love. It's impossible. It's like screaming and screeching and begging a rose to unfold faster, better, or differently.

Love is an energy—an active, living force that runs its threads through all of life, through all of the universe. But we can't control love. It is not its nature to be controlled. It's futile to stand with our hands in our pockets and heels dug into the ground saying, *I shall control the course of love,* or *I shall allow another to control me because I'm afraid love will go away.*

We can open our hearts and let love run through us. We can open our hearts and receive love. We can open our eyes and see universal love all around us, in places we never saw it before. We can awaken our souls and see that all these experiences have been lessons of love. Learning courage, faith, patience. Learning to love ourselves, when it looked and felt as if no one else did. Learning to express our creativity, express our emotions, and experience joy. Each one has been a lesson of love.

We have learned to let love be and be open to what that is and the new direction it may lead us in. Love is a powerful living force that permeates the universe and funnels through us. We don't lead it; it leads and guides us.

Honor the guidance of your heart, and
you will be honoring the guidance of love.

FEBRUARY 22

Magic Is in the Air

I left Washington's Hoh Rain Forest, pausing near the moss-covered trees. My walk through Moses Park had indeed been a trip to an enchanted forest.

Centuries-old trees, trees covered with mossy hair, shared their stories with me. Felled trees lying on their backs beckoned me to touch, to sit, to rest a while. Sunlight glistened through the entangled underbrush. The air smelled of nature's sawdust. The ground was warm, moist. Nature sprites danced and played along the path. The birds serenaded me with calls, whistles, and songs, like sounds emanating from a flute. Magic was in the air.

We can visit places that are magical to us, enchanted forests that remind us of life's wonders. We can visit them knowing that when we leave, we take their magic with us.

We'll see more and more of life's wonders in ourselves, in others, in the world we live in. People will appear in our lives at just the right time, saying the very words we need to hear. A book will speak to us. A new way to earn money will be revealed. A loved one may leave to follow his or her own path, and a new love will come into our lives. Old issues will be resolved. Healers will show up on our path. Ideas will come to us, seemingly out of the blue. They're gifts from the universe. We can have them whenever we want and wherever we go.

Come with me to the enchanted forest.
Trust the magic in the air; it is real. Take it
with you wherever you go, for the magic you
feel and want is yours if you simply believe.

FEBRUARY 23

Let Power Come Gently

Let your powers emerge gradually, gently.

Go gently on your path and look around. See what you have learned to define as power. See with the eyes of your heart.

You used to think you were powerful when you resisted your emotions, when you held back and didn't express yourself. You thought power came from being who you thought you should be, instead of who you are. Now you have learned that only when you are who you really are, can true power emerge.

The powers you've discovered are many. Your power to be decent, loving, and kind. Your power to heal, to be gentle, to comfort others. Your power to see and know the truth, and at times to see more than you can see with your eyes. Your power to take your place in the dance of universal love, and let the universe dance for you.

These powers have been gifts.
You've seen them. You understand
them. You know they're real. The
choice to embrace and use them
is yours.

FEBRUARY 24

There Is Power in Stillness

Our miracles and life's magic don't appear when we're restless and frantic. The miracles and magic happen when we're still, quiet, calm, and trusting.

Each of us has favorite items and places that help to calm and quiet us. What stills our mind? A walk in the park, a special place in the city, a quiet room? An old chenille robe? A rock, a cross, a picture, a lit candle?

Use these places and things to find that place of stillness in yourself. Find the power in stillness. It's a power that comes gently, like the morning sunrise or the evening stars.

Take time each day to seek out stillness,
to find that sacred spot. Let your mind
and soul be at ease. Don't grasp and grab

for the magic and miracles. When you reside in that place of stillness, the joy, miracles, and magic you're seeking will find you.

FEBRUARY 25

Learn to Help Heal Yourself

I feel a heaviness in my lungs, almost a pain; the next day, I find myself crying, discharging old grief and sadness. On another occasion, I feel sharp pangs in my stomach; within days, denied rage begins to surface and the pain subsides. My head aches, pounds, throbs; hours later, I feel the fear I've been running from. I feel the energy in my body shifting, moving, taking new shape; over the next months, I'm led into a new cycle, a new season in my life.

Some of the pains and illnesses we suffer from are indications of acute physical problems. They're signs that our body has broken down and we need medical attention. But many of the aches and pains we experience are symptoms of a deeper process—a process of healing and cleansing our heart and soul.

As we go through our daily experiences, circumstances will trigger this healing. Someone says something that makes us feel angry or afraid, which triggers a feeling similar to one we repressed years ago. Or a conversation causes us to remember something that hurt us long ago, and our body begins to release the pain of that old emotion. Sometimes, our aches and pains are signals that some emotion is ready to surface. We need to acknowledge the feeling, feel the energy, let it pass through us, then watch for the lesson to appear and the pain to dissipate.

If we are committed to a path of spiritual growth, our bodies will soon begin to use everything that happens as a vehicle for healing. Trust yourself and listen, and you'll know what to do. You'll find healers and help that will support you as you continue to discover and trust your soul.

Remember to trust the simple everyday wisdom of your body. It's a barometer for your soul.

FEBRUARY 26

Embrace the Lessons of Night

I reached Wyoming's Yellowstone Park late, much later than I had planned. The park was sprawling. I wasn't certain how to find the lodge. I couldn't find anyone to ask for help or directions. Tired and exhausted, I couldn't make sense of the map. I found myself driving around and around, becoming almost frantic.

Suddenly, beyond the treetops, I spotted a bright light. Good, I thought, it must be the lodge. I drove a little farther, then stopped the car and stared in awe. What I saw stilled my heart, and calmed my frantic pace.

Above Yellowstone Lake, nestled between two mountain peaks, glowed a huge, white, full moon, the largest I'd ever seen it. The pines stood guard, quiet and still. A light layer of snow and ice frosted the lake's surface. I pulled to the side of the road and watched the moon set. It was the single most beautiful, breathtaking scene of the journey.

I would never have seen this scene in the daytime. I would never have seen this moon, had I not gotten lost. I would never have seen it, had it not been this particular time of night. So maybe I'm not lost, I thought. And maybe I'm not late. Maybe what I'm really doing is taking a beautiful evening drive.

When we're lost, when the way gets dark, sometimes we see things we never would have seen in the daylight. Sometimes, the lessons we learn in the darkness are breathtakingly beautiful.

Enjoy the sunshine, but trust the darkness, too. It is more than to be endured. It is to be experienced, and later cherished.

FEBRUARY 27

Open to Life's Magic

"I will never forget my mother's words to me the first time she took me to the Hoh rain forest," a woman told me, when she learned I was going there. "We were at the edge of the forest, about to enter. My mother stopped walking and turned to me. 'There's magic here,' she said. It wasn't her words that impressed me. What struck me was the absolute certainty and matter-of-fact way she said it. It was like she had just told me, 'Dinner's ready.'"

There's magic in the air. It's the next place on the journey. It's inevitable. We have been clearing the path so we could do more than merely trudge down the road. The road leads to magic—a magical way of living. A magical way of being here. The magic in the air isn't an illusion, isn't a trick. You have done your work. You have stuck with the journey. Now is the time for fun, the time to see and know more of life's magical ways.

Walk lightly. Enter the enchanted forest. Look around. Keep your eyes and ears open. Tell others what you see. The journey to the heart is a journey of wonder and awe.

"The ancient ones, the trees, are waiting for you," the woman said. "When you get there, tell them I said hi." Open to life's magic. It's been waiting for your call.

FEBRUARY 28

Let Life's Rhythm Find You

I sat in my room, a small cabin in Chimayo, New Mexico. The clock whizzed through the hours, but I didn't whiz through my morning. I felt overwhelmed. Lost. I had more to do than I could handle. I didn't know where to begin. So there I sat. Stuck.

Genera, who ran the hostel, knocked on my door about noon. "Are you okay?" she asked. "Come have coffee and fruit with us." Her quiet kindness, her gentle concern, and the simple act of having coffee and fruit with a friend brought me back to balance.

There's a life force, a movement, a momentum that transcends our fears and hopes, our limitations, our overwhelmed feelings, and even our confusion. There's a heartbeat, a rhythm to life and the universe. It's gentle, easy, natural. It's in us; it's around us. It comes gently, naturally, like a friend knocking quietly on the door, asking if we are okay, if we have lost our way.

There is purpose, meaning, and rhythm to each step, each beat of your life. Each step, each feeling, each beat of your life is another mile traveled on your journey, your journey to your heart.

If you've lost your way and can't find life's rhythm, don't worry. Keep your heart open and it will find you.

FEBRUARY 29

See All the Landscape

Climb to the top of a mountain. What do you see? Valleys as well as mountains.

When you're on top of a mountain, you don't think, *This is all there is.* Or when you're driving through a hot, dusty valley, you don't think, *This is all there is.* You know there is more. You know the truth. Both exist, and more besides.

Life isn't an either/or situation. Don't work so hard forcing everything to be only good, delightful, joyous, or pleasant, for when you reach the valley, you'll become as miserably certain that life is only pain, sadness, and tragedy. You're wasting energy when you try to convince yourself that life is only one or the other.

Look around. See all the landscapes—valleys, oceans, plains, and, yes, mountaintops. That's what life is: all of it.

Enjoy the view.

March

MARCH 1

Find Healing and Magic Within Yourself

She was an Osage shaman. Her land, next to Cathedral Rock in Sedona, Arizona, was landscaped with a totem pole, a fire pit, a bridge leading to her house, and gardens of flowers and rocks. A river ran across her property, singing to all who quieted themselves enough to listen. A teepee stood close by, one used to house the sweat lodge ceremonies.

It was during one such ceremony I had met her. I returned later to talk with her for a while. She welcomed me back, welcomed all who had visited her to return to her land. She didn't call it *her* land, she called it *the* land. She said it belonged to us all.

"You don't have to take this journey," she said. "You don't have to travel around searching for spiritual spots. All the wisdom, the experiences, the spiritual places you seek on this quest are within you."

While it's fun to go on a trip, and trips often coincide with going to new places in our personal lives, we don't have to load up the car and hit the road to find what we're looking for. The places of power we seek are within us. Places of comfort, joy, wisdom, silence, healing, peace. The places we visit often reflect those qualities, reinforce them, remind us that they're there. But the places, the locations we visit, are only mirrors, extensions of ourselves.

The healing and magic we seek are not someplace else. They are within each of us.

MARCH 2

Value Your Past

Value your past and all the lessons you have learned.

How easy it is to diminish the importance of our past and look on our history with a critical eye. We see the mistakes, we see what we think we should have known, we see what we could have done better. What we forget is that the reason we are able to see so clearly is because of the past and because of what we have learned. Often, it is the very experiences we regret that have created this clear vision.

Value what you've learned in your past. Each lesson has led to the next. Every person and event in each part of your life has been invaluable in shaping and forming you—in creating the person you are today. Each part of your past, each person who has come into your life and shared experiences with you has helped you to open your heart more to life, love, God, others, and yourself. Even those experiences you think of as wrong, or mistakes, have been an important and necessary part in creating you. Sometimes, those experiences formed the most important parts of you because they created in you compassion and understanding for others. Often the most painful events of your life are the ones that opened you to your ability to bring healing, help, and hope to others. Your past taught you to love—others and yourself. It has helped you become a channel for Divine love and a force for good in this world.

When you look back at your past, look tenderly and gently at all you have been through. Look with the eyes of the soul. See that each experience was necessary to bring you home to your heart.

MARCH 3

Treasure Your Experiences

Gather experiences. Treat them as precious jewels.

The purpose of the journey is not to guard and restrain yourself. The purpose is to learn. You do not teach and lead your soul. Your soul leads and teaches you. It takes you wading across streams, strolling through meadows, deep into valleys, and high onto mountaintops. It takes you down winding, narrow roads and along fast-moving, four-lane highways. It takes you into tiny cafes, bustling cities, and out-of-the-way hostels where people break bread and tell what they have learned.

Let yourself have all your experiences. Don't limit or judge yourself or the adventures you have had. All were necessary, all were important, all have helped shape and form you. Your heart will lead you, guide you where you are to go. Don't worry about getting lost or off track. Don't worry about being wrong, or in the wrong place at the wrong time.

Gather experiences. Go through them. Select the gems from each. Listen while others tell their stories, their adventures, and show you their jewels, the truths that they have learned. Then, when you break bread and sip soup with others, open your heart and joyfully share what has happened to you along the way.

Having experiences is called living.
Sharing experiences is called loving.
Let yourself enjoy both.

MARCH 4

One Step at a Time

One step at a time. That's all you can take. That's all you have to take.

Yes, you have visions you've created of where you want to go. But you don't get there in one leap. You get there one step at a time. That's how you receive your guidance. That's how you respond to the guidance you've received.

Let your faith be strong. Your faith will keep you going through those moments in between steps. When your faith is strong, you don't look in fear at the journey ahead, wondering if you will get all the guidance you need, or if you will get to where you're going. You know you will, so you take the simple steps, one at a time, that lie ahead. You take them in joy, because you know you're being guided. You have faith that the simple steps you are led to do will take you to your destination.

One step at a time. That's how you will get where you are going. You are being led, each step of the way.

MARCH 5

Operate from Desire, Not Will

There are times when we need to force ourselves to put one foot in front of the other and do what needs to be done. But when we operate that way for too long, we can be separated from our heart, separated from our desires, instincts, and healthy inclinations. Separated from that part of us that lives and loves naturally. Separated from joy.

After years of grieving the loss of my son, I needed to come back to life. To do that, I had to force myself through the motions of living, those acts that I knew would create a good life for myself and my daughter. I was operating from sheer will, and that will was struggling hard to overcome the desire to give up. After a time of doing that though, I noticed that forcing myself forward had come habitual. Somewhere along the journey, I had forgotten about relaxing, trusting my heart, trusting my desires to carry me through. I became tired. Tired of forcing myself. Tired of pushing through.

I realized something else. It was safe to let go of willing my way through life. I had climbed the mountain. I was over the top. I was coming alive again. I had survived the toughest time. It was okay to relax and trust the guidance and desires of my heart. It was safe to relax and enjoy life again, to celebrate being alive.

If you've been operating from will, that was probably what you needed to do at that point in your life. It helped you survive, learn the lessons, get to the place you are now. But it no longer fits, not on a journey of joy. Not on the journey to the heart.

Let desire and inclination replace will. Let your heart and soul lead you forward. Then trust that they will, and trust where they lead. Let living from your heart's desires reconnect you to joy.

MARCH 6

Let Your Sexuality Be Connected to Your Heart

He was a handsome man. An actor. "Something's happened to me lately," he shared. "It's about my sexuality. I used to be sexual when and where I felt like it. No more. And it's not connected to fear of disease, although that's certainly a concern. What happened to me is that my sexuality has become connected to my heart."

Let go of sexual shame. Embrace your sensuality. Value your senses, all of them—touch, smell, taste, seeing, and hearing. Value your other senses, too—your intuition, your spirituality, your spirit's reaction to the world that dances around you. Open up to colors, textures, scents, and sounds.

Open up to your energy, all of it, including your sexuality. Let yourself see that all expressions of your love and your being are beautiful. Let yourself learn to express and receive love in sensual ways, ways that work for you.

Be done with sexual shame. Trust your body and what it likes. We aren't disconnected parts. Open up. Discover your sexuality. Let it be connected to your heart.

MARCH 7

Redefine Service

Service is a key, an important one. It's a key to joy, to love. And a gold key to the journey.

How long we thought service meant doing everything for everyone. How long we thought service had to be hard, taxing, boring—that it meant doing something we didn't want to do to help someone who didn't want to be helped.

Now, we're defining service differently. Service is joyful. It's an attitude, a belief, a way of looking at ourselves and our lives. Our very life is service. Our being is service. Service arises and springs naturally out of self-love. It arises from being who we are and from doing the things we want to do and are led to do. The things that bring us the most joy will bring the most service to the world. Doing things we don't want to do will leave us and the world around us cold, untouched, unmoved.

Service is love and joy. Service is being who you are. Bask in self-love. Service will flow naturally from that. It will be freely given and freely received. And now what you do will really help.

MARCH 8

Your Dreams Are Important

A woman told me about a dream she had, one that was bothering her deeply. "What do you think it means?" she asked.

"I don't know," I replied. "Besides, it doesn't matter what I think. The important thing is what you think. What's it telling you?"

We dream two kinds of dreams—waking dreams and sleeping dreams. Both are powerful forms of consciousness. Our sleeping dreams, the images that dance in our minds while we sleep, hold many clues to life, growth, the future, the past, healing, and our connections with others. They may reveal suppressed emotions. They may be bits and pieces of prophecy. They may be symbols of truths we're about to learn.

Our waking dreams are important, too. We go about daily with our expectations, wants, desires, hopes—our heart's plan for the future. We may not express these dreams. We may not even realize we are superimposing them on our lives, much the same way we can forget what we dream when we sleep.

There's power in allowing ourselves to become conscious of our dreams. What are our dreams telling us about what we want, fear, hope for, desire? Expressing our dreams will connect us to our consciousness and a higher consciousness. Expressing them will connect us to the creative force. Tapping into our dreams helps us tap into creativity—creativity for our lives, creativity for projects, the powerful creative force of the universe.

There's power in dreaming, whether we're asleep or awake. Take time to honor and express your dreams.

MARCH 9

Let Your Visions Guide You

Visions are different from dreams. A vision is a picture that comes from the soul and comes out through the heart.

A vision is a small glimpse of light that shines and shows us our path. It is a quick flash of something that hasn't happened yet. It may tell us something about today or ten years from now. Visions occur when our souls look at the map for our lives, get a sense of where we're going, and tell our hearts how to find that place. The more conscious and clear and direct we are, the more we can tune into and help create the highest vision for our lives.

What do you want? What would feel right? What do you see yourself doing? Be clear and concise, then let it go. Sometimes when we run out of dreams, we have to rely on our visions, these small glimpses of light, to lead the way. Learn to see the visions in your heart. Learn to trust them. Learn to help create them. Allow them to manifest themselves. When the path is dark, learn to be comfortable with these small bursts of light.

Let your visions guide you home.

MARCH 10

Beware of Gossip

Gossip is a seductive pastime that can be harmful to others, harmful to ourselves. Some gossip is innocent. We chatter about the experiences of others lightly, joyfully, in a way that doesn't hurt. Other gossip isn't so innocent. It's rooted in anger, jealousy, betrayal, and sometimes hatred. We feel deprived and cheated—hurt—so we want to hurt another.

Would you stand and throw darts at someone? Would you pick up a knife and stab that person in the back? I think not. Yet, when we gossip, we do the same thing. Words, especially those coated with emotion, carry energy, sometimes potentially damaging energy. When we hurt another, we hurt ourselves. Both are injured. We need to deal with our feelings of anger, hurt, betrayal, or jealousy before they wound through gossip.

While walking this journey,
you must learn of the dangers.
Gossip is one of them. Heal
the feelings underneath so
you can speak lightly with
words of love.

MARCH 11

Enjoy the Changing Scenery

How easy it is to think, *I will be feeling like this forever.* But look at how quickly the scenery changes!

In the space of a few hours while driving down the highway, we can see mountains, deserts, a petrified forest, and iron-rich mesas. In the space of a day we can see courage, faith, despair, desolation, anger, healing, and joy. If there's one thing that's true, it's this: the universe is always changing. It is constant, continual evolution.

The same holds true for the minutes, hours, and days of our lives. We are continually changing and shifting. Each emotion, attitude, and experience—each piece of scenery—leads into the next. Put them all together and what do you have? A grand journey—an exciting trip that leads to someplace worth going and someplace worth being, each moment you are here.

Look at how quickly the scenery
changes. Learn to enjoy the view.

MARCH 12

You Have the Power to Redefine Your World

One power we gain on our journey to the heart is the ability to redefine what we believe. We learn to see things in a new way.

We usually have a definition for most areas of our lives, particularly important areas such as work, love, money, and ourselves, but we're not always conscious of it. The experiences we go through can help our definitions surface, help us see more clearly how we define these areas. That's called growth. This growth, this process of redefining, will happen naturally on our path. But we can also consciously, actively work on our definitions.

Ask yourself if you're defining something or someone right now in a way that you'd like to change. Perhaps a work relationship, a love relationship, a project, or an issue is causing you distress. You may find you have the power to redefine this area in a way that minimizes or reduces your pain.

A healing professional and friend once taught me a technique that can be used on any subject you're trying to define. On a sheet of paper write down everything you currently believe, including and especially everything negative, about the subject or issue. Include all the "I Can'ts" and the "Why Nots." That's your current definition.

On a clean sheet of paper write down how you want to redefine this area and your involvement in it. Write down everything you want it to be, what you wish for it, what you think the highest truth possible about this subject could be.

Burn the paper with the old definition. Let the smoke clear away from your eyes. Save your new definition. Then watch how the new definition comes to life and takes shape.

You don't have to let past definitions of life, love, God, and yourself limit you anymore. You are free to redefine and help create the life you choose; you're free to see life in a new way.

MARCH 13

Connect to Creativity

The more open and connected you are to the world around you, the more creative you will become.

You will become more creative in your own growth and in how you live your life. You will be more creative in problem solving in work and in play. You'll be more willing to try new things—whether it's learning to play a flute, build a stone fence, ride a horse, or create a Japanese garden in your front yard. You'll find yourself more open in solving problems with loved ones, trying less traditional approaches than you might have considered in the past. You'll find yourself gaining insights, information, and healing from sources you may have previously overlooked. Your participation in all your activities will be less controlled and more spontaneous.

You will hear the universe prompting you more. You will imagine more. You will recognize the quiet voice of intuition, the voice of your heart. You will see possibilities. And because you are open to your heart, the guidance of your inner voice, you will know what to do, and when to do it.

The more connected you are to the universe, to life, to yourself, the more you creative you will be.

MARCH 14

Observe Yourself

Watch yourself. That's not a grim admonition. It's a call to observe yourself and is a helpful tool on the journey.

When you get stuck in a behavior, stuck in a pattern, stuck in a place, a thought, a feeling, a job, or a relationship and you don't know how to get unstuck, watch yourself. When you've tried everything you know and your feelings and old ways of reacting still come to the fore—even when you don't want them to and especially when you've made an effort to do things differently—watch yourself. When it feels hopeless, when it seems things will never change or shift, when you can't help yourself and it doesn't look like those around you can either, look at yourself.

The act of watching ourselves, neutrally observing ourselves without judgment or reproach, can be a powerful tool for change. If you've tried and tried to change but it hasn't worked, then watch yourself. Watch what you say, what you think, how you feel, how you act, how you react. Don't try to stop yourself. Don't judge. Just observe. Do it as long as you need to, although it may not take long.

Watch yourself. Then watch how you grow and change.

MARCH 15

Learn to Say Good-Bye

Sometimes we need to say good-bye. Some good-byes come suddenly, without warning. Others are anticipated. Sometimes they're a relief. And sometimes they hurt deeply. We say good-bye to things, people, and places. We say good-bye to beliefs and behaviors that become outdated.

Occasionally along the journey we need to say good-bye to something else, too—our dreams.

Dreams are precious. They become embedded in our minds and our hearts. When they die, it can be painful to let go of them. But if we're not careful, dead dreams we haven't released can sabotage our lives and hearts. We will continue to try to place people and things in the vacant roles in our dreams. Our dead dreams will, in fact, be controlling our lives and blocking our hearts. Living with dreams that are dead closes the door to finding new visions and creating new dreams.

If you can't see today or tomorrow clearly because of yesterday's dreams, it may be time for a funeral. Tenderly take your dearest dreams, your highest hopes and aims—the ones from yesterday that are now never to be—and place them gently in the ground. Tell them how dear they were, and are. But tell them also, it's time to say good-bye. Cover them up. Dry your eyes.

And open yourself to the new hopes and dreams of today.

MARCH 16

Become Willing to Heal Your Heart

We don't open our hearts by being a tower of strength. We don't open our hearts by glossing over things in our head. We open our hearts by feeling what we feel. We open our hearts by being vulnerable, honest, and gentle.

We've become so strong, so self-sufficient. *I can deal with that,* we say. *No big deal. I'll keep moving on.*

Yet many circumstances we've been through, and some we're going through now, cause break lines in our heart. Some of the fractures are small. Some are big. They really hurt. Maybe certain people in our lives weren't there for us, aren't there for us now in a way we'd like them to be. Maybe some deceived us unconsciously or betrayed us deliberately. *I can deal with that,* we say. *I understand. They have their own issues. I forgive . . .*

Yes, people do have their own issues. And we do forgive. But now it may be time to learn gentleness, compassion, understanding, and forgiveness for ourselves as well.

We don't open our hearts by ignoring the break lines. We take our hand, knowing it's held by God, and gently run our fingers across each crack. Yes, it's there. Yes, I feel it.

Yes, I'm ready to heal my heart.

MARCH 17

Cherish Hope

It was a beautiful city in Idaho. The lake that ran alongside the highway was so clear and blue, I pulled the Jeep to the roadside just to stop and stare. The air was clear. The city felt light, airy, buoyant. It's name was Hope.

I didn't stay long. I didn't need to. But I needed to drive by, drive through, pause for a moment to remember another important power to discover and cherish on our journey. Hope is airy, almost intangible, yet if we don't have it, we know it. Hope is simple. Clear.

Light. Our hearts, our souls, need a good glimpse of it every so often, just to keep us going.

Even those times we can't have what we want, we can be open to seeing its light shining unexpectedly in another direction, like this small town that caught my eye.

Cherish hope. It adds buoyancy
to the spirit, lightness to the day.

MARCH 18

Heart Connections

I went into the office at the lodge where I stayed in Sedona. I turned in my room key, then pulled out my camera and took a picture of Marianne. We had only known each other for eight days, but I felt deeply connected to her. We had been through a series of experiences that would probably stay with me for life. They had changed my life.

When we hugged and said good-bye, I told her not to cry—but she did anyway. So did I. "Call me whenever you want," she said. "I'll be there for you." I knew what she meant. She didn't mean for me to call her on the phone, although that was okay, too. She meant call her in my heart, call her to me in spirit.

For a long time, our connections to people and places may have come from someplace other than our hearts. We may have been connected out of need, fear, unfinished business, or simply the unwillingness to leave—to know there was any other way to be connected. Or we may not have even felt particularly connected to the people around us.

Now is a different time. It is time now to let your connections come from your heart. Open up. Listen. Does someone have something to say, maybe only a sentence or two, that's just what you need to hear? As you're going through your day, does someone come to mind, someone you think about getting in touch with?

Don't shrug off the things you know and sense. Be open to your inner voice. Do what it leads you to do. Love isn't bound by time or space when our connections come from our heart.

MARCH 19

Get Back in Your Body

Whenever you find yourself drifting away, losing touch with yourself, jumping from the present moment to some far-off point in the future, get back in your body.

Instinctively, when we become afraid or find ourselves in a painful situation, we may leave our bodies temporarily. We may shut down, move our consciousness out, abandon or ignore ourselves.

Sometimes, it's natural to go numb, to just go through the motions until things calm down. It's easier than feeling. But shutting down our bodies and emotions—disappearing—as a way of life won't get us where we're going—to the heart. Living with an open heart means we stay present for ourselves and feel as much as we can, as much as we need to. We feel the feelings that come our way.

You are safe now. You know how to own your power. You know how to lovingly care for and nurture yourself. You know how to trust

God and the universe to help you. You know you can trust yourself. You are safe now, safe enough to feel.

Deliberately, consciously, get back in your body. Feel your feet, head, arms, legs. Feel your heart; listen to it beat. Rub your shoulders. Massage your feet.

You're powerful now, and powerfully connected to yourself. Get back in your body. Come back to life.

MARCH 20

Learn to Heal Yourself

Sometimes we trick ourselves. If we feel unhappy, troubled, or scared, we race toward what we think will make us feel better. In desperation, in fear, we grasp for something, anything to stop our pain. Finding that job. Making more money. Getting married. Having a relationship. *If I get that one thing I need, then I'll be happy. Then my pain will stop.*

Sometimes it's true that finding the solution to a problem improves the quality of our lives. Having enough money enables us to fix the furnace when it breaks. Having people in our lives we love and who love us can be an important part of our happiness. Having work to do that we enjoy and that we feel is worthwhile helps us feel good about ourselves.

But when we're in pain—no matter what's causing it—the way to heal that pain doesn't come from outside of ourselves. External circumstances don't make internal emotions disappear. Even if we get what we think we want, the painful emotion we haven't had the strength or courage to face will still be there.

The way to heal pain, the only way, is to feel and release it. Your pain is your pain. Your fear, desperation, and resentments are yours, too. All these emotions belong to you. Feel them, learn from them, and let them go.

Walk courageously each step of the path on the journey to the heart. Enjoy when the universe sends you its gifts—a lover, some money, a good job. But know the ultimate key to happiness lies not in external things, but within you. Feel all your feelings. Learn to heal yourself.

MARCH 21

Nurture the Seasons of Your Soul

Study nature's ways. Learn her rhythms, her seasons, her cycles. See how she hibernates and rests during the cold winter, using that time to replenish and heal. See how she bursts forth in a slow crescendo of green and bright colors over the spring, rejoicing in the inevitable new growth. See how she gives her all, her grandest performance, over the summer months before gradually descending into a final burst of changing colors in autumn. Watch her cool down, return to her depths, and again take time to replenish.

These same seasons are within us. There are times to take action, to be busily involved with creating and doing and participating and giving. There are quieter times when we are being prepared for those times of activity. We cannot give and give without taking time to replenish ourselves. There are times of gentle growth when the first blades of grass, the first signs of spring begin to emerge in our lives—whether those signal a new stage of personal growth, a new stage in a love relationship, or the first buds of life on a project we're creating.

And each season, each time, leads into the next.

There is purpose and value in each day of your life, in each season of your life. Nurture your times of action, of creating, of doing, and value your quieter times of going within. The more you study nature, the more you will learn about yourself. Nurture and trust the seasons of your soul.

MARCH 22

Don't Be Controlled by Love

Using love to control and manipulate is heartbreaking. It can break the heart of the person doing it; it can break the heart of the person it's being done to.

So often, controlling through love is done almost unconsciously. It's a dance people do out of habit to get their needs met. Their reasons don't matter, although it's easier to have compassion for those who control unknowingly than those who use the power of love maliciously and viciously.

What matters is how you respond if it's being done to you. What matters is that you don't do it to other people.

Open your heart and see the truth. Set yourself free. If someone is controlling you by using your love for them or your need to be loved, acknowledge it. If you are doing it to someone else, acknowledge that, too. Once you see the truth, you can set yourself free.

So much of what we need to do to free our hearts and souls is simply to acknowledge the truth. The rest will happen naturally.

Love has no price. It's only love if it's free.

MARCH 23

Comfort Yourself

I was driving through Montana, on my way to a town on the Flathead Indian Reservation. I was going there because an old hotel, opened in 1928, noted for its medicinal mineral waters had caught my attention. As I pulled off the highway and began the drive down the side roads, I felt an environmental ambiance I hadn't experienced before.

The hills were huge mounds, covered with a soft-green, grassy moss. Not steep sharp mountains; comforting, rounded hills—one after another. A gentle energy emanated from them. It was more than love. More than kindness. I felt comforted, embraced, almost held by Mother Earth in her bosom. My body relaxed. My spirit soared. I felt warm. Cared for. Nurtured. Comforted.

Comfort is a place we can visit often, as often as we need to. Although certain places and objects help comfort us, it is really a place within each of us. Some of us may have thought that comfort was a waste of time, but now we know that there is tremendous power in comfort, the power to heal. We no longer have to deprive ourselves of comfort, of that warm feeling of being nurtured. We can visit it for ourselves; we can take others there with us.

What brings you comfort? What makes you feel safe, cozy, warm, loved? What places? What people? What events? Learn to comfort yourself. Learn to accept comfort, and learn to give it. Go to that special place of comfort whenever you need to. Stay as long as you wish. The healing power of comfort will make life better.

MARCH 24

Tap into Life's Energy

Life is not something separate or apart from you, as you once believed. There is a power, a life force, that moves, guides, directs, and inspires you. You are one with life, with life's energy.

Do things that energize you, charge your soul. Soak up the sun. Soak up color. Soak up beautiful sounds. Immerse yourself in nature, in a world that refreshes, restores, and renews. Don't worry about the task or the day that looms ahead, the work and love and play, the problems and choices that are on the way. If you energize yourself, restore yourself, the power to take action will come naturally like water from a spring.

Look around. What do you see that feels right to do? Which direction do you see as the right way to go? Trust the smallest glimmer. Give in to the urge, to the guidance that's there. Do it once. Do it again. Soon you will find yourself in harmony.

You will have all the guidance, energy, ideas, creativity, power, and ability you need to do all you're meant to do. And you will be given the power to enjoy it.

Break Through Your Blocks

I was walking at a good clip down sandy Colony Beach when it happened. Without warning, I began running. I ran the longest distance I had ever before run. Instead of collapsing in a panting heap, I kept running. Another stretch. Then another. By the time I tired, I had run a mile. The furthest I had ever before run in my life was about a quarter block.

I didn't intend to make this breakthrough. I was so blocked in this area I didn't think I could. Running wasn't even a goal. I had simply incorporated regular walks into my lifestyle as a way of exercising my body. This event surprised me because I'm not a physical fitness buff. I hadn't been allowed to participate in any physical education or sports activities as a child or teenager because of chronic health ailments. I spent many of my adult years neglecting my body. Lately, I had put some effort into connecting with my body and working out in an amateurish fashion. But running? Not me. Or so I used to think.

The next time I went walking, I felt timid, almost afraid to even try running. I wondered if what I had experienced was a fluke. It wasn't. I ran again, and again. Now, running is a regular part of my physical activity, one I truly enjoy.

Sometimes, we're so blocked in a particular area we don't even consider a breakthrough a possibility. We're so blocked we don't even see our blocks. Stay open. Don't limit yourself. Something that yesterday seemed entirely unfeasible and forever beyond your grasp may tomorrow, next month, next year—or today—become something you can do naturally, something that's available to you. It can come as a total surprise, in an area you hadn't considered. Your breakthrough may happen in an area you've been struggling with, and working on.

> *Life is more than setbacks, and it's not static. Appreciate and respect where you are now. But let yourself move to the next level when it's time. Celebrate your breakthroughs when they come. Listen to that quiet voice, that fleeting thought that says,* Why don't you . . . ?, *even if it's something you've never done before.*

MARCH 26

Make Each Moment Count

"A picture isn't taken *in* a moment," stated the brochure for the Cottonwood, Colorado, hotel. "It's taken *of* a moment."

It took me a long time to learn that important truth. I spent years trying to get my life together and keep it together, as though it were a solid chunk that could be arranged in a certain place, then made to stay there. It took me a long time to learn about moments.

In many ways, our lives are like a movie reel, made up of individual frames and single moments each one leading into the next. It is a waste of energy to try and hold on to the moments of the past. By the time we begin reaching for them, they're gone. It is just as poor timing to try to jump into moments that have not arrived yet—the future.

Stay in the present moment, the frame you're in now. That's the only moment where happiness, joy, and love can be found. And remember to make each moment count.

M A R C H 2 7

Resentments Hurt Everybody

Resentments only hurt ourselves? Not true. Resentments can hurt others, too.

When we brood and allow resentments to brew and fester, we send negative, mean, hurtful, spiteful energy to others. The more consciously and vividly we do this, the more pain we can cause everyone. The more bonded we are with others, whether they're business associates, friends, lovers, or family members, the more powerfully our resentments can impact them as well as us.

So if you're busy thinking resentful thoughts about someone close to you on the job or at home, consider the harm you are doing to him or her. The more powerful the emotions connected to these thoughts and the closer you are to the person, the more damage you can do. You can sabotage the other person, help keep him or her down. Even if you don't speak your resentments aloud, even if you try to hide the way you feel, the energy is there in the air hurting both of you. Just as we focus on clearing the air we breathe of toxins, we need to cleanse the air around us at work and at home from the toxic fumes of resentment.

Remember, when we harbor hate, jealousy, or rage, we connect to others in ways that hurt us all. Let's set others free. Let's release our resentments. Along the way, we'll set ourselves and our hearts free, too.

MARCH 28

Discover New Beliefs

The drive from Zion National Park to Bryce Canyon in Utah was a short one. I had traveled the same route several times. At a certain pass, no matter how sunny the day and cloudless the sky, it was raining there every time. Although it was hard to see, a small dark cloud seemed to hang over this one particular place, this one area of the road, all the time.

It may be like that in a particular area of our lives. A certain belief seems almost stuck to us, stuck to one area of our lives, and no matter how sunny the rest of the drive, it's raining there all the time. What cloud is hanging over you? Could it be one you're helping to create?

Some beliefs—*My choices are wrong, I make bad decisions, I'm wrong*—can create a dark heaviness that hangs over us like a cloud. These beliefs may be so subtle we don't notice them. What we do notice is a lingering pain or anxiety, a cloud that seems to follow us around. What we don't see is that we're helping create and maintain our own cloud with these beliefs.

The lesson may not be to make better decisions or be a better person. The lesson may be much simpler: change your beliefs. Make some new decisions. Let yourself discover some new, better, sunnier beliefs about yourself and your life. Allow yourself to believe that the decisions you make are fine.

Who you are is okay.
You always have been.

MARCH 29

Move Gently into Forgiveness

"I never knew how much I blamed and hated myself. I never knew how much shame and self-contempt I picked up from situations I'd been through until I really forgave myself and felt how that feels," one woman said to me.

Loving yourself, forgiving yourself, accepting yourself—all of these feel different from judging yourself. Many of us have lived with so much judgment of ourselves that we take these feelings for granted. We just think that's how we're doomed to feel. Until we do forgive ourselves, we don't realize how much we need to, and how good, how great, how absolutely terrific that feels.

I was leery of forgiveness for many years. I thought forgiving implied judging. And because judging was wrong and I shouldn't do it, I didn't need to forgive. The problem was, whether right or wrong, I had judged myself. And now I needed forgiveness.

Self-judgments set us apart, separate us from the rest of the world in an undesirable way. Forgiving ourselves reconnects us to the world, to God, to ourselves.

We can forgive ourselves for what we've done wrong, what we've done badly, and what we think we could have done better. We can transcend our judgments of ourselves.

Move gently into forgiveness. Love, forgive,
and accept yourself. See how connected you

feel. See how free you really are and always have been. See how much better you feel!

MARCH 30

Who or What Is Pulling on You?

Learn to become sensitive to the quiet as well as the clamorous pulls on your energy, your time, your emotions. You are becoming connected—to yourself, the universe, God, others—in a way you have never been before. To deny these pulls is to deny the connections.

A quiet tug on our consciousness may be telling us what we need to do. We think about an old friend and contemplate calling her, but we don't. *Don't be silly,* we tell ourselves. *Why would I do that now?* But maybe that friend is calling out to us. Or we have a problem we haven't known how to solve. That situation begins working on us, bothering us, interrupting our day. Maybe our instincts are telling us it's now time to do something about it.

We are living differently now, more magically, more at ease, more at one with our actions. One way we know it is time to do something not on the calendar or the clock is to pay attention to the quiet pulls on our energy. Being conscious of these impulses, then trusting ourselves to naturally know what to do and when to do it puts us in harmony with the universe and our soul.

Who or what is pulling on you? What do you think you should do? Now, take it to the next step, the next level. What does your heart lead you do to?

MARCH 31

Take the Pressure Off

Sometimes we need a little pressure to get moving, but sometimes we put too much pressure on ourselves. *I must do this,* we think, *and I must do it better and faster.* We begin to believe that only by worry and fear and pressuring ourselves can we get the job done—whether the job is spiritual growth, making a particular decision, or accomplishing a task.

That kind of pressure doesn't get the job done any better or faster. It simply makes you tense and fearful, and stops the creative juices. Too much pressure can take you out of the present moment. It can inhibit the life force, the flow of life within you. That kind of pressure can make so much noise in your mind that you can't hear your heart.

We have responsibilities. We have time frames and commitments to others. And there are times when we need to get the job done. But the most pressing job can be done best when we're relaxed. The most urgent decision can be made most clearly when we're at peace. It doesn't help to force ourselves to go faster, be somewhere else, or be someone we're not. There are few things we need to do that can be enhanced by becoming tense, fearful, and worried. The more pressing the situation, the more pressing the need to be present for ourselves, and be present for each moment.

Let off some steam. Release your emotions. Clear the pathway to the heart. The answer will come. The job will get done.

Give yourself some relief.
Take the pressure off.

April

APRIL 1

Learn to Clear Your Path

I met a woman at the mineral springs in Ojo Caliente, New Mexico. She had a gentle, open way. She talked to me about rituals, about miracles, about change. "My husband and I badly wanted a child, but I couldn't get pregnant," she said. "One night, I decided to go to a mikvah, a Jewish ritual bath. My decision felt powerful. But every obstacle you could imagine happened when I tried to get there. I could barely get out of my house. Then when I did, I got lost and had to go back home for directions. When I finally got to the bath, it was just beginning, but I knew I needed to be there. The night was electric. The air felt as if it were charged with lightning. It was a full moon. I went through the ritual and returned home. That night, my daughter was conceived. She's now seven years old."

There are often obstacles on our path. Roadblocks, barricades, detours. Things to go over, around, or under. Sometimes, the roadblocks are telling us no, this door isn't opening. Find another way.

Other times the roadblocks are telling us that the road we have chosen is very special. If we want to go down it, we will have to try. We will have to focus. We will have to muster our energy and show the world how badly we want it. We will have to overcome each and every obstacle, one by one, as they appear.

What do you want badly? Are you willing to go through an obstacle course, if need be, to achieve it? Are you willing to be tested by the universe? Are you willing to focus, push forward, go the distance?

Sometimes, the road ahead is blocked, but clearing the way becomes part of our journey. Learn to tell when it's time to let go, to surrender, to search for another road, a different path, another dream. But also learn to tell when it's time to move forward, through obstacles if need be, because the dream is electric, charged by Divine energy and love.

APRIL 2

Discover the Power of Meditation

I saw Spirit Rock Center, a meditation center, as I drove along the highway in Northern California. I turned into the parking lot and watched as people moved about the grounds very slowly. They were practicing a walking meditation.

Meditation teaches us to relax, to connect with our body, to let spirit and body become one. Many of us spent years abandoning ourselves, our emotions, and our bodies. We've been present for others, and now is the time for us to stay present for ourselves, fully and completely.

Meditation helps us leave our routine for a bit and slow down. We deliberately exhale stress, tension, and fear. Then we inhale light, beauty, peace, and love. We slow our minds and slow our bodies until we reach that quiet place. Meditation can renew us and help us return to our lives refreshed.

Meditate. Take time to inhale peace and exhale fear. Then take your meditation back to your life. Walk slowly. Stay present for yourself, more fully and completely than ever before. You too can turn your life into a walking, waking, deliberate meditation.

APRIL 3

Value Your Connection to Creativity

Creativity is a force—a living, real force. It's the power of love, the power of life, a gift of the Divine. You're connected to that force.

Open up to your creative powers—in work, in play, in love. Make creations that are beautiful to look at. Make creations you like to see, creations that are pleasing to you. Creativity comes in many forms—cooking, decorating, speaking, drawing, writing, or building a castle in sand at the beach. How you choose to create is up to you.

"I used to love taking pictures when I was a child," one man said. "Then one day, in a rage, my father smashed my camera to the floor. He told me taking pictures was nonsense. It was twenty years before I let myself take a picture again. Now, I can't stop."

Who told you you weren't creative? Stand tall, speak up, and tell them they're wrong. Own your creative powers. Allow your creativity to heal and flourish.

Value your connection to creativity. Value the way you choose to express your creative power. It's your expression of love.

APRIL 4

Wait for Timely Action

Watch the surfer as he works his way out to sea. See him watching the waves, waiting for the right movement, the right timing, the right swell. Sometimes the wave comes quickly. Sometimes he has to tread water patiently for a long time, waiting and watching before he can ride the wave.

Learn to ride the waves of energy in your life. Learn to wait for the right time to take action. Learn to wait until your senses, your emotions, your body, and the universe give you the signal you need. Yes, you have a list of things you want to do. But as soon as you have made that list, visualized what you want, you've already begun a powerful force. You've already begun to engage the universe in helping bring you want you want. There are moments that are more perfect than others to initiate action, to make that phone call, to finish that task.

Untimely action will not get the job done any sooner. It will simply waste your energy and send you back to sea, waiting for the right wave. Focus on your goal, muster all your forces, and head out to sea. Then wait patiently for the right time, for the right energy, for the right wave.

The right wave will come. When it does, grab your board, jump on, and ride it for all it's worth.

APRIL 5

Develop a Sense of the Sacred

During my stay in New Mexico, I found myself repeatedly—almost magnetically—drawn to the Ojo Caliente Hot Springs. The grounds weren't fancy; soaking cost only $8.00. But I felt so safe, healed, spiritually connected when I was there. At times, I felt almost an electric energy coursing through my body when I roamed the grounds. On my third visit, I noticed a small marker hidden on the side of the parking lot and I began to understand my feelings. The ancient spring was actually a Native American sacred site. The energy I felt there was real. I was standing on holy ground.

Develop a sense of the sacred. Develop a sense of what is sacred to you. Allow yourself to see and feel the holy grounds in your life as you go through your days and years. Many times what we're going through, what we're seeing is sacred, but our minds diminish that idea. So much in life is holy, but often we don't make the connection. Listen to your soul as you experience life. Let yourself connect with what is holy and sacred to you.

Stop chattering for a moment. Be still. Experience. Ask your soul to show you what's holy. The electric energy will rise through you. Your soul will come to attention. Learn to feel, see, and know the beauty of thc journey you're on.

Develop a sense of the sacred.
Where you're standing is holy ground.

APRIL 6

Be Present for Yourself

Learn to be present for yourself, fully present in a way that's new and delightful. Be present for your thoughts and emotions. Be present for the gentle way in which your heart and body lead you on. Learn to be fully present for each step of your growth, each step of your journey.

Value yourself, who you are, what you think and feel, and how you grow. For many years you neglected yourself. It was as though you were unconscious of who you were, how you felt, what you believed. You believed that kept you safe, protected you from feelings you didn't want to feel. You believed it was how you should live. Now you are learning another way. Survival is no longer enough. It does not meet the needs of your heart and your soul. Now you want to live fully and joyfully. To do that, you must be present for yourself.

Be fully present for others, too. Be present for their spirits, their emotions, the words they have to say to you, but especially be present for their hearts. You no longer have to fear losing or neglecting yourself if you are present for others. You can do this safely now. You will not be consumed by their needs; you will not become trapped in the workings of their lives. And if you're present for yourself, you'll know how much presence to give to others.

Be present for life—for the starlit skies and the chirping birds that sing to the morning sun. Be present for the earth and grass under your feet, for the feel of a snowflake in your hand. Be present for all the magic and mysteries of the universe.

But most of all, be present for yourself. Then your presence for others and life will naturally follow.

APRIL 7

What Are You Resisting Most?

Be open to the whole journey, all parts of it.

Is there a feeling, a person, a thought, a project that you have been avoiding? Is there some part of your life that you're refusing to deal with or open up to? Is there something you're resisting, something that makes you stubbornly say *no?* Ignore the voice that says, *This is how I decided it will be, so I will close off to that part; I will not consider it.* That is the voice of resistance.

Be open to everything. Your most valuable lessons may well come from the things you're resisting most.

APRIL 8

Enjoy the Adventure

It was a cold night in Sedona, Arizona. An unexpected snowstorm had passed through the usually warm city, dumping several inches of snow in a short time. The electricity was off. The cabin I was staying in was freezing.

Great, I thought. *I get to spend my last evening in Sedona fighting off hypothermia alone in the dark.* I put on a heavy sweater, then wrapped myself in a blanket, trudged to a phone booth, and called a friend to complain.

"Change your perspective," he said. "Pretend you're four years old. Get your flashlight. Then make a tent in your bed out of all the pillows and blankets you can find. Enjoy the adventure!"

At first I balked, then I decided to try this idea. I made the tent. Bundled up. My complaints quickly turned to memories of what it was like to be a child, to play with life, to play with all the experiences life brings. Soon I fell asleep.

When I awoke in the morning, the heat was back on. The lights had returned. The snow had stopped falling. Capped in a frosty layer of white, the breathtaking city of rust-iron mesas looked like a wonderland. I had learned another lesson, practical and simple.

Change your perspective and
enjoy the adventure. Let the child
in you come out to play.

APRIL 9

Take Better Care of Yourself

Take better care of yourself than you ever have before. That's what your heart is telling you to do.

Those times of driving yourself, depriving yourself, not being gentle and loving with yourself will no longer work. Punishing, criticizing, repressing, and denying won't bring the feelings, the growth, the result you're seeking. The harder you push, the more you relentlessly demand perfection, the worse you'll feel.

Fall in love with yourself. Be gentle, loving, kind, and attentive. Take time throughout each day to tend to your needs, just as you would tend to someone you loved deeply and dearly. Loving and caring for yourself this way won't waste time. It's not a delay. Take better care of yourself, and life's magic will return. Your life will improve. You'll feel better, too.

Taking care of yourself is a simple act with profound consequences. The better and more often you care for yourself, the more you'll align with the universe and God's love.

APRIL 10

Be Aware of the Energy Around You

I stopped at a quaint little store in the mountain city of Solvang, California. It was filled with clocks, tick, tick, ticking away. Some sang, some chirped. Some just ticked. "If you wind them and leave them together long enough, they'll all soon begin ticking together in harmony," the shopkeeper told me knowingly. I listened. What she said was true.

We are energy and vibration. When we're open, how easy it is to begin ticking to the rhythm of those around us. If we had kept ourselves locked up and put away, it would be different. But since we've chosen to be open, to be sensitive, to open our hearts and souls, we'll connect with, tick to, the vibrations of those around us. Our energy fields will touch and merge. We'll begin to feel, and sometimes visibly take on, the characteristics, rhythms, and vibrations of those in our field.

Pay attention to, choose carefully, those with whom you live, eat, and play. There may be times when you can handle their energy, and times it isn't right for you. Sometimes, when we're feeling off balance, it may be that we're around energy that just isn't right for us.

Stay conscious of who you travel with on this journey. See who you're attracted to and notice who is attracted to you. See how much better you feel when you surround yourself with the energy of love.

APRIL 11

Learn to Listen to Silence

Driving into Yellowstone Park, I switched off the radio. The sun was setting. The mountains on either side of the road framed my view. Snowcapped mountains, their peaks touching the clouds, reflected the peach, pink, and orange of the setting sun. The clouds were beginning to change color, the way they do at twilight. Evergreens lined the road. Some stood tall. Some stooped. Some bent, as if peeking at or beckoning the travelers on the road. The smell of pine gently filled the car.

Because I'd been driving all day, I had kept the radio on to keep me alert and entertained. Now, I shut it off. As I drove, I let the silence fill the car, fill my mind, fill my soul. Before long, the colors of the sunset began to almost sing. The trees, the mountains filled me with their energy, rhythm, vibration.

Certain sounds can be healing—music, the voice of a friend, the laughter of a child. But there are other times when we need to turn down the sound and listen to silence. Silence can be healing, too.

As the sun set and I drove through the gates of Yellowstone Park, I realized this: the sounds of silence aren't silent. Each creation that lives sings its own song. It takes a quiet mind, a quiet soul, a quiet heart to hear these songs.

Learn to listen to silence. Listen to
the world around you. And the silence
will sing you a beautiful song.

APRIL 12

Open Yourself to the Wealth of the Universe

We all have sources we turn to for support. We may turn to special people in our lives—family members, friends, a lover. We may turn to nature—the mountains, trees, oceans, rivers, sun, moon, and stars. But we no longer have to limit ourselves to just one person, one source for love, energy, comfort, and guidance.

Certain people come into our lives for a short while to help us through particular times. Other people come to stay for a longer time. Sometimes we love people and are so deeply committed to them that they will be sources of energy and love for us, and we for them, for most of our lives. That's good. That's how it should be.

But while it's good to have people who are special sources of support for us, allowing one person to be our sole support can mean trouble. We may begin to drain that person. We may become overly dependent. He or she may move away from us. Or we may become angry, as we usually do, at whomever or whatever we are dependent on. For many reasons, we may find ourselves in conflict with the one we have deemed our source. Something may happen that causes our source to no longer be available to us. It's important to be conscious of what our needs are and to get our needs met. But it's also important not to make one person responsible for doing that.

Open to a larger, more abundant source. That source is God. And God's supply is the universe. When we look to God and the universe, we open ourselves to a never-ending supply of what we need—love, energy, teaching, support, information, guidance, and nurturing. Certain people and places may help us along our way, but God is our source for love.

APRIL 13

Give Freely of What You've Been Given

Learning not to overcare, overgive, and overdo are the lessons of the past. We have learned them, learned them well. There was a time when we needed to monitor our giving because we were giving compulsively, almost addictively, with no thought to what felt right in our heart, with no understanding of loving ourselves. But that was yesterday.

This is now. We can trust ourselves to know when it's time to stop or when our giving has become destructive. We can trust ourselves to know when it's not our job to give, because now we are connected to ourselves, listening to ourselves, on track.

Give freely of your time, your heart, your joy, your wisdom. Share your experiences, your strength, your hope. Share your weaknesses as well as your strengths. Share your money, your gifts, your laughter. Share your hope. Share yourself.

Give freely of what you've been given, and the universe will provide you with exactly what you need. Give freely and the universe will give freely to you.

APRIL 14

Relax

Too often out of sheer habit we tighten up, tense up, and then approach life from that stance. When we have something to do, our automatic response may be to tense up—shoulders and neck strained, back bent and cramped, breathing shallow. But anything that needs to be done can be done better if we're relaxed.

Learn to relax. Program your body, each part of it, to let go and be at ease. Allow yourself to come into your natural posture and alignment. Learn to relax until moving, acting, speaking, being all come naturally from this relaxed place.

Find activities that help you do this. A hot bath. A steam bath. A massage. Sunning. Walking. Meditating. Teach yourself to become aware of how your body feels during these activities. Memorize that feeling. Practice relaxing until you can recall that memory and carry it throughout your day.

Periodically throughout the day, take a few moments to check your tension level. If you find any part of your body tense, take a few more moments to consciously relax that part. Visualize warmth and ease flooding any part of your body that has become tight or is in pain. Let the tension, the stress, the blocks drain out from top to bottom. Your body wants to relax. It wants to become comfortable. It wants to heal itself.

Empty your mind of tense thoughts, and let it follow your body into relaxation and calm. Allow your mind to become still. Quietly accept each thought, then release it. Breathe in comforting, healing energy. Breathe it into your mind, into each cell of your body. Breathe out stress, strain, discomfort, and fear. Don't resist what you are feeling or thinking. Accept it, then release it. Just as water cannot pass naturally through a pinched hose, your vital life force cannot flow freely through you if you are cramped and tense.

Honor the life force that is in you, that flows through you. Honor it by relaxing, opening to it, and inviting it to surge through your body.

The techniques of relaxation will
refresh, restore, and recharge you, so
that you can do all you need to do
with more power and vigor than before.
Anything that needs to be done can be
done better if you're relaxed.

APRIL 15

Imagine What You Want

What do you want? What do you want to create in your life? What situation do you want to live in? Describe the scenario. Imagine it. We can often have what we want, but we rarely take the time to imagine it. And imagination is the first step toward creativity.

What do you want? What would it look like, feel like? Is what you're working so hard on what you really want? That relationship? That job? That home? If it is, go for it. If it's not, imagine and create something different.

Begin with imagination. Imagine what you really want in your mind, and you've taken the first step toward creating it. If you don't know what you want, that's okay too. Ask the universe for help. Ask God and the universe to bring you your highest good.

Ask the universe to help you create exactly what you want and need. Trust the universe, and you will be trusting an honorable and benevolent friend.

APRIL 16

You'll See the Answer

The answer you are looking for may be right before your eyes.

Have you asked the question? Have you put it out to God, the universe, yourself, and the world?

What do I need to do now? What do I need to do next? Where and why am I stuck? What am I not seeing? What's the answer? I need a clue.

Often, asking the question means the answer is trying to find you. Follow your heart, then open your eyes. You'll see it.

The answer may be right in front of you.

APRIL 17

Listen to the Voice of Your Heart

Cultivate the art of listening to your intuition, your inner voice. This is the guidance of your heart. It's a voice that speaks differently from the one in your head. The heart whispers softly; the head prattles loudly.

The head has an agenda for our lives. It chatters away boldly, but its vision is limited. It leaves no room for the mysterious workings of the universe, nor does it take into account the side trips we need to get where we're going, where our souls need to go. It's the voice that says, *This is the way it's going to be.*

The heart, the inner voice, speaks differently. Sometimes it whispers. Sometimes it pulls. Sometimes it pushes. It's spontaneous, in the present moment, and often a surprise. The heart takes into account what has to be done and the best way to do that. The heart takes emotions into account—the way things feel, the way you feel, the wisdom of your soul. The heart leads us into and through the lessons we're here to learn.

Cultivate your inner voice. Practice listening to the whispers of your heart. Practice trusting your intuition, what you really feel, what you really know. Practice until that voice is the one that you hear.

Be patient. Be gentle. Let yourself
learn to hear the gentle and trustworthy
words of your heart.

APRIL 18

There's Magic in the Unknown

Sometimes we're out of ideas. We think and think but nothing comes. We don't know what's next. It feels like we're at a dead end. But we're not. That void, that dreaded blank spot is really a glorious magical place.

Sometimes we have to run out of our ideas before we can open to any new ones. The reason we can't see any further is because our ideas are limited by the past, by past experiences, by what life has been like before. Our future doesn't have to be limited by our past. Life knows that. Now we can learn it, too. We're not at a dead end. We've reached a new beginning.

Now is a time of magic. Let the universe take
your hand and show you things you have never
seen before. Now, at last, you're open and
vulnerable enough to begin. Celebrate the magic,

the mystery of the unknown. Celebrate the miracles that will certainly come.

APRIL 19

Release Old Emotions

Our emotions and experiences sometimes lead us out of the present moment. Something happens—someone says something, we hear something—and a feeling crops up. Often, underneath it is an old feeling, a feeling from the past, an old chunk of energy that's hidden in our soul, stored in our body.

We aren't off track when that happens. We're right where we need to be: off center and out of the present moment. We can use moments like these to heal ourselves.

Let yourself feel the feeling. Let yourself release the energy. Talk it out. Jog it out. Do what your heart leads you to do to release that bubble of emotion from your soul. Take as much time as you need—an hour, a day, a month.

When it's gone, you'll find a surprise. You've advanced on your path. You've learned something new. A new cycle has begun. An issue arose that provided an opportunity for healing and growth, and that healing and growth turned into a pleasant and welcome surprise.

Yes, sometimes experiences lead us out of the present moment. But if we stay present for ourselves, we'll always come back. Changed. Lighter. Healed. And more ready to love.

Loving Yourself Will Make It Better

Are you feeling powerless? Have circumstances taken a turn you don't like? Do you feel there's nothing you can do to make today better? One power that's always available to you is the power to love yourself.

Sometimes we feel powerless. We have circumstances in our lives we simply cannot change, no matter what we do to create something different, to move the situation along. We can't get another person to behave differently. We can't seem to change something at work. We can't do much about our money situation, at least not at the moment. Nothing in life seems to be going our way. It's not that we're doing anything wrong. We aren't off our path or neglecting a particular lesson. The energy of that particular time in our lives is frustrating. There is no action we can take to change our circumstances. All we can do is surrender to the circumstances, accept what's happening, and stay in the moment.

During those times, there is one action we can take that will help. We can love ourselves. When we can't do anything about the world around us, when we can't even seem to do much about ourselves, we can always, always love ourselves. When all our other powers seem stripped away, we can practice the power of self-love. It's one power no one can take away.

Self-love will always make things better.
And perhaps when a difficult time is past,
you'll look back and say, That's what I was
really learning all along—the ever present,
healing power of learning to love myself.

APRIL 21

Trust What You Know

As you grow, as you evolve, as you continue on this journey, you'll discover many special abilities, gifts, and powers. One is an increased sense of knowingness. We will begin to understand events and people on a level much deeper than we experienced before.

We will begin to know the feeling of a person, place, or thing. We will begin to feel its energy, not just its matter or physical form. We'll talk to a person for a while and know if that person feels trapped, feels like a victim, or feels free. We'll know if a place holds energy that's good for us. Or we'll know that the energy isn't right for us, doesn't currently complement our needs. We won't judge. We'll just know. And we'll know what to do.

Powers appear when we open the heart. We find the powers of love, comfort, faith, joy. There are other powers, too, that come along the way. One of these is the quiet power of trusting what we know.

Open your heart. Let it show you what
it knows. Learn to trust what you know.
You're wiser than you think.

APRIL 22

On the Other Side of Fear Is Joy

Climb over the wall of fear.

Fear can be like a brick wall on our path. We may say we want to move forward—we want to feel better, do something new, live differently, go to the next place on our journey—but if we have unrecognized fears about that, we may feel like we've hit a wall. We don't know we're afraid; the fear is tucked and hidden away. All we can see is that, for some unknown reason, we can't seem to move forward in our life. We're in the dark.

Or we may be conscious of our fear, but be refusing to deal with it. We have talked ourselves out of honestly addressing the fear by telling ourselves to be strong and brave. While there is much to be gained from pressing forward at certain times in our lives, there simply are other times when we cannot do that because our fear holds us back. There are times in life when real power comes from being vulnerable enough to say, *Yes, I am afraid.*

Gently face your fears one at a time as they arise. Let each fear surface into consciousness. Tell yourself you know it's there. Then release its energy; let it dissipate into the air. Don't be afraid of what you'll find; the feeling is only fear.

There's a magic I've learned over the years. It happens when I feel my fear. My life changes. I become empowered to move on. Barricades I have not been able to penetrate crumble and disappear. And all I had to do was simply face and feel my fear.

APRIL 23

Give Yourself a Break

Learn to appreciate yourself and others.

Knowing we desire growth and improvement is one thing. Constantly driving ourselves and others is another. Maybe the answer isn't that we need to do better, try harder, push more. Maybe the answer is recognizing and appreciating how well we already do things. How hard we try. How much we have done. How well others are doing, too.

Pushing ourselves can become so habitual that we deny ourselves any feeling of satisfaction. No matter how well or how much we do, the urge to try harder, do better, do more keeps pushing us on. It doesn't let us rest. We still feel it isn't quite good enough.

If you've been pushing yourself that hard, you may need more than a coffee break. Take a real break. Give yourself permission to put that drive aside. Quiet that part of you that wants to do more, be more, accomplish more. Learn to value how well you do things, even if no one else sees or appreciates your efforts. Applaud your own efforts and the efforts of those you love. For today and for one week, instead of demanding more from yourself, tell yourself how well you've done. For today and for one week, instead of demanding more from those around you, tell them that they are doing well, too.

Tell yourself how well you do. You may discover you're doing better than you thought.

APRIL 24

Change Your Perspective

Sometimes a slight difference in where we stand can dramatically change how we see things.

One morning, shortly after sunrise, I climbed to the top of a mesa in Sedona. I'd been there the day before, staring at the shapes and forms of the other mesas, and gazing down upon the city. Now this morning I sat in a different place to meditate and to look around. The spot where I sat this day was only a few feet from where I'd sat before, but the view looked entirely different. I saw different shapes and forms in the mesas. I saw a different view of the city, the world below.

We often need to change our position so we can see things differently. We don't have to make a dramatic change; we just need to move around a little. Perhaps an unresolved issue is blocking our vision, blocking us from seeing the beauty that's there. Maybe a bit of anger or self-contempt is interfering with our vision. Maybe the changes we need to make are minor, much less than we thought. Maybe we simply need to look at whatever we are viewing without fear, to change our mood and see it with the eyes of love.

Take a break. Move around. Learn to change your perspective. Maybe you don't need to change what you're looking at. You just need to change where you stand.

APRIL 25

Connect with Peace

Om ah hum vajra guru padma siddi hum.
Om mani padme hum.

—A BUDDHIST CHANT

Hail, Mary, full of grace; the Lord is with thee; blessed art thou among women, and blessed is the fruit of thy womb, Jesus. Holy Mary, Mother of God, pray for us sinners, now and at the hour of our death. Amen.

—A CATHOLIC PETITION

God, grant me the serenity to accept the things I cannot change, the courage to change the things I can, and the wisdom to know the difference.

—A NONDENOMINATIONAL PRAYER

People have many ways of seeking and finding peace. Mantras—chants or prayers that align the mind with peaceful thoughts, with the river of peace that runs through our universe—are one way of returning to our center. Do you have a favorite prayer, a religious chant, or a saying that helps you? That puts you back on track? That takes your mind to that place of peace within your soul?

Value the mantras that touch and heal your mind, the sounds and thoughts that align you with peace. Find and value the words and prayers of your religion, the thoughts that work for you, that connect you to your center. These will help you discover your connection with the universe, the flow of life, the certainty that all is well. You and your life are on track. Know you'll be given all the guidance and grace you need.

Find rituals that help you believe that peace is yours, rituals that connect you to the Divine in the universe. Ask for peace. Ask in a way that works for you.

APRIL 26

Change Is in the Air

Just as the world around us changes and evolves, so do the circumstances and situations in our lives. We live in a universe that is alive, vibrant, and constantly evolving. Change is the way nature, the universe, and the Divine move us through each period of our lives and into destiny. We are led to our next lesson, our next adventure. There's no need to deny change, to fear it or fight against it. Change is inevitable. Just as the earth is constant motion and transformation, so are we.

Take your place in the universal dance, the universal rhythm. Allow change to happen. Work with it as your life unfolds. Sometimes change comes in one smashing moment like a volcanic eruption. Other times it happens more slowly, the way the winds and rain sculpt bridges out of canyons.

Learn to trust your body—its signs, signals, warnings, and excited proclamations. We let the gathering clouds warn us of impending storms, and we learn to study and predict tremors in the earth. In much the same way, our body can function as a barometer for our soul and its place in the constantly changing and evolving universe.

You are open now, more sensitive than you've been before. Change is coming. It's here. You can feel it in the air. You can feel it in yourself.

Thank your body for helping you.
Thank the universe for what it is about
to do. Then thank God because change
will bring you closer to love.

APRIL 27

Love Sets Others Free

One of love's most challenging lessons is freedom.

Much of my life I thought love meant restraint. *I couldn't do this if I loved you. You wouldn't do that if you loved me.* Certainly there are times when love asks us to make choices. But love doesn't limit, it doesn't confinc, as I once believed.

Love brings with it the gift of freedom. Love teaches us to allow the person we love to do as he or she chooses. It teaches us to encourage the people we love to freely make their own choices, to seek their own path, to learn *their* lessons *their* way in *their* own time.

Love that restrains isn't love. It's insecurity. We may tell others how we feel about something they do or don't do. We may make decisions as a reaction to others' choices. That is our right and our responsibility. But to restrain another in the name of love doesn't create love; it creates restraint.

Love means each person is free to follow his or her own heart, seek his or her own path. If we truly love, our choices will naturally and freely serve that love well. When we give freedom to another, we really give freedom to ourselves.

APRIL 28

Reward Yourself

Take time to reward yourself. Let it become a deliberate and practiced habit.

Many of us grew up in families, or with people, who didn't reward us. We weren't rewarded for good behavior; we weren't rewarded or loved unconditionally, just for being, and particularly for being us. Although many of us may strive to change that behavior by rewarding the people around us, we may have neglected the importance of rewarding someone very important—ourselves.

It is one thing to mentally congratulate ourselves for a job well done. It is another to take the time to actually, deliberately, and specifically reward ourselves. How many years do we have to live before it's time to treat ourselves? How much good do we have to do before it's good enough to give ourselves a gift? Maybe it's time right now—today—to begin practicing the habit of rewarding ourselves.

Our souls can become tired, very weary, of striving to grow, to do things well, to do our best at life, love, and work if there is no reward. Our passion can wane if good is never good enough, and if the rewards and pleasure are always, always at bay—somewhere out in the distant future. If you find yourself beginning to resist working hard, doing well, striving for spiritual growth, maybe it's because you're neglecting to reward yourself for all you've already done. If you feel like the world offers no reward to you, maybe it's because you're not cooperating by rewarding yourself.

Stop punishing and depriving yourself. Don't let others punish you for a job, a day, or a life well done. Instead, reward yourself. Take a break and do something especially nice for you, something that would make you happy. Buy yourself something. It can be a little gift. Or you can splurge. Take yourself somewhere you want to go—in your home town, or in another country. Do something fun, magical and exciting, something that makes your heart sing and your spirit soar. Reward yourself by allowing yourself to enjoy what you give yourself, or what you're doing. Make rewarding yourself an *attitude*.

Reward yourself often. When you accomplish a particular task. When you've gone through a grueling part of your healing process. Reward yourself during those frustrating times, just for being so patient. Sometimes, reward yourself just for being you.

APRIL 29

Comfort Makes Everything Better

With comfort comes nurturing, genuine acceptance, and love. Comfort doesn't involve any expense. It comes from the heart. It goes right to the heart.

Look at how much better you feel when you receive comfort, when you comfort yourself, when you allow the universe to comfort you. Look at how those around you respond when you give comfort. A comforted person feels renewed. Healed. Genuinely okay. When you're comforted, the pain and stress that has awakened you each morning dissipates. You open your eyes and feel happy to be here. Happy to be you. You know, really know, that all is well. Finally, you feel safe.

When many of us were young, we ran to our mother, grandmother, or aunt to make a skinned knee, a hurt feeling, a bruised ego better. Now we are grown, but there's another mother who can do that, too. Some call her the nurturing, feminine side of God. She is all that is in the universe, and in each of us, that is loving, tender, and gentle. And her comfort really does make everything better.

Comfort heals. It brings joy to the spirit. Comfort renews power, vitality. Comfort opens you up like the sun unfolds the petals of a fragrant and beautiful flower. Simply put, comfort will make you and those around you happy.

APRIL 30

Awaken Your Healing Powers

From the traditional to the alternative, healers and healing energy can take many forms. Masseuses. Hypnotists. Chiropractors. Medical doctors. Herbalists. Each may have a touch of healing to bring to us at just the right time and place. But the power to transmit healing energy isn't limited to those who work in hospitals or have mastered the ancient Chinese art of acupuncture.

We each have the power to transmit healing energy to others and ourselves, regardless of our profession. We each have the ability to awaken that power and use it in the world around us through our chosen field of work. The man at the deli knows his customers' names and the details of their lives, then greets them with a warm, sincere, and healing smile. The woman who decorates homes takes time to get to know enough about her clients so that the colors and objects in the home reflect where they are on their spiritual paths. Friends and family members heal by using their gifts of intuition and speech to gently encourage and empower, their gift of thought to transmit healing messages, and their gift of touch to rub a stiff neck or sore shoulder.

There are many ways each of us can creatively figure out how to incorporate and channel our healing powers into our daily life. See your favorite healers when you need to. On your path, be open to discovering new healers and combinations of practices that work for you. But don't limit who can bring healing into your life. Remember that you're a healer, too.

Healing energy is the energy of love.
Learn to let it flow through you.

May

MAY 1

Learn to Release Old Toxins

Just as splinters can get embedded in our body, old emotions and beliefs can act like toxins and become embedded in us, too. We may have picked up residue along the way—beliefs we didn't consciously choose, feelings we weren't safe enough to feel, toxins from the world around us.

Now is a time of cleansing. Now is the time to heal your body and emotions, your mind and soul.

What beliefs and emotions do you need to heal? Look around at your life right now. What are you thinking? What are you talking about? What issues are cropping up in your life? Who are you talking about? What are you remembering? Who has come back into your life? What hurts? Is that feeling familiar? When have you felt it before?

Once you've identified what you're feeling and thinking, release it. Let the energy go. Let it leave your body. You can chatter all you want about what's going on with you, but that doesn't release the energy from your system anymore than talking about a splinter takes it out. Sometimes the process will sting just a bit when you pull out the splinter. But don't worry. It won't hurt for long. And soon you'll feel better than you've felt in a long while.

Often the process of releasing old toxins can be as gentle and natural as the way a flower or tree grows with sunshine and rain, a bit of fertile soil, and a little pruning and weeding.

Growth can be gentle now. Growth can be fun. Breathe in new air. Breathe in new energy. Exhale the past, its feelings, beliefs, and toxins. Let it go. Let yourself be transformed.

MAY 2

See the Divine All Around You

The woman was old, perhaps ninety. She had the frailness we sometimes see in the elderly, but her life force was strong, vital. She sat in the cafe eating breakfast with a younger woman. "You've been through a lot," the younger woman said. "It must be hard since your husband died. How are you doing?"

The older woman chewed a bite of toast, then responded. "I'm okay," she said. "Everything that's happened has brought me to a closer walk with the Lord."

"What do you mean by that?" the younger woman barked.

"This is what I mean," the older woman said. "I see God more in everything. In people. In things. In the world. In myself. It's just a closer walk."

I smiled to myself, quit eavesdropping, and finished my breakfast. Every religious faith has its own language. Each has its own frame of reference. But most roads lead to the same destination: taking our place in the Divine rhythm of life, recognizing Divinity in all that is—in others, in ourselves, and in all the creations of the universe.

Open to your connection to the world around you. Know that we really all are one. The connection is God. The connection is the Divine as each of us understands it. The connection is love.

MAY 3

Say Good-Bye with an Open Heart

On our journey, we meet many souls with whom we interact, exchange energy, in a way that enhances our growth and theirs. We learn lessons together. We break bread. We share love. But there often comes a time to say good-bye.

A good-bye can come suddenly, unexpectedly, without much warning. Or a good-bye can be expected, planned on, and take a while to work out. The length of time doesn't matter. What matters is how we handle our good-byes.

We can do it with our hearts open, saying thank you for all we've learned. Or we can close our hearts and bitterly say we've lost again.

We can say good-bye with an attitude of trust, faith, and love, believing our hearts led us together, for the time we were close, to celebrate life and further our journeys. Or we can do it with harsh judgment, asking what's wrong with us that our paths didn't let us stay together. We can say good-bye with our hearts open, feeling our sadness, our longing, and our joy. Or we can say good-bye with emotions walled off, saying that's just the way life is.

Sometimes, it's time to say good-bye. We can't always choose timing, but we can choose the words of our heart.

And sometimes it's not good-bye.
It's till we meet again.

MAY 4

Cherish Each Moment

Stop waiting for the one moment in time that will change your life. Instead, cherish all the moments. A desert cactus that blooms briefly only once a year does not consider all the moments it is not in bloom wasted. It considers them necessary and important. It knows the rest of the year, the rest of its life, it is beautiful, too.

All the moments count. The quiet moments. The moments of boredom and solitude. The moments of sharing. The exciting moments of discovery. The moments of grandeur. The agonizing moments when we feel sad, angry, and upset. Each moment in time is equally important. Don't wait and hope for the one thing, the one person, the one event, that will change your life, plummet you into the future and the life you desire. Instead remember that each moment in time brings change, evolution, and transformation.

Most of us relish the magnificent spiritual experiences, those tremendous discoveries, those important times of change. But those moments don't happen that often. The truth is, each moment in time is a spiritual experience, an important time of change. Cherish all your moments. Soon you will see the beauty and power of each.

Let each moment have value. Let each day of your life be the spiritual experience you seek. The power to change and evolve lies within you. The life you desire is happening right now. Your destiny is here.

Cherish all your moments.
Embrace the beauty and
importance of each one.

MAY 5

Value the Power of Clear Thought

Value your mind, and the power of conscious, clear thought. All this talk about opening the heart has not been to discount or devalue the power of conscious clear thought, or of opening our minds and expanding our consciousness. A gift, a benefit, from opening our heart is increased clarity of mind and thought.

As we clear the pathway to the heart by feeling, expressing and releasing old emotions, we will clear the path to the mind. Just as the body is connected to the mind, so is the heart. A cramped body can cause fuzzy thinking, but so can a clogged heart. To attempt to think clearly and consciously with the heart closed may not work. It may even prove frustrating and difficult.

"Don't think so hard," the wise old man gently instructed me. "You're hurting your head and your thinking isn't become clear. Relax. Stop trying so hard. Open your heart. Then your thinking will clear. The mind," he reminded me, "is connected to the heart."

If you're feeling cloudy and confused and can't get the answers, stop trying so hard. Move your body and clear your physical energy. Then try opening your heart. You may see a delightful result. Without trying or forcing, your thinking clears. And it becomes clear without the frustration of trying to force thoughts, ideas, or thought patterns. It happens almost magically, and quite naturally.

The mind is connected to the heart. Value the power of conscious clear thought. Value your mind, and its power, by valuing the power and wisdom of an open heart.

MAY 6

Stay Open to Life

I have a tendency to be dogmatic. If I have an experience that's unpleasant, I take a firm stand and say, *I'll never go through that again. I'll never do that again.* If something frightens me or I don't understand it, I'll push it away. Won't even consider it. *That won't work for me,* I say, sometimes before I know whether it will or not. Being dogmatic shuts us down and can shut life out.

The universe will challenge our prejudices, though. Without being certain how it happened, we may find ourselves doing the very thing we thought we never would, liking it, and hearing a quiet voice, the one that comes from our heart ask, *What do you think now?* When we're open, we'll find ourselves doing things, sharing things, experiencing things, and liking things we never thought we would or could.

Open your heart. Open your mind. Open to life and all it holds for you. Let the dogma dissolve.

MAY 7

Are You Angry?

Anger ranks high on the list of perplexing, troublesome emotions. We want to be kind and loving, but then suddenly we feel a jolt in our heart, an edge to our voice. Something has been tapped deep inside. It could be a chunk of old anger, something we weren't conscious of or safe enough to feel back then. It may be current. Something has come into our life today, and our reaction is anger.

Oh no, we may think, *this isn't what I need*. But denying anger will not bring us joy. Hiding it, tucking it away deep inside is not the answer. We may even turn it upon ourselves. Not feeling anger won't make it go away. Its energy will still be there, pounding away inside us and, in subtle ways, pounding away at others, too. Until we acknowledge our anger, feel it, and release it, it will keep us off balance, on edge, and irritable. We need to give ourselves permission to feel all our emotions, including anger.

But allowing yourself to feel angry doesn't mean giving yourself permission to rage, to hack and cleave at the world, to verbally abuse those around you. Find ways to express your anger with grace and dignity. Park your car, roll down the windows, and yell. Find a solitary place, a spot where you are safe, then speak loudly about how you feel. Write it out. Shout it out. Pound it out. Go to the gym and work it out.

Anger can be a guide. Used creatively, it can help us decide where to go and where not to go. It can help us get to the next place in our lives. Feeling and expressing our anger in appropriate ways will take us forward to a place of power within ourselves.

Let yourself feel angry when anger is what you really feel. Then get the anger out of your head and out of your body. Once that's happened, you'll feel clear. You'll know what to do next. The path to your heart, to your inner voice, will be opened. Sometimes getting angry is exactly what we need to do next.

MAY 8

Love Yourself

No matter what, love yourself.

Love yourself, even if it feels like the world around you is irked with you, even if it feels like those you've counted on most have gone away, even if you wonder if God has abandoned you.

When it feels like the journey has stopped, the magic is gone, and you've been left sitting on the curb, love yourself. When you're confused and angry about how things are going or how they've gone, love yourself. No matter what happens or where you are, love yourself. No matter if you aren't certain where you're going or if there's anyplace left to go, love yourself.

This situation will change, this time
will pass, and the magic will return.
So will joy and faith. You will feel
connected again—to yourself, God,
the universe, and life. But the first
thing to do is love yourself. And all
the good you want will follow.

MAY 9

Trust Each Step

Stay present for each step of your journey. We don't go from one place to another in a gigantic leap. We get there in increments, by going through each feeling, each belief, each experience one step at a time.

Sometimes when we pray for miracles, what we're really praying for is help in skipping steps, for shortcuts. The simple act of acceptance, of returning to each step of our path, can often bring us the miracle we need. Then we see the truth. The real miracle is one always available to each of us: it's the miracle of acceptance. We can go where we want to go, one step at a time.

Stay present for each step of your
journey. Trust each stage. Many things

are possible for you if you accept that
the fastest way is one step at a time.

MAY 10

Go for the Ride

Not all sections of the road we travel are smooth, paved, easy riding. We may prefer the smooth sections of highway, but sometimes the road gets rough. And the rough section can go on for miles and miles.

That's okay. It doesn't mean you've lost your way. It doesn't mean the rough section and bumpy spots will last forever. You're still on your path.

Relax. Wiggle your shoulders a bit. Get ready, for you just may be in for the ride of your life. Don't try to ignore the bumps or pretend they're not there. Not all roads are paved and smooth. Not all roads are meant to be. Slow down a bit if you need to, but don't stop.

Accept each part of the journey
as it comes. Let each stretch of your
path be what it needs to be.

MAY 11

Love Yourself Enough to Relax

Our bodies react to the world around us—and within us—in many ways. Our bodies act like sponges—they can soak up healing energy or they can absorb and trap the negative energy of stress and tension.

Some of us are so used to keeping our bodies tense and bound up we don't even notice how much they hurt, how strained and tight our muscles are.

Connect with your body. Learn to tell how tense it is. Take a few moments throughout the day to see what hurts, what aches, what muscles are being strained. Although tension can affect the entire body, many of us have favorite places in our body to store stress, places that usually become tense, rigid, and full of aches. Necks, shoulders, lower backs are favorite traps. Become familiar with your body and where it stores stress and tension.

Then, learn to relax. Explore different options. Therapeutic massage. Self-hypnosis. Meditation. Soaking in a hot bath. Sitting in the steam room. Exercise. Visualization. Taking time to do activities that bring you pleasure. If you make the effort to explore relaxation techniques, you will find ways to relax that you like and can afford.

If you've been soaking up too much stress, give yourself a break. Let your body start soaking up some healing energy, too. Love yourself enough to help your body relax.

MAY 12

Discover Inspiration Points

Sometimes, we become so caught up in the daily grind that we forget how much beauty and inspiration our world offers. We forget about the power of inspiration.

My favorite inspiration point in Colorado is a small stand next to the Royal Gorge Bridge, the highest suspension bridge in the world. The stand overlooks the gorge, offering a magnificent overview of canyons, mountains, peaks, and plains. In Bryce Canyon, the place called Inspiration Point overlooks massive canyons. From that vantage point, you can see delicately shaped spirals, in the orange iron color so prominent in the canyon, surrounded by the lighter sandstone and sulfur peaks.

What inspires you? Discover inspiration points—those high places of the spirit from which you can see more, see more clearly, see more beautifully. Spend time taking in a grander view of life. See how calming and inspiring it is. See how you return to life with vigor, enthusiasm, and passion.

Visit places that invigorate your soul, help you see the larger picture. Find places in your home, your community, your state. Look for that place in yourself, that sacred inspiration point within you, where your soul and heart see the larger picture, where you and your ideas come to life, where you make the connection between your soul and the world around you. Seek the power of inspiration.

Inspiration points abound. Open up. Look around.
When you seek inspiration, it will come to you.

MAY 13

Forgive Yourself

Doesn't it feel good to forgive yourself? You don't have to be afraid or reluctant to do that anymore. Forgiving yourself doesn't mean you're condemned. It means you're setting yourself free.

We can gather so much guilt as we go through life. We may blame ourselves for the experiences we've had and how we've handled them. We may build up resentments against ourselves. We may even resist forgiving ourselves because we think that means saying we were bad and wrong. But not forgiving ourselves when we need to often leads us to return to situations that are unhealthy for us.

Forgiving yourself means you can leave places that feel bad, you can end relationships that no longer work, you can avoid situations that cause you continual pain and grief. Forgiving yourself means you can stop punishing yourself for what you've done and what you *think* you've done wrong.

You don't have to hold your mistakes against yourself any longer. You don't have to deprive yourself of comfort, joy, love, and acceptance. It's much easier to say, *I made a mistake. This isn't right for me. I don't like this. This is wrong.* Then forgive yourself.

Forgive yourself if you've done something wrong. Forgive yourself even if you haven't done something wrong. Then see how good forgiveness feels. Forgive yourself and be free.

MAY 14

Stay Open to Surprise

On my journey, I have often been surprised. Sometimes, pleasantly surprised.

Some of the places I was told to visit, places I was told would bring me joy, didn't. Occasionally, they left me cold and confused. I would reach out to grasp something from an experience, only to find it wasn't there, at least not for me. I was left wondering why it didn't work, why it didn't feel right for me, or why it didn't do for me what others said it did for them.

Then other places, other experiences—the ones I had the least expectations of—surprised me. They riveted my soul, opened my heart, touched me, changed me in ways I didn't expect. In ways that still surprise me.

To have certain expectations is natural. But stay open to surprise. Don't let your dreams and expectations color what you know to be true for you. Trust your perceptions. Trust how a thing feels to you. If you expected something to work and it didn't, trust that. If something has opened your heart and produced growth, love, and joy, trust that.

Don't let your expectations or prejudices color and distort your *experience. You may be pleasantly surprised to find joy where you least expected it.*

MAY 15

Lighten Up

The time for heaviness is past—heaviness of body, mind, spirit, and heart. That heaviness many of us felt was part of a time now gone. It's time to lighten up.

"He was a different person," she said. "Cheerful. Happy. Fun to be around. Things that used to bother him no longer did." The woman was talking about her husband of only three years. She had dated him for a long time. Then after nearly dying of a heart attack, he was changed, transformed. They married and had the best three years of their lives before he died.

Those years were possible because he had learned to enjoy life, learned the value of love.

We don't have to wait to open our hearts and enjoy life. We don't have to wait to lighten up. We can do that now. We know that we can trust, that we can journey through each stage of our lives with open hearts, loving and living freely.

Let go of heaviness. Seek that which is light.
Gravitate toward joy. Your soul and body will
lead you, if only you will listen. Walk lightly.
Speak and laugh lightly, as much as possible.
Go lightly along your way.

MAY 16

What You Believe Is What You Will See

We can call things into play by what we believe, what we say, what we envision, what we speak. This is one of the powers we're learning about.

Much of this dance of life, this universal rhythm, is out of our control. But while we don't choreograph it, we can work within the part that is ours, with the power that is ours. We do this by what we believe. If we believe that we have to fight the entire world, that we're separate and apart, and that for the most part those we meet will be our enemies, out to hurt us, then that will most probably be true.

Our beliefs about what we deserve and who God is will change as we journey through our adventures. But there is also much we can do now to participate in changing our beliefs and creating a more desirable world for ourselves.

What are your beliefs? Listen to yourself. Listen to what you think, what you say, how you react. Listen to yourself talk about other people, about what life is really like, and about what *always* happens to you. Listen to what you say about what you can and cannot do. What you hear yourself say is what you believe. And that is probably what you are used to perceiving as happening.

Try believing something different. Try asking the universe and God to help you change and correct your beliefs. Take an active part in creating your world. Say your new beliefs. Say them aloud. Write them down.

Believe that you deserve love. Believe that universal love is there for you. And you will begin to see exactly what you believe.

MAY 17

Happiness Is Within Reach

What we need to be happy is a question we often forget to ask ourselves.

Is there something you could do for yourself that would make you happy, put a spring in your step, a smile in your heart? Many of us haven't asked ourselves this question enough. Some of us haven't asked it at all. Or if we have, we haven't answered it. Instead we diligently search for our path, for the way through our lives, through our current situation or circumstance, never taking time to ask ourselves what would make us happy and what would feel good to us. Then we wonder why life feels so hard, so difficult and unrewarding.

Discovering what would make us happy can help us through any difficulty in life. It can help us through the quieter moments of our day. It can help us make larger, more significant decisions. It can help us in our work. Especially if we look in our hearts and answer honestly.

What would make you happy? It's a simple question, but one with profound consequences. Asking and answering that question, then acting on it, is often our path—a path that will lead to the next step, a path that is in our best interests. We will be choosing our destiny. And the destiny we're choosing is joy.

What would make you happy? Ask yourself often. Think about your answer. You may well find that the answer is within reach.

MAY 18

Love All of Yourself

Do more than just accept yourself, tolerate yourself, put up with yourself, endure who you are. Love yourself.

There came a time in my life when I simply could no longer put up with putting up with myself. I had talked about self-love. I had said out loud that I loved myself. The words were good, but they didn't ring true. I had to actually begin experiencing and practicing love for myself. It became the next step on my path.

To live in a magical way, one in which you connect with the universe, loving yourself isn't optional. It comes first. To hear the quiet voice of your heart so you know when you're being led, to hear your thoughts so you can see what you really believe, to trust and open your heart, you must first experience love for yourself.

Have you abandoned yourself? Let yourself see if that's true, feel if that's true. Then learn to experience love for yourself.

Learn to love the way you handle things. Love your unique way of learning, growing, and seeing things. Love where you've been. Love what you've done. Love where you are, and what you're doing now.

Love how you look, smell, and feel. Love the color of your eyes, the color of your hair, and the radiance in your heart. Love how you laugh. Love how you cry. Love your mistakes, and love all the good you've done. Love it all. Love all of you.

Step into love for yourself, and the universe will reflect that love back to you.

MAY 19

Don't Be Afraid of Making Mistakes

Don't be so afraid of making a mistake. That energy can create more mistakes. It can stop us from enjoying what we're doing. It can block us from creating freely and making something beautiful.

Sometimes it's necessary and important to make mistakes, to fumble around and do something poorly so we can learn to do it better next time. No matter what we're doing or what we're learning, we have to start somewhere. Look back at the past. We learned by trying, stumbling, falling, getting back up, and trying again. But we wouldn't be where we're at if we hadn't begun where we were.

Jump in, begin, and do the task as best as you can. Stop worrying about mistakes, and let yourself do it as well as you can right now. If you do it wrong or poorly, you can do it over again. And when you do it in an attitude of love, you won't fail. You'll learn something new about yourself, life, and the task.

Love yourself enough to try. Let yourself make mistakes. Tell yourself you don't have to do it perfectly. Let yourself have fun while you're learning. Start where you are, and do what you can. Learning and getting better will happen from there.

You may not always know the best way in the beginning, but if you keep trying, you'll quickly learn to tell when you're on track.

MAY 20

Value the Fragrances of the Universe

I stopped at the small gas station to fill the tank and get a cup of coffee en route through northern California. "Did you know that the world's largest manufacturer of aromatherapy products is right here in town?" asked the attendant. His remark reminded me of the power of our sense of smell to affect how we feel. We are surrounded by odors, but unless one is particularly noxious, we tend to ignore the effects of the scents we are inhaling. And we tend to underestimate the power of certain scents to help us heal.

Nurture your sense of smell. Let it comc alive. Use its power to help you heal. A bundle of white sage burning in a sea shell on the table. The wisp of cedar smoke from the fireplace. A cone of incense filling the air. Lavender oil in the bath. Drops of eucalyptus sprinkled in the shower, its penetrating aroma mingling with the steam. A vanilla candle on the nightstand next to your bed. The smell of a forest, fresh with rain. Ocean air, salty and damp. The rich sawdust smell of redwood. Comforting smells from childhood—bread baking in the oven, freshly baked chocolate cake on the counter, chicken frying in the pan. The smell of our favorite people, their hair, their clothes, their cologne.

Value your sense of smell, the way it connects you to yourself, to memory, to emotion, to the universe and the world around you. Use your sense of smell to help you discover what's right for you. Surround yourself with the fragrances of the universe. Let them help you heal.

MAY 21

Listen for the Music

The woman at the campground in Olympic National Forest extended an invitation to me. "Some evenings when the soaking pools are closed and the guests are in their cabins, the members of the staff build a campfire, gather 'round, and sing. Listen for the music. You're welcome to join us. You'll have a great time."

The universe has invited us to join in, too. How often have we heard the music and for some reason been fearful to join in? We don't have to stand in the shadows, watching others make music, watching others laugh and have a good time. Whether it's a group of friends doing karaoke or simply a good time of love and laughter, when we hear the music in our lives, it's okay to join in. Some of the best times in my life were spent around a piano making music with the people I love. Some of the most memorable times have been when I forgot my fears and self-consciousness enough to relax and have fun with the people I was with.

> *Music is all around us. Listen for it. Seek it out. Know you're welcome to join in. Don't worry about how well you carry a tune or whether you know all the words. You've been invited to the campfire. Come. Sing along. You'll have the time of your life.*

MAY 22

Learn the Art of Joyful Living

Let's pretend for a moment we have a friend who's with us much of the time. This friend watches us, watches our lives and circumstances, and comments: *Oh, that's too bad. That's terrible. That's awful. You could be doing better. You're not doing very well. What's wrong with you? Why did you do that?* This friend isn't very pleasant, but many of us have brought such a friend with us through much of our journey.

Now, let's imagine something different. Let's imagine a friend, a constant companion, who laughs a lot. This friend laughs at traffic, laughs at delays, laughs at long lines. Even laughs at setbacks. Of course, this friend doesn't mock us or laugh at us when we're in pain. This friend is compassionate and gentle, and has an open heart. But he or she helps us laugh, even when we hurt.

This friend has learned the art of joy, the art of living, and the art of living joyfully.

Let's bring along the friend
who knows the art of joyful living
to help us learn the same.

MAY 23

Trust That Guidance Will Come

Trust and act on the guidance you have now.

Some parts of our lives appear like a long, paved highway. We can see exactly where to go; we have a panoramic view. Other times, it may feel like we're driving in the dark with only one headlight on a winding road through the fog. We can only see a few feet in front of the car.

Don't worry if you can't see that far ahead, if you only have a glimmer of light to guide your path. Slow down. Listen to your heart. Guidance will come. Trust what you hear. Do the small thing. Take that one step. Go as far as you can see.

Then go back to your heart, and you'll hear the next step. It may be a step of immediate action, or deliberate inaction. Sometimes you may have to quiet down, wait, and prepare yourself to hear what you're to do next.

Trust and act on the guidance
you have now, and more will come.

MAY 24

Rituals Connect Us with Faith

I stopped in at the Franciscan monastery, a short visit to look around. I bought a keychain, returned to my car, then realized I had misplaced my keys. I went back inside and talked to the receptionist. Just then a short priest joined our conversation. He had a bald head encircled by a short fringe of hair and he wore a flowing black robe. "Let me show you what I do when I lose something," he said. "I ask St. Anthony for help."

The next moment, the priest was spinning in a circle, clapping his hands in a joyful prayer. "St. Anthony, St. Anthony, please look around. Something's been lost and cannot be found." He stopped, looked at me, then smiled. "Now you'll find your keys," he said. He was right. Within thirty seconds, we found the keys. They were on a counter in a place we had looked twice before. For some reason, we just hadn't seen them.

But I found something more wonderful than my car keys. I had witnessed a delightful man expressing pure, innocent joy in a ritual that helped him and others through the days.

What are the rituals that are important to you, that awaken joy, innocence, and faith in you? Do you allow yourself to use these rituals freely? What were the rituals you enjoyed as a child, the ones that brought you comfort? Do you remember them? Engage in these rituals. Use them freely. Share them with others, as the priest did with me.

Rituals connect us to faith. They're faith in action. Rituals are reminders of our connection to God. They bring us back to God and ourselves.

MAY 25

Embrace Life's Mystery

Embrace the mystery of life. You don't need to know everything in your head. You don't need to figure everything out. You don't need an instruction sheet or a set of rules. You don't need all the answers.

Let yourself experience life. Hang on to the handlebars when you must, but as much as possible put your hands in the air and enjoy the ride. Feel everything you need to feel along the way. Feel the fear, the joy, the exhilaration. Feel the wind in your hair and the sun on your shoulders. Feel the vitality of life surge through you. See vitality and life in all that's around you.

Watch the magical journey of your life unfold with all its ups and downs. Feel the awareness surge up from deep within. Grasp the insights that come. Grab the brass ring whenever you can.

Embrace the mystery of life. Embrace the mystery and magic of you.

MAY 26

Awaken to Your Heart's Contentment

One day, you'll awaken to discover your life is all you wanted and hoped it would be.

Oh, you'll not find everything just the way your head said you wanted it. It might not be the way you planned. But you'll awaken to your dreams—your dreams of joy, love, and peace. Your dream of freedom.

You'll see beyond the illusions. You'll transcend your old limiting beliefs. You'll wake up and notice that your past is just as it needed to be. You'll see where you are today is good. You'll notice that you laugh a lot, cry a lot, smile a lot.

You'll look at tomorrow with peace, faith, and hope—knowing that while you cannot control some of what life does, you have possibilities and powers in any circumstance life might bring. The struggle you have lived with for so many years, the struggle in your heart, has disappeared. You're secure, at peace with yourself and your place in this world.

One day, you'll awaken to your heart's contentment. Let that day be today.

MAY 27

Stop Punishing Yourself with Fear

It's time to stop punishing ourselves. Time to stop beating ourselves over the head with fear.

This is the scenario. A fear enters our mind. Our mind takes it and runs with it. *Something bad is going to happen. Something terrible and traumatic is on the way.* We quickly review the traumas of our past and make the determination: *Yes, it is very possible that this devastating event will happen.*

So we sit crouched in the present moment full of fear and dread. We worry that the worst that could possibly happen, probably will. We begin to believe that it is most likely waiting at our doorstep, ready to pounce on us and steal our joy, our peace, our place and rhythm in the universe.

Because we have harbored the fear so intensely, it has already manifested itself. The thing we fear doesn't need to happen; it already has—or it might as well have—because we are already forcing ourselves to live through it.

Yes, many awful things have happened to you and me that we are very sorry happened. But that doesn't mean that we have to give up the beauty of the present moment to something that hasn't happened yet. Even if it does happen sometime in the future, by harboring the fear we will have lived through it twice as long as we need to.

Recognize and acknowledge your fear. Then release it. Let go of the energy. Stop punishing yourself. While life's seasons may not always be fair, they are trustworthy. And within each day, each moment of each season, there is a way of peace and joy.

Do not allow fear of what if *to*
ruin the joy of what is.

MAY 28

Let the Universe Support You

Who or what is your source of power? Who or what are you connected to?

Watch yourself as you go through your days. Where do you get your nurturing, your support, your empowerment, your energy? Does it all come from one person? Do you have a multitude of sources? Do you consider God, the Divine, your ultimate source?

There was a time when many of us made one person our only source. That time is past. Although special people are in our lives to be of special support, one of our lessons has been to broaden our connections, to connect to the universe, to open up to all the love and support that is there for us. If we use for our source only one person, one job, one place, one situation, we may encounter problems. Searching for many sources of support is a sign of our growth, a sign that we are continuing on our journey.

Value and cherish the people in your life who feed your soul and nurture your heart. Value and cherish the people who are special to you, who you hold dear, who help support you. But don't limit your connections. Open your heart to a living universe. Open your heart to Divine love.

Know that if you can't get what you need from one person or place, it is because the universe has something or someone better for your needs and your growth.

Who and what are you connected to? Are you willing to become connected to the universe?

Open your heart, your mind, your soul, and let the universe teach you about Divine love. Stop limiting your source to only one person. Open to a limitless source of support and energy. Open to the universe.

MAY 29

Let the Past Slip Away

Gently, lovingly, leave past moments behind.

You can't lose love. You don't need to hang on so tightly. If the lesson has been learned, if it is time to move on, let the past slip away. Come into the present moment. Discover all that's there for you.

Clinging to the lessons, people, and feelings from yesterday will keep you tired, confused, and afraid.

Shed the tears that need to be shed. Feeling your grief will help bring about your transformation.

Then say your good-byes. Be glad you had the experiences you did. Be grateful for all you've learned about yourself, about love. Then gently move into today.

Stop believing in loss. Start believing in life.
Let the past slip away. Come gently into now.

MAY 30

Open Your Heart

She laughed so much she made me giggle. "Do you laugh and smile all the time?" I asked the woman. "Are you this happy all the time?"

"My heart is open and healed," she said. "I laugh a lot. But I cry a lot, too."

An open heart feels all it needs to feel. Cry when it hurts. At the end of your tears, you will see more clearly. Tears clear our eyes and our heart. Cry whenever you need to.

Laugh often, as often as you can. Laugh with friends. Laugh out loud. The discoveries, the growth, the insights, the closeness, the sharing, the learning don't have to be such serious, somber events. Truth is discovered most often in laughter. Bonds are formed. Love becomes unveiled.

Cry a lot. Laugh a lot. Let life reveal its mysteries to you. Let love find you, course through you, touch all you meet through your laughter and tears. The fortunate person is not the one who wins the lottery. That's luck. We find fortune when we open our hearts and learn the secret of life.

Laughter and tears are the signs of an open heart.

MAY 31

Let Yourself Be Alive

In Sedona, as I drove from the sweat lodge back to the room I was renting, I felt exhilarated. My excitement wasn't only about the experience I had just been through. For so long I had limited my choices, limited my freedom. I was thrilled that I was finally giving myself permission to live more fully.

Have you been limiting your choices, telling yourself there are only a few options available? Have you been limiting your choices, saying you've seen and done everything you can in this world? Have you been limiting yourself and your life, then wondering why life is so limiting?

Set yourself free. Give yourself permission to experience and taste more of life. You are here to live your life—fully, richly, passionately. The journey has been about more than cleansing, healing, and spiritual growth. You have a body, emotions, passion, and thought. You are here to bring all parts to life, to connect the parts, and to fully live your life.

Partake of the abundance of the universe.
You're sitting at a banquet table. Let yourself feast.
Move on from monitoring, watching, limiting.
Experience all of life that you can.

June

JUNE 1

Let Your Body Lead You

Our bodies can help provide us with direction.

Many of us have heard the expression *I'm leaning toward that* or *I'm leaning away from that*. When we're centered and balanced, our body will help show us what we really want to do. We will literally lean toward or away from what we like or don't like. We've spent much of our lives forcing our body into situations, into energy fields and circumstances that it leaned away from, resisted, moved back from. Then we wondered why we hurt and felt uncomfortable.

The more we honor our body, the more it will help lead us. And the more it will become a natural guide helping us on our path, reflecting the desires of our heart and soul. The more we learn to trust our body, the more we'll come into harmony with our natural rhythms, the cycles and movements of our lives.

Learn to open to the subtle guidance and messages your body sends to you about what it likes, what it dislikes, what it leans toward, and what it leans away from. Learn to see where it's leading you. Talk to your body. Ask it what it wants. Then let it show you. Respect it enough to listen.

The more we connect to our bodies, the more we will live connected to our hearts, our souls, and be guided by the Divine. The more we practice listening to our bodies, the more naturally and easily this guidance and connection will flow.

Trust the wisdom of your body, for it often reflects the wisdom of your soul.

JUNE 2

Why Hurry Through?

Why hurry through a day, an hour, a life?

Hurry never catches up with itself. It misses out. It strains. It stresses. It doesn't trust the natural rhythm, the natural order, of the universe. Slow down. Tap into the rhythm of the world. Tap into your rhythm as you dance through life, as you dance through eternity.

When we hurry, it is as if we are dancing out of step to the music. We become out of sync. Our body strains and stresses. We stop enjoying life. We are too busy hurrying, racing blindly to somewhere, anywhere. We hurry so fast that when we get there, we don't take the time to enjoy it. We simply hurry on to the next moment.

Step in time to the music—the rhythm of your soul. The rhythm will lead you where you want to go. It will take you through all the tasks that need doing. It will take you down the road to spiritual growth, healing, fulfillment, and joy.

And you'll have more fun
going there because you
weren't in a hurry.

JUNE 3

Transcend Your Judgments

"Not judging people is really a practical issue," a friend explained. "Everybody does something they could be judged for. If we start judging, we'll spend all our time doing that."

My friend was right. But not judging is more than a practical matter, it is a spiritual issue as well.

I used to spend a lot of time judging other people. I used to think the world was divided into right and wrong; I thought judging others would help me stay clear on the difference; I thought judging was my job. Now I've learned something new about judgments and about myself. Judging others is what I do when I feel afraid, insecure, and limited. Judging others is something I do when I am afraid to love, when I can't accept love because I can't accept myself. And most important, I've learned that judging others is not my job. When I judge others, I judge myself.

Yes, there are issues we need to work on. Many of us have quirks we may live with most or all of our lives. But judging doesn't help. Judgments limit us. Judgments condemn. They say, *My past is not as it should be. I'm wrong. My life is wrong.* Judgments put us in prison, no matter where we are.

Judgments come from the head. Freedom and love come from the heart. Transcending judgments will set you free. Learn to look at yourself in love—who you are, where you are, where you've been. Learn to look at others with love, too.

When we accept others with freedom and love, we accept ourselves.

Judgments put up barriers.
Transcend your judgments,
and you'll be free.

JUNE 4

Let Joy Find You

Somewhere along my journey it happened. Quietly, imperceptibly, almost without my knowing it. I relaxed. Got comfortable with myself. I began enjoying myself, accepting myself, accepting life. Liking life. I found joy.

Somewhere along your journey, it will happen to you.

Joy is a gift. It appears almost imperceptibly, without warning, like a morning sunrise lighting our bedroom while we sleep. And it is almost as predictable. Keep doing the activities that bring healing and growth into your life. Keep loving yourself. Keep walking your path. Continue loving.

Don't worry about finding joy.
Because somewhere along your
journey, joy will find you.

JUNE 5

What Are You Trying to Prove?

You don't have to prove anything to anyone. Not even to yourself.

A subconscious desire to prove ourselves may be hiding at the root of our fears, the root of our tension, the root of our need to do and be more. Accompanying it can be a burning belief that we aren't good enough, that we need to compensate for some deficiency in ourselves in order to take our place on this planet.

We may feel like we have to earn our place, earn our right to be here. Like we're being watched and judged, graded.

You don't have to prove anything to anyone. You're fine just the way you are. You have energy, vitality. You have particular gifts and talents. You have been learning your lessons just right in your life.

Let go of the need to prove yourself to others—to parents, people from the past, people in your life today. Could it be the one you've really been trying to prove something to is yourself? The answer is simple: learn to approve of yourself. Love and accept yourself the way you are today. Then step right up and take your place in the universe.

JUNE 6

Learn to Change Your Energy

The simple act of moving around can change your energy. When your mind starts to flag, move your body around. Go for a walk, take a bath, get a drink of water, work out at the gym. You're doing more than moving your body; you're changing and rearranging your energy field.

Listen to your body. It will say what it needs, what it would like, what would be helpful. If you let it, it will even move quite naturally to what would do it good. Stretch your legs. Stretch your arms. Go outside. Do some deep breathing. Call a friend. Meditate. Tell a joke to a co-worker. You don't have to stay stuck in the energy you're in. You don't have to be a victim to the way you feel right now.

One of the powers we learn we have is the ability to shift, refocus, and rearrange our energy. When we get stuck in a particular emotion or reaction or mind-set, when we get toc bogged down or too fired up, we can save ourselves a lot of time by changing our energy, instead of hammering away at a change in the situation. Learn to tell when it is time to do that. Then discover what works for you—the little acts as well as the big ones.

Be gentle with yourself when you get stuck, when you need a fresh viewpoint. Learn to change and rearrange your energy as needed.

JUNE 7

Never Say Never

On my trip, I stayed at several state parks. The lodging was usually fine, but the ambiance and setting often weren't what I wanted. I needed smaller, quieter places. At one point in my journey I said, *Never again will I stay in a state park.* Shortly after, I found myself nestled in a room at Olympic State Park in Washington. It was one of the finest, quietest, most healing places I had ever encountered. I laughed at myself. By saying *never*, I had nearly cheated myself out of this experience.

Please don't say *never*. It sets up resistance. Challenges life. Challenges fate. And closes doors.

Never is dogmatic and judgmental. *Never* means limited thinking. And *never* usually means *probably*.

When we say *never*, it is sometimes because we have prejudged a thing without experiencing it. Other times, we say *never* because in the past a particular experience with a place or person was unpleasant. To say *never* means we're expecting all similar experiences to be unpleasant. It doesn't leave room for change or new and different experiences.

Learn from the past. Trust yourself. Trust your experiences, even the ones that haven't worked for you. But please don't say never. *Stay open to all the universe holds.*

JUNE 8

Be Gentle and Loving

As I drove into Utah, past Zion National Park, I began to feel the oddest sensation emanating from the earth, emanating from me. It was soft. Lovely. Light. All evening, deer had been crossing my path, coming to me from out of the woods. That's when I remembered. In the Medicine Cards, deer are the symbol for gentleness and love. The feeling coming from the ground, through the air was gentleness, kindness, and love.

The universe was reminding me of something. It was a place inside me, one I had discovered before, a place of gentleness and love. Somewhere along my life's journey, with all its trials, moving about, business, and experiences, I had let gentleness slip away. Now it was time to go there again. It was a reminder to be gentle and kind to others, be gentle and kind to myself.

Gentleness, kindness, and love are more than places to visit. They are places we can take with us wherever we go.

JUNE 9

Believe in Life, Not Loss

Believing in life means we can trust—trust in the nature and rhythm of life with all its constant change. We believe in transformation, change, and purpose.

Believing in life means we're not in bondage to the past. No matter what we've done, what decisions we've made, we set ourselves free to trust ourselves now. We trust what we feel, we trust what we know, we trust what we think we need to do next. Believing in life means we trust that the lessons we're learning are real. They're valuable and Divinely ordained—even when learning a lesson means feeling pain.

Believing in loss means we focus on the grief, on the pain, on the tragedy, on the inescapable reality of certain events. Believing in loss means we get fixated on what was taken from us, what we did wrong. We judge ourselves and our lives harshly. Believing in loss often means we stay stuck. We're afraid to let go of a person, place, or thing that's no longer right for us because we're afraid to lose anything more.

Do you believe in loss? Or do you believe in life?

Believing in life means it's okay to let go. We can trust where we've been. We trust where we're going. And we're right where we need to be now. Believe in life.

JUNE 10

Enjoy Summer

Learn to enjoy summer, that wonderful warm time when everything is in full bloom.

Summer isn't forever, but don't ruin it by fussing. Forget about the winter just past, the autumn that lies ahead. Immerse yourself in the good times, the fullness of summertime.

We may have gotten so used to the other times, the colder times, that we've forgotten how to enjoy the sun, the warmth, the play times. The good times. Each moment of our lives is important. Each moment of our lives is a spiritual experience. To live fully in joy, we need to learn to enjoy the good times as well as weather the storms. Most of us are proficient at hunkering down and getting through the winters of our lives. Now, it's time to learn something different.

Take off your heavy wrap. Grab your straw hat and go bask in the sun. Tomorrow's lessons will take care of themselves.

Today the lesson is learning to enjoy summer.

JUNE 11

Be Honest with Yourself

What are you feeling deep down inside? Under the anger. Under the rage. Under the numb *I don't care, it doesn't matter.* Are you really feeling scared? Hurt? Abandoned? Go more deeply into yourself and your emotions than you have ever gone before. Be more honest with yourself than you have ever been before. The way to joy, the way to the heart is tender, soft, gentle, and honest. The way to the heart is to be vulnerable.

You don't have to be so brave. You don't have to be so strong. You don't always have to walk away with your head held high saying, *I can handle this. I've been through worse before.*

Become angry if you must. Feel your rage if it's there. Go numb once in a while, if you must. Then take a chance, and go a little deeper. Go way down deep inside. See what's there. Take a look. Risk being vulnerable.

Love yourself and all your emotions.
Be as honest with yourself as you can be.
Say how you really feel.

JUNE 12

Recharge Your Battery

Rest when you're tired. Take a break when life stales. Take time to recharge your battery.

Energy isn't something you have—it's something you *are*. To give and give and give, to put out without taking in, depletes your battery. It drains you, runs you down. Running on a low battery is no longer necessary, because now we know how to live differently.

Taking time to rest, renew, and refresh yourself isn't wasted time. Recharge. Choose what energizes you. Nature. A song. The voice of a friend. A nap. A hot bath. A cup of tea. A favorite program. A movie that makes you laugh or cry. A walk. A run. A prayer. A poem. A book that speaks to your soul.

Actions that emerge from an energized source are easier, go further, accomplish more. Let your work and love come from a vital spirit.

JUNE 13

Trust the Process of Growth

Be patient with yourself. It takes time to work out issues, to work through things. It takes time to learn lessons. The more important the lesson, the longer the cycle to work it out and work it through.

We may live in a technical age, but our souls aren't technical. They're still connected to nature. We grow and change as nature does. Learn her ways. Study her seasons and cycles, and know those same seasons and cycles are in each of us. The process of change is like planting a seed and watching it grow and bloom into a flower.

What are you trying to develop? A project? A change in yourself? Is there something new you're learning, trying to do? Are you trying to adjust to a major change in your life? Is there an old habit you're struggling to let go of? A love relationship or friendship you're hoping to begin or attempting to end?

Each stage of the process of growth and change is important. From those first moments when we see the idea, or the change begins, to those long moments of nurturing and nourishing the idea, each stage counts. Is there a change in your life that's begun, one you've started to notice? Are you thinking about it a lot, talking about it a lot, but not quite ready to take action? That stage is important too. You're nurturing and nourishing the seeds of change.

It takes time for nature to change things into
what they're becoming. It takes time for things
to develop. Be patient with yourself and life.
Trust the process of growth.

JUNE 14

Learn the Power of Respect

I watched as my journey unfolded this spring. Each place I visited gave me a lesson. People would show up at the right time and place with exactly the words I needed to hear. Sometimes the lesson would be announced loudly, clearly. Sometimes an awareness would surface softly when I least expected it, when I was beginning to wonder if any lesson or purpose was there at all. Everything I saw and experienced ultimately reinforced my trust in God, the universe, and the power of my heart to lead me on. After all, I had taken this trip on just a moment's notice with no itinerary, and a magical adventure had unfolded. By the time the journey ended and I pulled into the driveway at home, I had learned more than just to trust the process. I had learned to respect it.

Do more than trust the process, the journey you're on. Become so awestruck by it that you respect it, too. Respect your feelings and the timely manner in which they surface, heal, and lead you into new discoveries. Respect your experiences, the places you've been, the scenarios you've been through. Respect the way you've gained gold and jewels, the treasures of the soul, from each one.

Respect the darker moments, the more difficult times when you're uncertain and don't know what to do next. Respect the timing as your life and journey unfolds. Don't murmur about why such and such has to be the way it is. Don't limit how your growth can happen.

Learn to respect the path of others.
Learn to respect your own.

JUNE 15

It's Okay to Not Know

Sometimes we don't know what we want, what's next, or what we think our lives will look like down the road. That's okay. If the answer is *I don't know,* then say it. Say it clearly. And be at peace with not knowing.

Sometimes the reason we don't know is that what's coming is going to be very different from anything we've experienced before. Even if we knew, we couldn't relate to it because it's that new and that different. It's a surprise.

Sometimes the reason we don't know is that it would be too difficult, too confusing for us right now. It would take us out of the present moment, cause us to worry and fuss about how we could control it or what we have to do to make it happen. Knowing would make us afraid. Put us on overload. Take us away from now.

Sometimes our souls know, but it's just not time for our conscious minds to know yet. Sometimes knowing would take us out of the very experience we need to go through to discover the answer we're looking for. And sometimes the process of learning to trust, the process of going through an experience and coming to trust that we will ultimately discover our own truth, is more important than knowing.

The process of moving from what we don't know to what we are to learn is a process that can be trusted. It's how we grow and change. It's okay to not know. It's okay to let ourselves move into knowing. The lesson is trusting that we'll know when it's time.

JUNE 16

Seek Freedom and Equality in Love

Are you deferring to someone in your life? When we relinquish control of our lives to someone else, we also relinquish responsibility for our happiness, our well-being, our joy, our growth, and our choices.

It's healthy and normal to want to be nurtured. A partner can make our lives easier, take some of the load off. We are sent helpers, friends, and lovers. The Divine arm of love reaches out through people, through our loved ones, to bring us the support we need. Opening to and receiving that support are essential to well-being, to joy, to happiness. But there's a difference between receiving help and support and being controlled. There's a difference between surrendering to love and surrendering to control.

Relinquishing control can happen subtly, but its effects are powerful. We begin to believe we've lost our freedom. We begin to believe that someone has taken it away. We feel stifled, repressed.

Don't make other people responsible for delineating your boundaries. It's your job to take responsibility for your choices, your comings, your goings, your well-being, your path. If you feel you've relinquished your power, your freedom, take it back. Take responsibility for yourself. You don't have to defer to anyone. The times of being controlled are past. You can accept nurturing without being manipulated. You can accept love without being controlled.

Set yourself free. Love exists only where freedom exists. Create relationships that are equal. There you will find love.

JUNE 17

Learn to Report Instead of Judge

There is a world of difference between reporting and judging.

When you report, you merely say what happened. *I am going through this. I did this. She did that. I feel this.* But when you judge, attitudes and feelings are added on. *I am going through this; therefore I'm deficient. I did this; therefore I'm wrong. She did that; therefore there's something wrong with her. I feel this; so I must be bad.*

Reporting brings clarity and helps move us forward. Report on what is happening in your life as often as you like. But try not to judge. Judgment limits, confines, brings condemnation down on others and ourselves. It says who you are, where you are, what you are doing is wrong. That leaves little room to move, and even less space for acceptance. It diminishes the freedom to grow and evolve.

Reporting without judgment doesn't mean we approve of what's going on or that we don't have feelings about the situation. Nor does it mean we have to tolerate whatever comes our way. But when we can report without judgment, we can accept. And acceptance sets us free. Acceptance is the place from which all growth and change occurs.

When there is truth and acceptance
without fear of judgment, there is love.
Create your own world of love.

JUNE 18

Don't Worry

Worrying doesn't help. Our worries haven't prevented one disaster along the way. At times, the only thing they've prevented is our joy. Our worries are fear. We say, *I will worry and be fearful until things have worked out; only then can I relax and enjoy.* Our worries are self-punishment, a form of not forgiving ourselves, not loving ourselves, not trusting.

We may think that worrying helps ward off trouble, but that's an illusion. Sometimes worrying brings troubles upon us, because we're so caught up in our fear that we don't take the responsible steps we need to take. By neglecting our lives due to worry and fear, we may bring needless consequences upon ourselves.

The lesson is trust. When we're trusting, we let go of our fear, confident that what we want and need will come. We trust that if what comes appears to be trouble or hardship, we will get what we need to get through that, too. When we trust, we get peaceful first, before we get what we want, before we see what the future brings.

Worry and fear are the opposite of love.
Love yourself more than you ever have.
Love yourself enough to stop worrying.
Love yourself enough to give yourself
the gift of peace.

JUNE 19

Your Heart Will Guide You Through

If you feel confused, alone, unsure of what to do next, go back to a place you can trust—your heart. In matters of work, money, love, play, go back to your heart.

The issues that arise in your life can be dealt with from the heart. You will be guided through gently, safely, with love and truth, along the path that's best for you. Are you feeling upset? Do you wonder why things aren't working out? Are you unsure of the map, uncertain of the next step, wondering how to untangle the mess of the past?

The answer isn't in your head, it's in your heart. It's not outside of you, although sometimes we receive guidance from others. The answer you're seeking, the guidance you're looking for needs to feel right to you. It needs to resonate with your heart. Your heart is the center, the balance point for your emotions, your intellect, and your soul. Your heart is safe.

Go back to your heart. It will
always lead you home.

You Are a Perfect Balance of Yin and Yang

I trudged to the top of the mesa in Sedona. A woman I'd met had told me what to look for. There it was: a rock formation, a naturally formed statue. On the left side, the formation looked like a woman, an Egyptian goddess with necklace and breasts. On the right, it had taken the shape of a male. I found it immediately. A statue with two sides, two faces—one male, one female.

For many years, I denied the feminine part of God, of the universe, of myself. I thought my strength and my power had to come from other parts, other sides. I resented my femininity, raged about it, because I thought being feminine meant being helpless and powerless. But I've learned something along the way. There is power in the feminine and power in the masculine. Both parts are in us. Both parts are valuable.

Our strength, courage, protectiveness, and the ability to decide, organize, plan, order, and choose reflect masculine energy. Our creativity, sensitivity, emotions, vulnerability, intuition, and instincts for nurturing and caregiving are the wisdom of the feminine side.

Honor and respect the masculine and feminine energy, the yin and the yang in yourself, the universe, the people around you. Both parts are important. Both can be trusted. Learn to let them work together in harmony.

Climb to the top of the mountain.
Look around. See the perfect balance
of masculine and feminine. Let that
balance come alive in you.

JUNE 21

You're Right Where You Need to Be

You're right where you need to be—on your path, guided, in just the right place for you today.

Many times on my journey I stopped short, convinced I would never find the place I was trying to find, only to discover that it was right in front of me all the time. I had gone there instinctively. Gone right where I needed to go, right where I was heading.

There is a part of us that knows where we need to be and understands where we really want to go. There's a place in us that has the map, even if our eyes and conscious mind can't see it, can't figure it out, or aren't certain it's there.

If you're spinning in circles, feeling lost and confused, trying to figure out where you need to be and not all that certain where you're going, stop. Breathe deeply. Look around.

You're right where you need to be.
Maybe you've been there all along.

JUNE 22

Forgive Your Inner Child for Being So Afraid

No matter how much work we've done on ourselves, no matter how committed we are to healing, there may be part of us that's four years old when we deal with certain people. There may be a part of us that still feels frozen, frightened, powerless, and abandoned when we face certain situations.

We may be all dressed up, look grown up, have our professional hat on. But the person wearing it is four. And scared. Afraid to speak up, relax, be who we are—a powerful, sensitive, creative, competent, intelligent, wise adult.

Watch for these four-year-olds. Be gentle, kind, compassionate. Forgive them for being so frightened. They have reasons that are valid, understandable, and sometimes noble. But their reasons come from a long time ago. This is now.

We're grown now. We're strong. We're free. We can walk away, speak up, laugh, say how we feel. And we can't be abandoned anymore, because we know how to live on our own.

Watch for your four-year-old. This child may never completely leave you, but you don't have to let him or her run the show.

JUNE 23

Discover the Power of Stillness

I will forever remember Yellowstone Glacier Lake at midnight. A large full moon—the biggest I have even seen—was resting atop the lake. The lake was frozen over, a still mirror between the mountains. Even the pines stood motionless. At that moment, I saw stillness—quiet, motionless stillness—and I began to understand its power.

Be still and know that I am God. How often I heard that verse from the Bible. How well I knew it, but how little I understood stillness. Stillness is different from solitude, different from aloneness, different from turning off the stereo or speaking softly.

Stillness is a place. You can find it in the desert or in the mountains. You can find it when you're alone or when you're in the midst of people. You can find stillness wherever you are, whatever you're going through. Stillness is a place within you. Slow down. Breathe deeply. Get quiet. Become familiar with stillness. Take time to learn its power.

From that place of stillness, the right action
will emerge and you will find your next step.
From that place of stillness, you can move
into the present moment. There you will find
your power, and there God will find you.

JUNE 24

Restore Your Natural Balance

Seek healing, a refilling of energy and spirit, as soon as you see that you need it. You don't have to push yourself to give, do, or perform when what your body, mind, soul, and emotions need is to heal.

Seek and support your natural balance. Listen to your body, listen to your soul, and both will tell you what they need and when. If you aren't certain what you need, ask. Ask your body what you need. Ask your heart what to do next. Ask God and the universe to help.

Find the balance that's right for you. Become sensitive to your needs. When you become stressed, depleted, out of sync, in need of healing, seek help immediately. Nurture and care for yourself until you're in balance once again.

Inhale, receive. Exhale, give back. Your natural balance is as necessary as breathing. The inhaling is the breathing in of life's energy. The exhaling is the sharing of your resources. You wouldn't expect to exhale if you hadn't inhaled. So it goes with healing, with our life force, with our energy. You cannot give it out if you don't take it in.

Find the balance of receiving and giving, of the taking in of energy and the giving out of energy, that works for you.

Let the balance become natural.
See how much more you do and are.
See how much better you feel when
you keep your life force vital.

JUNE 25

Ground Yourself

So much of our growth is spiritual. Sometimes we fly so high, our soul soars into the heavens, touching life's magic, sailing into the high spiritual realms. That is as it should be. But we need to be grounded, too. Even the tallest tree, the one that reaches hundreds of feet into the sky, has roots that go deep into the earth. The higher we want to travel on spiritual planes, the more we need to learn to ground ourselves. Our roots need to go deep into the earth, too.

Touch things that grow in the earth. Walk on the grass. Sit on the ground. Feel its presence, its solid grounding energy, rise up into you.

You are a soul, a spirit, but you have a body, too. Remember and nurture your spirit, but take time to attend to your body. Connect with what is physical, connect with the energy of the earth. Do the simple tasks that connect you to life on this planet—the day-to-day chores that connect you with your body and the rhythms of this world.

Grow spiritually, but let your spiritual growth be grounded in daily life and the things of earth. That is how you stay grounded; that's how you honor your body and stay connected to it. Grow spiritually, but let that growth reflect and honor embodied life. Just as the body and workings of an airplane give shape to the idea of an airplane and allow it to fly, your body gives shape, form, and freedom to your soul. But even airplanes need to land sometimes.

Learn to tell when your body and soul
need to come back to earth. Take time to
get grounded. Then you'll be able to soar.

JUNE 26

Say Good-Bye with Love

When traveling with another person, we sometimes come to a junction. It may be in the best interests of one person to go one way, to see certain sights, gain certain experiences, learn particular lessons, and for the other to go in another direction. This is a difficult time of challenges, maybe hard choices.

Blending journeys sometimes is not always best, or even possible. We can accompany another on his or her journey, but there may be a price to pay for that. We may forgo our own journey and become passive observers. We can ask or insist that the other go along with us on our journey. But for the most part, he or she may be as bored and restless as we would be if the situation were reversed. Sometimes we need to let go. Sometimes we need to say good-bye.

These junctions can surprise us. They can appear early on or after years and years. They can occur in friendships, professional relationships, love relationships, or with family members. Although arriving at these junctions may be a surprise, it's usually not an accident. Often it's an important part of the journey.

Feel all your feelings. Although you may need to feel angry for a while, clear all resentments from your heart as soon as possible. Say good-bye with blessings and love toward the other, thanking that person for all he or she has helped you learn. Remember that any curses you place on another will ultimately come back to harm you, too.

Grieve your losses. Say your good-byes. Then let each travel down the road that he or she needs to go. Holding on won't help. Let both be free to plan their own journeys, map their own trips, and embrace and enjoy their own destinies.

Set others free to achieve and experience
the path that leads to their highest good and
you, too, will become free to find yours.

JUNE 27

Learn to Be Calm

I felt strained and tense when I began the drive along the Redwood Highway in northern California. I had wanted to take another road, one quicker but less scenic, to get to my destination. At the last moment, I decided to drive through the trees.

Thousands of redwoods grew hundreds of feet into the air. Some stood tall and proud. Some seemed to have their necks craned, so they could peer down onto the highway. Some grew with roots connected, like families. Some stood alone. Mile after mile after mile, for as far as I could see in any direction, thousands of trees surrounded me. Their power and message became inescapable. It was one of calmness, patience, and growth.

For hundreds of years they have been here, patiently seeing things through. Little ruffled them. They just kept on growing for all those years—steadily, patiently, peacefully, calmly. They have been through enough, seen enough, to know not to worry. Things work out. Change happens. Life continues to evolve.

I didn't see one tree hurrying or worrying. They have been here long enough to learn life's lessons well.

Learn a lesson from the redwoods. Let them teach the power of patience and calm. Life goes on. Things happen. People change. Times move along. There are stories to live and stories to tell, but we can be calm and know that, always, all is well.

JUNE 28

Feel Your Feelings

You don't have to *do* anything about your feelings. Understand that. Believe that. They are only feelings. Emotional energy is important. It's important not to block it, stop it, deny it, or repress it. It's important to discharge it. To value it. To value ourselves.

But you don't have to *do* anything. You don't have to act on every feeling. You don't need to control every emotion or let your emotions control you. Doing something is the old way, the way of control. Simply feel whatever you need to feel. Become fully and completely conscious of what you feel. Take responsibility for the way you choose to express your feelings. Then let your feelings go. Release the emotional energy.

Soon you will know what to do next, know what lesson is under way. You will naturally take the action that's right for you to take.

All you have to do about your
feelings is feel them.

JUNE 29

Stay Clear

Sometimes we don't tell other people what we're feeling. Sometimes we don't tell ourselves.

Often on this journey, provocative events happen. We may become resentful. Angry. Or frightened. Emotional energy builds up within. If we don't take the time to work it out, the emotion becomes a block. It blocks the channel to our heart; it blocks our channel to ourselves; it can block our connection to others and to God.

We may think we're being polite and appropriate by not saying what we feel. We may think that most thoughts and emotions are so minor it would be a waste of time to acknowledge and express each and every one of them. It's true that some aren't worth mentioning, but many are. We need to take the time to feel and release the thoughts and beliefs that are important to us.

Is a relationship blocked? Are we feeling something we're unable to discuss? The feeling won't disappear. The energy of the unexpressed feeling will be present, blocking our connection until we take the time to get it out. We may not tell the other person what we're feeling, but all of us are wiser than we think. And our bodies and emotions will begin reacting to what's denied, despite what we say.

Many of us experiment with the technique of using affirmations to try to further our growth. The same principle applies. If we say we love ourselves, but we've got a chunk of self-reproach tucked down deep inside, we'll continue to act as if we dislike ourselves until we clear the other energy out.

What are you feeling? No, what are you *really* feeling? Ask yourself as often as you need to. Then take the time to feel and release the emotion, thought, or belief.

You've connected to yourself. You're
connected to the world around you.
Now, keep your connections clear.

JUNE 30

Cherish Your Connection to the Universe

My relationship with the universe used to be different. I felt separate, apart, disconnected from the rest of the world. My vision of God used to be different, too. I used to see God as sitting on a throne, separate and apart from this world. I still see God as the supreme creative force, but the separateness is melting, changing, transforming into something new. Now I see God, the energy of God, and Divine love as a part of all that is, the breath of life in every living thing.

I used to see the world as made up of individual and separate components. I used to see people as disconnected and essentially powerless in a world separated from God. Each thing, person, and action a distinctly different operation or event from any other, from the whole. Now I see a planet full of people connected to the Divine. Now I see a universe connected by a Divine thread that weaves throughout all that is, was, and will be. A living universe that is alive, magical, connected by universal love. Connected by Divine love.

Enter into a relationship with the universe,
a relationship as alive, as active, as vital as any
other relationship. Then know that you are
connected to the world and everything in it.
Know that universal love, Divine love, is real
and you are an important part of it.

July

JULY 1

Embrace Each Cycle of Your Life

It took me a long time to accept wearing glasses. I am still surprised when I need my spectacles to read a menu or scan the telephone directory. Sometimes I look in the mirror expecting to see the body, the face of my youth because I remember her. She's still in me.

Now I'm learning to welcome aging, as each decade of life brings its own challenges, joys, sorrows, and teachings. I'm learning to trust the lessons of each cycle of my life. I don't fear aging, for I know that it's as much, and as important, a part of life as my youth.

"My mother just had her seventieth birthday," the woman at the lodge told me. "My sister and I asked her what she wanted. She wanted a wet suit for diving because waterskiing had strained her back."

What does getting older mean to you?

Young and old. All part of the same.
Each moment is a moment of life,
your life. Each cycle has its lessons.
Dig out your glasses, if you must, but
laugh when you do it. And remember
to make each moment count.

JULY 2

What Would Make You Happy?

Why don't you make yourself happy? Did someone tell you you couldn't be happy, couldn't let life help you out? It doesn't matter who told you you couldn't have what you wanted. What matters is if you're still telling yourself that now.

Yes, there are many situations in life in which we need to go without, do what needs to be done, get the job done. There are times when a particular purpose is served by depriving ourselves. But there are also situations—many more than we think—in which we can have what we want. There are moments when what we want matters.

Look into your heart. Ask yourself what you want. What would feel good? What would bring joy? Is anything to be gained by depriving yourself a while longer? Get creative. Look around. What are some ways you could give yourself what you want? What could you do to create your life more to your liking?

Giving yourself what you want isn't selfish. It teaches others they can have more of what they want from life, too.

Use your imagination. Set yourself
free. Let yourself see the pictures

and feel the emotions of what would make you happy. Then take a moment, pause, and smile. You're beginning to get a glimpse of all you can have from God.

JULY 3

Cherish Your Heart

A woman I met in Washington gave me a gift. It was a beautiful heart, sculpted by her son, an artist. It was a mosaic of broken pieces, a heart covered with break lines that had healed over and mended together.

"My son made this," she said. "I want you to have it." I thanked her for the gift. Now I keep it close. It's a reminder to keep my heart open.

Keep your heart open. Take care lest life's problems shut you down. When you close down, your passion, enthusiasm, faith, and zest will disappear.

Open your heart to all you meet. If it's not safe, you'll know. But don't close your heart. Just move in another direction. Don't worry about getting your heart broken. Sometimes that happens. Sometimes it's the price you pay for opening your heart, for taking the risk. But if it does happen, you can allow your heart to heal, then open it once again.

Remember the sculpture. Let it remind you that, once healed, a broken heart is a beautiful work of art.

J U L Y 4

Learn to Relax

We need to learn how to relax, how to unwind.

Find something that's relaxing, healing, soothing, and available to you. Sit in the sun. Sit in the tub. Take a trip to a nearby hot spring or mineral bath in your state. Perch atop a mountain or hill, taking in the view from above.

Let yourself sit and soak it in for as long as you can. Let yourself be still for as long as you can. Move around a bit if you need to. Then go back and try again.

Don't just do it once. Try it often. Allow yourself to relax. Give yourself opportunities to unwind. Soon you'll learn how.

Pay attention to what you think and feel when you try to relax. Watch, as a neutral observer, without judgment or reproach. What thoughts come to mind? How do you feel? What do you feel?

Go as deeply into your thoughts and feelings
as you are able. Sit quietly for as long as you can.
When your body is done, it will tell you.

J U L Y 5

Become Excited About Life

I woke up one morning and found myself in a strange place. Instead of waking up to pain, I felt a new feeling coursing through my veins. I felt happy, at peace, and excited about being alive. This feeling had come around before, but never to stay or last. Now I knew that it was mine for good. It was where this journey had led.

Let excitement course through you. It is vitality; it is healing, life-giving energy. It is the life force. Feel it course through your veins. This excitement you are feeling is different from the pain of years past. It is a different feeling, but your birthright, my birthright, the birthright of us all. It is your reward for staying committed to your process of learning and growing.

Continue to clear out old, negative feelings and outdated beliefs. Stay committed to healing and discovering your soul, even when you wonder if it's worth it. Even when you wonder where your path is going, or if it's going anywhere. Love yourself. Love others. Then love yourself some more. Love yourself until you feel the life force, this exciting new energy, course through you.

> *Stay committed to your growth process until*
> *you wake up one morning and ask yourself,*
> What is that strange thing I'm feeling? *Then*
> *know what the answer is. The answer is joy.*

JULY 6

See How Each Soul Has Touched You

Often in our lives, we don't realize the significance of a relationship until later, when the experience has passed. Then we understand how the person helped us along the way, took us to the next part of our journey, opened us up to begin learning the next lesson. And we see how we, in turn, helped shape that person.

One evening, as I was readying for sleep, I had a vision. I saw clearly before me a scenario of the dance we do with each other. I saw in my heart, understood deeply, the tangible, shaping impact each soul had on my life. Each moment, each interaction with another person, had been important—the quiet interactions, the ones I barely noticed, and the more significant relationships. Each moment—the moments that hurt, the moments that brought joy—had helped. We had touched each other. We were joined in an intricate dance, a dance in which our souls learned and grew.

And we had taken our places with each other on time, for the dance was perfectly choreographed.

I could almost see us waving gleefully to each other, happy for how we had connected, joyful that we had helped each other learn the lessons of the soul: courage, love, forgiveness, gentleness, self-love.

See how each soul touches you? See how you touch them? Ask your heart to guide you with honesty, love, and responsibility in all your encounters. Honor the sacredness of love. Honor the lessons of planet earth and the people who help you learn them.

JULY 7

Recognize the Signs

Sometimes, the universe gives us warnings.

I was driving down a local highway in New Mexico, a safe distance behind the car in front of me. Suddenly, the driver slammed on his brakes to avoid a huge puddle, a flood of water in front of him. I stopped short, but the car behind me was following too closely and rammed into the rear of my Jeep.

I got out and inspected the damage. My car was fine. The woman who rammed me had dented her bumper. No one was harmed. I got back in my Jeep, thinking it was over. But as I drove off, I began to wonder. Something about the incident still nagged at me.

Several weeks later, I was driving down a fast-moving two-lane highway. Behind me was a large truck loaded with cars. In front of me were several cars. In front of the cars was a school bus. The traffic was moving at at least fifty-five miles an hour.

Suddenly, I saw the brake lights from the cars ahead. The school bus had stopped to let a child disembark. I pulled to a stop behind the car in front of me. Then I remembered the lesson from the accident a couple of weeks ago: sometimes I can stop safely, but the driver behind me can't.

I looked out my rearview mirror. The truck loaded with cars was frantically trying to stop. I pulled my car off the road onto the shoulder, giving him an extra car length. He screeched to a stop, right behind the car ahead of me. Had I not noticed, not pulled out, we'd all have been piled up. And the children in the bus . . .

Sometimes accidents happen without warning, but sometimes the universe gives us a nudge, a little sign. We don't have to become paranoid, we don't have to think every event means something, but we can trust ourselves to recognize a sign when we see one.

JULY 8

Sometimes the Road Gets Rough

Don't be dismayed when you come to a pothole, a detour, a stretch of rough and rocky road. Don't be surprised. Slow down a little. Be patient. It's not the whole journey. It's not the way it'll always be. But it is part of your journey, too, part of your journey to your heart and soul. Even when we're living with joy and freedom, we continue to learn, grow, feel, experience. And the road can still get rough.

Happiness doesn't mean feeling gleeful all the time. Happiness doesn't mean the road we're traveling is always smooth. Happiness means feeling all we need to feel. And accepting each part of the journey, even the changes of course and direction.

Feel all your feelings. Feel your fear and frustration about slowing down, then settle in for the ride. You may not be going as fast as you'd like, but the journey hasn't stopped. You're not doing anything wrong. You are going slower, but you're still moving forward.

JULY 9

Learn to Focus Your Energy

"I've come to this lodge for one reason," the woman at Breitenbush Retreat in Williamette Forest said. "I brought my fiddle, and I'm not leaving until I can play a bluegrass tune. If I want to get out of here, I'd better learn how to play."

There is a time to be open, almost unfocused, as we take in what the world, the universe, is showing us. There is a time to get out of our heads and quietly take the journey our hearts lead us into—following with the openness and wonder of a child.

But there also comes a time to aim our attention and focus our energy on what we want to accomplish. Instead of floundering with scattered thoughts and possibilities, we choose one, then act on it. We stay in step with the natural rhythm, but we're pulling our scattered attention together and focusing it as part of that rhythm.

To do that, we may have to work through or push away inner distractions. Moving through our inner obstacles enables us to accomplish our goal—whether that's a task, a particular piece of work, or learning to play the fiddle.

Is there something you want to do? Is your heart urging you to learn something, accomplish something, go somewhere, do something? Make it a goal. Focus your energy. Learn to stay focused until you reach that goal.

Put yourself in the cabin and don't
let yourself out until it's done.

JULY 10

Trust the Timing of Your Lessons

Too often our first inclination when we learn a lesson, gain a new insight, have an awareness, or glimpse a new truth is to judge and criticize ourselves—for not seeing it sooner, not knowing it before, or being in denial too long. That's not necessary. It's not appropriate. We're not at fault because we didn't have this awareness or understand this lesson until now.

We don't need to see the truth one moment before we see it. Judging ourselves for not knowing sooner can close us off to what life has to teach us now. We're here to learn our lessons, discover our truths, have our adventures.

Let yourself have your experiences. Allow yourself to learn what you learn when you learn it. Don't judge yourself for not learning sooner. Be happy, grateful, and excited when your lesson arrives.

Trust your voice, that quiet inner voice,
when it speaks to you of truth. Be grateful
you can hear it; do what it tells you to do.
Trust the timing of your heart.

JULY 11

Clear the Path to Your Heart

I watched Old Faithful from my window. The geyser gurgled and spewed a low layer of steam. Then true to its name, Old Faithful erupted and sprayed thousands of gallons of steaming water into the air. Right on time.

A full range of gurgling emotions, reactions, and responses to life line the pathway to the heart. We need to feel them all—anger, hurt, sadness, irritations—in order to feel joy. To experience life and all its wonders, we must embrace all these feelings.

We need to experience the little angers as well as the big hurts, the painful wounds that life sometimes brings. To insist that we will only feel pleasant emotions means we're blocking the pathway to the heart. We're ignoring all the other gurgling emotions that need to be felt.

All our emotions are important; all need to be recognized. The energy of each needs to be acknowledged and released. This clears the way for love. All the emotions that precede love clear the heart so it's pure and free to feel joy.

*Trust your emotions. All of them.
You're not off the path. They lead to
the path you're seeking. They are the
journey to the heart. Let them flow freely.
And sure as Old Faithful, your heart
will come gleaming, shining through.*

JULY 12

Let the Universe Lead the Way

Feel and see how the life force, the heartbeat of the universe, leads you on, guides you, takes you on the way. Yes, there are times when we need to march forward, muster up our willpower, and grind through the motions. But those times are transitory. And that's not the magical way we're living now. Even when we stop, doubt, wonder, get tired and confused, the universe is there to revitalize us, move us along our path and lead the way.

If you're tired, rest. If you're sad, cry. If you're thirsty, take a long, cold drink of water. If you feel hopeless, feel that. But know it's just for the moment. If you feel confused, feel that. Feel it until clarity, desire, hope, and meaning break through. You don't have to trudge through on willpower, not any longer. You do not have to push your way through.

Rest until you feel healed, then gently go forward. Let the universe assist you. Open your eyes, the eyes of your soul, and see where to go. Feel where to go. Sense what to do next. See how the magical power of the universe carries you along, even when you get tired, even when you get confused. You are connected—to yourself, to the universal life force, to God.

Quiet the chatter of your mind. Renew your body. Replenish your soul. Take in all the healing energy of the world around you.

Then let the universe lead the way.

JULY 13

See the Snow on the Desert

I drove through Arizona's petrified forest, a land where dinosaurs once roamed, then headed across the painted desert. A light dusting of snow covered the sand and shrubs. I felt both awe and surprise at the scene nature had created.

Nature does many things. Tornadoes blow across the land. Hurricanes pound the shores. Bolts of lightning streak through the sky. Dust storms fill the air. Nature petrifies wood, turning trees into beautiful crystal rocks, glowing with brilliant red and orange fossilized patterns. Nature takes centuries to carve bridges out of stone, using only winds and rains and the flow of water from other rocks. And sometimes, she puts snow on the desert.

Many things happen in our lives. Some of them are probable, consequential. Some of them are flukes and seem to come out of the blue, from nowhere. All the events work into a pattern, helping to create us, create our path through life, create our destiny. Sometimes we're influenced greatly by a traumatic storm. Other times seemingly chance occurrences can change the entire pattern and course of our lives.

We don't have to understand everything. Maybe we aren't supposed to. We don't have to be prepared for all the storms. Sometimes the greatest learning occurs when we're caught off guard, by surprise.

Weather the storms. Let them pass.
Keep your balance, as best you're able.
Remember to be flexible and sway with
the winds like the tall trees in the forest.
Trust the flukes, too, those moments
when it snows on the desert. Let destiny
have its way with you.

JULY 14

Touch the Eternal

My friend, a clerk in a local bookstore, and I were sitting on a bench one evening about twenty feet from the edge of the Pacific Ocean. A few stars and a tiny sliver of moon softly lit the sky. We were drinking coffee and staring at the sea. "I like the ocean," my friend said. "I need to see it. It's nature's way of reminding us of eternity."

Sometimes, we zoom in on the details of our lives and all we can see is the small picture—the problems, issues, and specifics of what we need to do today. These moments are real. They're the heart of our lives. It's good to stay focused and attend to them, but sometimes we need to step back and see the big picture, too.

Visit places that remind you of
eternity when you can. See the
mountains. See the stars. Walk
among the ancient redwoods.
Stand at the ocean's door. Let nature
and life remind you of eternity in
ways that speak to your soul.

JULY 15

Delight in Yourself

Stop picking on yourself, worrying if you're good enough, wondering what people will see if you let them see your heart. This is what they'll see: that you are a lovable and delightful soul, a beautiful child of God.

Be yourself and accept yourself—warts, waistline, and all. You don't have to sit up that straight, be that proper, or fear what others may see. Let your imperfections show! Share them! Love yourself anyway! Relax, and be who you are! When you do that, your life will be fun and a joyful gift to others.

People who comfortably accept who they are—both their flaws and their good points—are healing, delightful, and fun to be around. Look at any work of nature: a canyon, a flower, a bird. A mountain or a forest trail. Where does the perfection begin and imperfection end? It's the combination that makes a perfect scene. So it is with you.

Relax. Lighten up. Let go of shame and fear.
The whole picture is perfect, and perfectly okay.

JULY 16

Go a Little Further

I arrived at Oregon's Willamette National Forest after dark. Suddenly I found myself at a fork in the road. To the right was a chained gate marked "Foot Travelers Welcome." To the left was an open road marked "Nature Sanctuary, Authorized Visitors Only."

I stared at both signs, then headed to the left. I didn't see anything that looked like lodging and I began to feel uncomfortable, like one of the unauthorized visitors the sign warned about. I backed the car out to the fork, turned around, and left.

Two hours later, I still hadn't found the retreat. I was tired and worried about running out of gas. I tried to remember what I'd been learning—that desperation attracts more desperation. I relaxed and visualized myself finding the retreat, being given a key to a room, and going to sleep in a bed. I visualized it until I could see the scene clearly in my mind.

Before long I found myself back at the fork. *I mean no harm,* I thought. So *I'll just drive down that nature sanctuary road again, the one for authorized visitors only.* I drove as far as I had been before, then decided to push ahead a bit more. I rounded the bend and there it was—the parking lot, the night office, and a man who could give me a key to my room. Within twenty minutes, I was in bed for the evening.

> *Sometimes we need to go further than we thought we could. We need to go past our fear, past our uncertainty, past the bend we can't see beyond. If we stay on the course, give it that extra push, and go round the bend, we may find what we're looking for.*

JULY 17

Put Yourself on Equal Ground

I sat in the booth across from my friend. I was fiddling with an empty soda can in front of me while we discussed the subject of power. Suddenly he snatched the can away from me and began tossing it in the air, catching it, then tossing it up again. "See how easy it is to take your power?" he said. "See how you just gave it to me?"

I watched, amazed at how quickly I had relinquished my power, how vulnerable I was to the world around me.

Then my friend smiled and stopped juggling the can. "Relax," he said. "It's an illusion. That's not really your power—it's an empty can. And it's an illusion that anyone can take your power away from you."

Each of us has an unlimited supply of power available—the power to think, to feel, to take care of ourselves. The power to open our hearts, love, be gentle, honest, and kind. We each have the power to be clear and to trust and follow the guidance of our own hearts.

Part of our journey to freedom, an important part, is equalizing our relationships. For many years, we may have believed the scales were tipped one way or the other in our work and love relationships. We may have believed that others knew a great deal more than we did, or we may have begun to believe that we had all the answers. But no one has our power. That's an illusion. So much so that sometimes the person we believe is more powerful than us may be looking at us thinking we're the ones pulling the strings.

Remember, if you give up your power or decide that someone has power over you, you'll begin grousing, sabotaging, and doing sneaky little things to equalize that relationship, to feel like you have your power. There's another way, a better way, one that will help you heal.

Put yourself on equal ground.

JULY 18

Find the Humor in It

I called home from my trip to talk to my friend. He was taking care of Max, my African Grey parrot, while I went on this journey. "How's Max?" I asked. "Is she doing okay?"

"Well," he said, "she's a little confused. I've got her outside on the patio. She says hi to all the sea gulls that come by and she can't figure out why they won't talk back to her."

My parrot makes me smile. My friend makes me laugh. I have many friends that make me smile. Together, we laugh a lot. Learning to laugh, learning to find humor either in what we're going through, or despite it, is a powerful tool on this journey.

Cherish the gift of humor. Life doesn't need to be so gloomy. Spirituality doesn't need to be so serious and somber. Work doesn't need to be that way either. Learn to see the humor in life. Look for it. Find it. Enjoy it. Surround yourself with people who like to laugh. Being around people who laugh can open us up to the power of humor in our own lives. Laughter can become contagious. There is something magnetic, something healing, about being around people who let themselves laugh often.

There is no situation in life that can't be improved by laughter. Sometimes humor can help us get through situations we couldn't possibly endure without it. Sometimes laughter isn't superfluous; it's essential.

Sometimes laughter is the next
lesson we need to be learning.

JULY 19

The Lessons Are Love

Lessons of love, that's what they are.

We usually don't know what the lesson is while we're learning it. Maybe we're not supposed to. Besides, if we knew it, really knew it, we wouldn't need to learn it. We'd already be practicing it in our daily lives. But even when we don't know what the lesson is, we can know one thing: it's a lesson of love.

Courage. Faith. Patience. Loving ourselves when it looks and feels like nobody else cares. Starting over again one more time, when we think we've already started over again more times than we should have had to. Forgiveness. Compassion. Gentleness. Joy. Each one is a lesson of love.

For many of us, the problem isn't that we haven't had love in our lives before. The issue is that we haven't understood love. Know this: not only are the lessons about love, the lessons themselves are love.

Feel your feelings. Struggle through your situations and experiences and emotions. The struggle to learn isn't incidental to your purpose. It's an integral part of your purpose, your destiny, your reason for being. Go through your moments of darkness and confusion, and trust that the light will come. Through it all, rest in one thought: you're on track. You're on your path.

You're connected to love. You're connected to God. And the lessons you're learning are lessons of love.

JULY 20

Value Your Connection to Creativity

For years, I had been storing my son's clothing, some of his favorite articles, in boxes in the garage. I didn't want to let go of the clothes, yet I had no use for them. One day an idea came. I was talking to a woman enthralled with quilting, with fabrics, textures, and the art of creating quilts. She was talking about how she was making a quilt out of her family's old blue jeans, because it created a use for the fabric and gave them a blanket that held the energy and memory of their experiences. It wasn't just a quilt. It became a special comfort quilt because of the energy the fabrics held.

That's when the idea came. My son had died years ago. His physical presence was no longer here. But the clothes held the memories of his physical presence and the energy of his spiritual presence. I could make them into a quilt, one that would cherish his memory and give me comfort.

How do we get our ideas? From other people. From certain triggers in the world, the universe. From our imagination. We are connected to creativity. It's a force in the universe, an energy that runs through us. If we're connected to ourselves, our intuition will guide us as to what to do and when to do it. If we love ourselves, we'll trust ourselves enough to act confidently and joyfully on that guidance.

Value your connection with creativity. Embrace your imagination. The universe will show you how, teach you how, help you along the way.

JULY 21

Value Work

We need to value the simple tasks of life and the work we do professionally to earn income, fulfill purpose, and bring our gifts to the world.

There are many tasks to be done in life—our personal responsibilities to others, our professional commitments, our responsibilities to ourselves. There is value and honor in work, in performing the tasks that make up our daily lives.

When we joyfully perform the tasks of life—whether we're taking care of ourselves or fulfilling a commitment to another—we connect with the very rhythms and workings of life and the universe. Many important spiritual lessons are connected with work. It's better not to use work as an escape, a way to avoid life. But work done with an attitude of honor, love, and joy can be a tool on our spiritual path.

Work can take us into the rhythm of life. Work can bring us back to service, back to our hearts, back to our souls. We don't have to leave ourselves behind when we do the tasks of life. We can take all we've learned into our work; then learn more lessons from the tasks we do.

Remember to honor and value the work and the tasks that are yours to do—from the smallest to the grandest. Wash the dishes, fold the laundry, hold a business meeting, rake the yard. Each task is important.

Value work. Let it connect you
to the rhythms of life.

JULY 22

Take a Trip

I met the three women at the Ojo Caliente hot springs in New Mexico. Two were in their fifties; one was in her sixties. They splashed around in the mineral water in the steam pool. They looked happy, alive. "We only live two hours away, but twice a year we come here together. It heals us, renews us, and sends us back to our lives changed."

Is there someplace you'd like to travel to? Do you have time off from work, time that you could use creatively? Do you have a long weekend coming up? How would you like to spend that?

Vacations and trips are important. They give us a chance to get away, see someplace new, rest, and refresh our spirits. Trips often synchronize with growth and change in our lives. They celebrate what we've been through or what we're going through. A trip can correlate with a new leg on our journey in spiritual growth. Often, when we feel the urge to travel, it's connected to a deeper urge, the urge to go somewhere new on our path.

Recognize the desire in your heart to travel and see new horizons. Then honor it, for it reveals your desire to touch new horizons in your life.

JULY 23

Make a Fresh Start

Sometimes we need to start over—in work, in love, in our place of residence, in creating our lives. Sometimes we have to start over again when we don't want to, didn't plan on it, and don't think it's fair.

We may end a relationship, move, start a new job, start a new career, or begin an entirely different part of our lives, a part so different we don't recognize it as being connected to the earlier ones. It's new. We're new. Life is new. We're starting over again.

Sometimes it feels like we're starting from scratch. While we may feel a sense of excitement about this new beginning, we may also harbor a sense of dread. *Not again. Not one more time. I can't. I don't want to.* That reaction is understandable. We become tired, frightened. We feel uncertain.

Honor all your feelings, all your emotions. Remember all your lessons. Clear the way to the heart. Then make a decision.

It's time for a fresh start.

JULY 24

Joy Is the Way

The woman was in her fifties, maybe sixties. She had retired from the big city and was now working as a waitress in Mary's Restaurant, a small cafe in a small Montana town. She looked as if she lived alone. She looked as if she had been through her share of disappointments, joys, and awakenings. She brought me a plate of bacon and eggs, set them down, and gave me a radiant smile. "It's a beautiful day," she said.

"Yes it is," I said. I looked at her. "Are you happy to be here?"

She thought a moment, then replied. "Yes," she said with joy in her voice. "Yes, I am."

Joy is the way. Joy in the morning. Joy throughout the day. Joy at twilight. Joy in our dreams, waking and sleeping. For so long we believed that our joy depended on specific outward circumstances, on a particular situation being a certain way, or on the presence or behavior of a particular person. While getting what we want and being with those we love can add to our joy, we have learned another kind of joy, a deeper kind of joy. A joy that abides and carries us through.

Joy doesn't come from the outside, although the energies of the universe and universal love can add to our joy and fill our wellspring. Joy comes from doing the Divine will each moment. Joy comes from living in harmony with ourselves each moment of each day. Joy is a choice that comes from accepting and living fully each moment of our lives, knowing that each day and each event is important.

Joy comes from trusting each moment.
That's the secret of joy. Receive it now,
then pass it on with a smile and a kind
word to all who come along your path.

JULY 25

Don't Get Ahead of Yourself

I pulled out the map. *I'll go here,* I thought, *and there. I'll visit this place, then that one.* My mind raced with excitement at all the places left to see. I felt overwhelmed, wondering if I could get to all the places I wanted to visit. For a moment I forgot to look around and appreciate where I was—in the forest at the foot of Mount Olympus in Olympic State Park.

Don't get ahead of yourself. There are many wonderful places left to visit, many experiences to have, many people to meet and enjoy. But you aren't there yet. There will be some trials, too. More lessons along the path. But you aren't there yet, either.

Stay in this moment. It contains the experience you need to have. This moment contains your happiness. Living this moment, being fully present for it, is the way to get to the next experience, the next person, the next emotion, the next adventure. Cherish the moment. Feel all there is to feel. See all there is to see.

Learn the lessons of today, and you will be prepared for the adventures and joys of tomorrow.

Be here now. This is the only place you need to be.
And from this place, all things are possible.

JULY 26

Find Places of Repose

I was driving down a Nevada highway feeling tense and agitated when the sign appeared: "To the Nature Sanctuary." I ignored the first entrance; then turned at the second one. In a few short feet, the road and scenery changed from barren, flat highway into a terrain of serene repose. A family of ducks bathed and swam in a small lake, surrounded by trees. Tiny wrens pecked at the gravel. A boy about thirteen sat fishing, a picnic lunch by his side. In only a few minutes, my agitation disappeared. I had found a place of peace.

Rest when you become tense, afraid, upset. Rest until peace returns. Stop what you're doing. Take a moment, take an hour. Take the time you need to restore peace. Breathe deeply. Breathe in the quiet beauty of the world around you. Let it be a sanctuary that soothes and calms your soul.

Places of healing and repose are moments away. Find them in the world around you. Then discover those places in yourself. The universe holds the antidote for your fears and agitation. It offers all the healing you need. That healing is right around the corner.

Take a moment, take an hour. When
you feel your peace interrupted, look
for a place of repose.

JULY 27

Be Vulnerable with Yourself

As we go through our days, we meet many people. We learn it's safe to be vulnerable with some, not so safe or wise to be vulnerable with others. But there is one person it's always safe to be vulnerable with. Yourself.

Share your deepest secrets with yourself. Whether you rise early in the morning and write your thoughts in a journal or take a few moments throughout the day to bring your deepest secrets to consciousness, you need to be clear, straight, and honest with yourself. Harboring secrets, ducking, dodging, and hiding from the truth will slow you down. It will block the pathway to your heart. It can even stop you cold if you get enough secrets tucked away.

Take time each day to recognize what you think, what you feel. You don't have to act. The sheer acts of recognition, honesty, and acceptance are all that are necessary to keep you moving, growing, going forward.

Be as vulnerable as you safely can with those you meet along the way. But always be vulnerable with yourself.

JULY 28

Acknowledge Your Fears

I never knew how afraid I was. Maybe I was even too afraid to look at my fears.

People speak of facing fear, of not being afraid of fear, of working through fear. How do we do that? Try this technique, recommended to me by a healing professional. Take out a sheet of paper and a pencil, and write down everything you fear. Take as much time as you need. Let it roll out. Don't be afraid of what you see. Some of your fears may be of the unknown. Write as much as you can about those, too.

We don't need to list everything we need to do about each fear. All we need to do is acknowledge, honestly, what we fear. Once we do, the way will become clear. Acknowledging our fears will give us power. Acknowledging our fears will help set us free. Often, it moves us to the next place. It is the barrier we need to pass through.

Although some of our fears may be real, may be grounded in reality, facing them won't make us more afraid. Facing our fears won't cause us more pain. Facing fear will bring us peace and power. The truth isn't the enemy. Fear of the truth is the enemy.

Be gentle with yourself. Let yourself have your fears; and let yourself face them.

Having the wisdom to face the truth
will bring us closer to peace.

JULY 29

What's Your Handicap?

"What's your handicap?" the golfer asked his partner. "My childhood," said his companion.

Some handicaps are physical, certain limitations placed on our bodies. Other handicaps are emotional, burdens of heartache from sad or abusive childhoods. Others may be dealing with current issues—perhaps facing a terminal illness or grieving an irreparable loss.

After losing my son, I found myself at a point where I simply could no longer stand the agony of waiting for my pain to disappear. I knew that all my life I would miss him, and I became absolutely despondent. *There is no way out of this,* I thought. *I'm spending my life waiting for this pain to disappear so I can begin living my life again. But the pain never will disappear. And I'll never begin living my life again.* That's when a gentle idea began to change my life.

I began to understand that I was living and working with a handicap. The loss would always be there. The pain and heartache would always be present. I could accept that, treat it as a handicap, and within that framework go ahead and live my life once more. The moment I made that decision, my attitude and perspective changed. I was able to go on, able to move forward.

Many of us are living with handicaps. Some will change over time, but others won't. If that's the case, stop waiting for your handicap to disappear. Instead, decide to live with it. Work around it. Treat yourself with care, with gentleness. Allow yourself to feel and experience all the limitations and emotions of your present situation. Accept them. Let them be part of you, part of your experience.

Despite living with a handicap,
go ahead and treat yourself to life.

JULY 30

Find Your Own Healing Places

When I arrived in Sedona, I met Marianne. She and her husband ran the lodge where I stayed.

"You'll like it here," she said. "You'll find the healing you need."

"Where should I look?" I asked. "Where should I go? What things should I be sure to do?"

"There is no map for that," she quietly replied. "You'll find your own places. They'll call to you or you'll call them to you. You'll be drawn to what you need."

Sometimes, along the way, people specifically point things out to us. We get a clear plan about where to go next. But we can also reach a place for which there is no map, no itinerary, no set agenda for how to find our way. That's because we're supposed to be trusting our heart.

This is an important place on the journey. It tells us we're now living from our heart, and that's the lesson. It tells us our heart can be trusted. It's a time of joy; a time of trusting what we've learned and what we know; a time of trusting the universe and discovering that that trust is well placed.

You don't need to be shown what to do next. Your heart and soul will lead the way. You'll learn to tell when something is right, when something works.

Learn to find places of healing. Learn to find people, places, events, and rituals that work for you. Don't worry about how to find them or wait for someone to point them out. They'll call to you, or you'll call them into your life.

JULY 31

You Are Complete

Look around at all that lives, at all that is. See how connected each creation is to the workings of the universe. But see also that the essence of all that is, the core, lies within each. From the tiniest purple wildflower to the tallest redwood in the forest, each creation contains its own energy system, its own energy core for living. And so it is with us.

We're intricately connected to the world. We receive energy, life-sustaining nourishment and support, from the world around us. But inside each of us is our own source for love, joy, and wisdom. Our ability to love, live, feel, and be happy comes from our own hearts.

Look inside yourself. Feel your vitality, your energy. Feel your essence. It is pure love. Everything you need in order to live and love is within you. Nurture yourself. Let yourself grow. Learn to grow and walk in the ways of love. Learn from all who cross your path. Value your connections to others and the world around you. Receive and give freely as you walk down the road.

Take your place in the world. Know you
are part of a complete universe. But remember,
you are a complete universe, too.

August

AUGUST 1

You Have It All

I was sitting at a camp in Washington's Olympic Forest, talking to a young woman. We were both enjoying the day.

"People forget that life and death are both part of life," she said. "They forget that young and old are both part of life. We live in a society that has everything separated. We live in a society that's forgotten the *whole* in holistic."

The whole. All of it. Male and female. Young and old. Life and death. Tears and joy. All part of the same. Parts of the whole. *I want to have it all . . .* We may have heard those words many times. We may have said them ourselves many times. *I want to have it all . . .*

Connect the parts. You do have it all.
You've had it all, all along.

What Do We Do When People Resent Us?

Even with our best efforts to detach, we may still have moments when the resentments and harsh feelings of another interfere with our peace. We react much as if someone were throwing darts or rocks at us. All the efforts in the world to ignore resentment may not help if we're feeling the impact of each harsh feeling thrown at us.

These are some ideas that might help.

1. Talk to the person. Reason things out. If that's not possible, send them a box of blessings through prayer or thought.

2. Protect yourself emotionally and spiritually. One healing professional recommends these techniques, which have helped me. You may have your own. Take some quiet time, close your eyes, and envision yourself encased in a large cube of mirrors. Totally protected, you can see out, but others can't see in. All they see when they look at you is themselves. Spiritually protect yourself by envisioning a flaming circle of fire around you, around the mirrors, too.

3. Look deep within yourself and find the emotional block, the unresolved issue, or the old belief that makes you vulnerable to that energy, to that person. Then release it. Heal it by acknowledging it, feeling it, and letting it go.

4. Take a closer look. The pressure and resentment you're feeling may be your own. Release them. Heal yourself.

Now thank that person for helping you heal, grow, and move along your path.

AUGUST 3

Learn to Be Present

"I haven't been able to give you much materially," he said. "Not jewelry, diamonds, gold. But the gift I've given you, what I've had to offer, is staying fully present for you."

Presence is a gift—staying fully present for friends, family, ourselves, our lives. Staying in the moment, with our hearts open, will change other people's lives and ours.

So often we've learned, out of habit or fear, to be only partially present, partially conscious, for ourselves, others, and our lives. We aren't certain what we're feeling; our attention and energy are diverted to the next place, the next person. We're there, kind of.

There's another way, a better way. One where we keep our hearts open and know what we feel. We take the risk of being vulnerable enough to share who we really are and to allow others to do the same. We become fully present for each moment and each person on our path.

Yes, there are times when it isn't safe to be open, when the energy of a circumstance isn't right for us. But that usually reveals a lesson and dictates a choice. It may be time to learn, time to leave, time to feel, time to choose.

Learn to release all that stands in the way of you and the present moment. Learn to let go of all that blocks you from being fully present for yourself and others.

Give the gift of presence to
yourself and to the world.

AUGUST 4

Value Passion

Value what ignites the flame within you.

Value what inspires and interests you, what enrages you, what tickles and exhilarates you, what sparks the fire within. Your strong feelings—what you love or hate—are not wrong. Your passions will lead and guide you in all you want to do. From the tiniest idea to the grandest scheme, what makes your flame burn more brightly is the light shining from above, gently guiding the way.

The universe and God will lead and guide you, tell you what to do. The message might come through a story someone tells you, a place someone mentions that they liked, or a problem someone's having trouble resolving that attracts your attention with a bit of extra force. A movie that sticks in your mind. A book you couldn't put down. Something you realize you hate, something you find you love after all, an idea you find interesting, something that makes you stop and think. Learn to tell how you react to what you see and hear. That's how you'll learn to listen to what the universe has to say. That place may be the next place you're to go on your path. The idea may be just what you're looking for to help you get unstuck.

When you know what you're feeling deep inside, you'll know what you like. If you've grown cold and bored, you can come alive again. Feel whatever you need to feel and you'll find your passion underneath. If you don't know when you feel sad and alone, you won't know when you feel good. Feel all the feelings that come your way. Each one has a lesson for you. And as you release that energy, you'll be releasing passion, too. Value your passions and the way you feel. Soon you'll find yourself knowing just what to do and when.

Stay open. Keep your fire burning bright.
When you recognize what inspires you,
you'll be recognizing the Light.

AUGUST 5

Respect Life

The message came softly, gently, during the sweat lodge ceremony I went to in Sedona. At the end of the evening, the shaman thanked the rocks—for glowing with heat, bringing their passion to evening, symbolizing passion in our lives. She thanked the wood that created the fire that heated the rocks—for giving its life so that we could have warmth, so that we could celebrate the event. She thanked the water for cooling our throats. And she thanked God for life, for each of our lives, for our lifetimes on this planet.

Respect life. All of it. The world moves so fast, it's so easy to forget to respect all that lives, all that is. We get so harried, so hurried, we take life for granted. Take time to remember that all life is sacred. All that is part of creation is a creation, and the same life force moves through us all. With all its trials, tests, worries, heartaches, and sometimes heartbreaks, life is a gift.

A few short years on this planet, then we are gone. Do not spend it worrying about all that has gone wrong. You will miss the lesson. You will miss the gift, the gift of life.

Respect life. All of it.
Respect and honor your own.

AUGUST 6

Find Neutral Ground

There is a town in Idaho, Lava Hot Springs, that overflows with quiet, inexpensive hostels offering hot mineral water soaks to all who pass through. Folklore has it that in days long past, warring tribes would put aside their differences when they came here to soak in the waters and heal. This sacred ground was neutral territory.

Although most of us are not at war with another tribe, or even another person, many of us have been at war with ourselves. I have spent years judging myself and my experiences. As I have opened up to my emotions, I have spent time and energy judging those, too. Often, I expend as much energy judging and labeling the experience or emotion, as I do living through it. I have run in terror from grief. I have attacked myself repeatedly for experiencing anger. I have put antagonistic labels on guilt and fear.

Now I am learning the power of neutrality. It speeds my growth process, the time it takes me to learn my lessons. If what I'm going through isn't wrong, then I am free to have the experience and embrace its lessons. Neutrality brings peace and the freedom to learn.

As we continue our journey, the journey of the soul, we can learn to find the peace offered by neutral territory. We let ourselves have our experiences, the ones we have chosen, the ones we've created, the ones we've been given. We let each burst of energy we need to feel pass through without judgment. Good or bad? I don't think so. Just energy. We learn to let others have their emotions and lessons, too.

Discover the power of neutral territory.
It is sacred ground that can help you heal.

AUGUST 7

Be All You Can Be

Step out into the cool night air. Look at the stars. See how they shine. Know that it is okay for you to shine, too.

Who told you you had to hold back? Who told you your gifts, your talents, your beauty—your natural, beautiful, loving, delightful self—was wrong? Who told you not to be all you could be? Maybe, as some suggest, we've gotten too comfortable focusing on our flaws, our errors, our dark side. Perhaps it's not our dark side we fear. Perhaps we're really afraid of our gifts, our brilliance, our light.

Now is a time of light. It's time for us to shine. We've worked hard on ourselves, dealt with our issues, gone back to the past. We've learned our lessons well. The reasons to hold back and hide away are no longer there. Enjoy the fruits of your labors.

Be all you can be, and enjoy being that. Don't hold back. Use your gifts with joy. Use your talents. Let your light shine for all the world to see.

Finally, you are free to be all that you are and can be.

AUGUST 8

Touch the Timeless Rhythms of Life

Chaco Canyon, New Mexico, touched me deeply, profoundly. It sang to my soul. I walked through the canyon viewing the remnants of the Anasazi culture, touching, seeing, experiencing what was left of their sophisticated society, a civilization over two thousand years old. I felt reverence and humility as I touched the stones of a culture that no longer existed. I could almost see the people who lived there, busy with their work, their relationships, their goals, their fears and hopes. Just like us. I wondered if they knew that someday their society would be extinct, gone, vanished. I wondered if they knew how important they were, how each of us plays a tiny part in the eternal dance of the universe.

It's so easy to become consumed by the details of our lives, to be impressed with the technology of our own society, to get lost in the business and busyness of our ways. But it's important to remember ancient cultures, other civilizations, other lives lived long ago—the lessons of our planet, the timeless lessons of love and life. I wept with wonder, awe, and joy at how important yet humble each of our lives is. My soul vibrated with the awareness of eternity, with the infinite rhythms of life.

I lingered at Chaco Canyon, not wanting to leave. A still voice whispered to my soul, reminding me that I could return as often as I needed and wanted, because this place was now part of me, part of my heart.

Allow your soul to awaken. Allow it to soar.
Touch the timeless rhythms and cycles of life.

AUGUST 9

Grow in Your Sensitivity to Toxicity

Just as we are becoming more careful about our earth and the toxins we put into the ground and air, so will we grow in our sensitivity to events, people, places, and substances that are toxic to us.

Our bodies will speak to us, tell us what they don't want, what they can't handle anymore. Our bodies will tell us what hurts, what we're allergic to, what we wish to move away from. Often, underneath the toxins are old, embedded emotions. Release the emotions and you release the toxins. Our bodies will gasp for clarity, purity, cleansing, and detoxification.

What is toxic to one person may not be toxic to the next. What my body wants and needs today may be different from what yours wants and needs today. The answer is in listening—listening to our bodies, listening to what they're saying, how they're reacting to the people, the substances, the world around us. Listen. What is your body telling you?

Grow in your sensitivity to toxicity. Trust
the messages from your body. Let yourself heal.

A U G U S T 1 0

Find Places of Healing

Find places of healing. Discover people, things, and places that nourish your soul, bring you back to center, help you heal.

Life is not an endurance contest. Not anymore. We are not in a race to see how long we can go without, how much we can go without, how much pain we can stay in. Although sometimes we go through dry spells and droughts, we are not cactuses.

There is a place in each of us that wants to heal, that can heal, that will heal. It's a peaceful place, one of nourishment, replenishment, peace, safety, comfort, and joy. It's a place of love and acceptance. It's a place of forgiveness, honesty, openness, nurturing, and kindness. You can find it quickly, if that's what you're seeking. You will recognize it instantly because of how it feels. It will bring you back to center. It will bring you back to calm. It will bring you back to joy.

Find places of healing. Then go there often. They are yours for the asking, yours for the seeking. Healing places are an important part of the journey.

A U G U S T 1 1

Trust Yourself

When you look around, feel insecure, and wonder who you can trust, know you can trust yourself.

We often stand like little children, holding out our hands, waiting for someone to lead us somewhere, anywhere. We hope that someone can show us what we need do to next. We think, *Maybe someone else knows better.* But that thought is often the beginning of trouble. If we choose to let others lead us around, we'll soon find out that they don't know what's best for us.

If we abdicate responsibility for our choices, we may become angry, sometimes full of rage at others for running our lives, for telling us what to do. We need to take responsibility. We need to trust ourselves.

Sometimes we do get clues or hints from others. Sometimes we get direction from outside ourselves. But it must resonate with our heart. It must resonate with what we know to be true.

And the direction we take, what we do next, needs to be our choice, because whether we see it or not, it *is* our choice.

Trust and respond to your
own heart. Trust the wisdom
and guidance within you.

AUGUST 12

Practice Forgiveness

He was an old man, sitting on the corner bench. "I don't know why we just keep on forgiving our brothers and sisters," he said, looking at the people walking by. "I suppose it's because when we do, we really forgive ourselves."

Is there someone we're judging, censuring? If we look more closely we'll see that when we blame others, we're chastising ourselves as well. If we're honest, really honest, we can see that often what upsets us is something similar to what we ourselves do. Other people can be mirrors of our own behavior.

Yes, there are times when another person does something absolutely outrageous. And we can stand there, hands on hips, saying, *I've been wronged. I can't understand how anyone could behave that way.* But often, if we're honest, we really can understand—we have behaved that way, too.

> *Practice forgiveness. Judgment without forgiveness causes us to feel isolated, separate, and apart, causes us to judge ourselves in the same way. Discover how much better you feel when you forgive others. Find out how much better you feel when you forgive yourself.*

AUGUST 13

Come Back to Center

Come back to center, that place in you that is still, calm, quiet, and connected.

Your center is a place you can trust. It connects the body, mind, heart, and soul. It connects truth, your inner voice, and the Divine. Your best work comes from there. Your most loving times come from there. Your insights, awarenesses, and guidance come from being there, at that place. Your best decisions and finest moments come from that place.

Your center is a place that is quietly confident, unassuming, spontaneous, and free. It is gentle and kind, but it has the power to defend instinctively against attack.

Your center is a place that is naturally joyful and at peace. It is accepting, nonjudgmental, and it channels the voice of your heart. It knows perfect timing. It knows the rhythm of the universe, the rhythm of all creation, and it delights in its connection to that rhythm.

If you must leave your center to learn a lesson, feel a feeling, or experience something new, do that. Take all the side trips you are called to. But come back to your center when you're done.

And go to your center first,
before you go anywhere else.

AUGUST 14

Value the Simple Tasks of Life

Simple tasks can take us back to the rhythm, the way of life we're seeking.

How often we think we don't want to be bothered with laundry, bills, dishes, the lawn. We have other things to do, more important tasks to accomplish on this journey we're on. But doing the ordinary tasks doesn't take us away from the rhythm we're seeking. They don't take us away from life's magic. These tasks are the rhythm. They are the magic.

The simple tasks are important not just because they need to be done. The simple tasks are the microcosm of how our lives work. They keep us grounded in reality, they remind us of what's real, they show us how life works. They will lead us into the way of life we're seeking, if we approach them the right way. Do the laundry. Do the dishes. Pay your bills. Rake the leaves. Do these tasks with respect.

Restore and maintain order around you, and you'll feel order in your soul. Create beauty around you, and you'll feel beauty in your soul. The magic will return. The simple tasks will lead you back to it.

AUGUST 15

Spinning Our Wheels Is Part of Getting Unstuck

When our car gets stuck in the mud or snow, we immediately try to get out. Sometimes we have to spin our wheels to get a rocking motion going. Sometimes we have to try harder, then try again before we can get out. Sometimes, spinning our wheels digs us in more deeply. Then in frustration, we let go, relax. Soon we find ourselves doing what we need to get unstuck. We ask for help or figure out another approach.

That's how it is on our journey. We may find ourselves in a situation we don't know how to handle. So we start spinning our wheels in frustration, confusion, or fear. What we know is we want out. Sometimes we need to get through that time of spinning our wheels in order to get to the next place, the place where we slow down and figure out what to do next. Sometimes our frustration helps generate energy to get momentum going in the general direction of solving the problem. Putting forth that energy gets steam built up, tells us and the universe we're ready to free ourselves.

If you find yourself spinning your wheels, be gentle with yourself. Slow down, get a nice rocking motion going, one that's rhythmic yet powerful enough to free you, then put the car in gear, step on the gas, and gently drive out of the muck.

Sometimes we need to spin our wheels. It helps us get unstuck.

AUGUST 16

Tap into the Creative Flow

Life is creative, and so are you. Let the creative energy of the universe come alive for you. Let it help you bring your creativity alive. Let it bring you the answers, the direction, the guidance you need to create. Let it bring you your ingredients.

What are you trying to create? A more loving, open relationship? More spiritual growth? A new job? A book? A new home? A friendship? A play? A song? A quilt? A meal? A budget? Ask the universe for the help you need. Ask it to help you find your ingredients; ask it to help you form your vision, get clear on your ideas, and produce the best creation you can.

Your answer may come quickly. As we grow and embrace our connection to the universe, as we embrace our connection to ourselves, we find many of our answers appearing almost immediately. If the answer doesn't come right away, don't try to force it. The help will come. The idea will come. The next ingredient for your creation will appear. Sometimes the answer will come softly, almost as a whisper. Other times the guidance will be loud and clear. You will see and hear the guidance clearly and easily when you continue to love yourself.

> *Tap into the creative energy of the universe. It will help you tap into your own. To tap into God and the creative force, just tap into your heart.*

AUGUST 17

Let the Shifts Happen

I listened as the tour guide explained the crack, the huge gaping rupture in the earth's surface as we traveled along Bryce Canyon. My mind traveled back to an earthquake that shook southern California in January 1994. Earthquakes are reminders that life shifts, moves, changes places. Sometimes the shifts are gradual and begin slowly, like the gaping hole in Bryce Canyon that started with a tiny split. Sometimes, as in the California earthquake, the shifts happen in an instant. We don't know in advance about, and can't plan for, the shift.

But there's one thing we can count on. Just as nature shifts and moves into new shapes and forms, so do we. Sometimes our shifts happen suddenly. Other times, they take place over years, beginning almost imperceptibly. As we move into increased self-awareness, we will become more aware of these shifts. We'll know, see, and feel when they're taking place. We may not know where they're leading, but we'll know something's afoot. The more we value and trust life, the more we can count on these shifts to lead us forward and trust the new shape being formed in our lives. The more flexible we become, the more we allow for these shifts and work with them instead of against them, the easier they will be.

Life is always moving, changing, shifting into its next shape. The movement is natural. It is how we evolve. Let the shifts happen. Take responsibility for yourself each step of the way. Trust the new shape and form of your world.

AUGUST 18

Throw Away Old Messages

Who told you that you were bad and wrong? Are you still letting others tell you that—after all these years?

Listen quietly. Whose voice do you hear telling you that? Is someone still putting you down, sabotaging your happiness, preventing you from living and moving in self-acceptance, joy, and love?

Inhale and breathe in love, peace, and joy. Exhale and breathe out negative energy and negative messages. Feel them loosen, disintegrate, release. Feel your soul, mind, and heart become clear. You don't have to let others take your power, rob your joy. Don't become so accustomed to living with the pain of old, negative messages that you don't notice how much they hurt.

Get rid of these old messages. Pull them out of your soul just as you would pull out barbs or knives. Pull them out one by one, then toss them away. You don't have to work around the pain from these messages any more. You don't have to figure out how to incorporate that pain into your life.

Allow yourself to heal. Find new messages that empower you with love, messages that set you free.

AUGUST 19

Your Destiny Is Now

The train seemed to move endlessly toward the horizon as I drove along beside it. To me, trains symbolize destiny. For a long time, the concept of destiny confused me. I wondered how to find my destiny. I hoped I had one. I wondered what it would feel like when I got there. But destiny doesn't bewilder me anymore. I enjoy seeing trains.

Destiny isn't some distant place, or a peak of fame and fortune. Destiny isn't one moment in our lives, one time when we shine for all the world to see. Those moments are nice, if they come. But there's more to destiny than that.

Destiny is now. Destiny is each moment of our lives, shining through, linking together, like the endless cars on the train. Destiny means embracing each moment, being present for it, cherishing it because it is our now. Whether it holds exhilaration, discovery, sadness, tough decisions, confusion, or tender love, each moment is our destiny. These moments of destiny link together in an endless chain to become our lives.

Let yourself live and be in each moment, with each person, learning each lesson along the way. Destiny isn't someplace we go. Destiny is where we are.

AUGUST 20

Your Soul Can Be at Peace

Peace is all around you.

If you forget to be peaceful, try some things. Forgive, trust, love yourself. Be still, be kind, be gentle. Do these things until peace returns.

Seek places of healing. Seek places of power. Come back to center. Breathe deeply. Breathe in the air, the energy, the loving resources around you. Fill up on life. Fill up until you find and feel peace. Work things out, work things through, release the past, take the steps your heart leads you to do. Do this until you find and feel peace.

Breathe deeply. With each breath, release your fear. If you know what's causing your fear, write it down. Speak it out. If your fears are unknown, let them go, too. Don't tangle yourself up trying to figure out or understand. Trust that your body, your soul, your heart, is healing and releasing.

Be gentle with yourself. A place inside you is healing its fears, telling you something, feeling something. Don't punish or abuse it for feeling afraid. That won't make your fears go away. That will make the beautiful, delicate part of you go away. Be tender and gentle. Rest until your fears subside. Rest until peace returns.

Peace is yours for the asking, the wanting, the seeking. Desire it with passion, and you shall see it, find it, have it.

No matter what you're
going through, your soul
can be at peace.

AUGUST 21

You're Free to Open Your Heart

Open your heart to the people you love. Open your heart to the world. Open your heart to God, to the universe, to life and all the creatures and creations in it. Open your heart as much as you can.

It's safe to open your heart now. There was a time when you believed that the only way to protect yourself was to shut down and close your heart. You have learned so much. You have learned the powers of honesty, compassion, forgiveness, and kindness. You will no longer become stuck or trapped if you open your heart. You can leave if you want to. You can say what you need to. You no longer need to protect yourself by guarding your heart with the heavy armor you wore in the past. Now you are free. Free to open your heart. Free to open yourself to the universe.

A woman I met in Sedona gave me a lovely visualization to use. Picture your heart. In front of your heart see a beautiful rosebud, tightly closed. Whenever you want your heart to open, picture the rose blooming wide, beautiful, alive, and fragrant. Whenever you want to retreat, turn the rose back into a bud.

Open your heart to the world, to the people who live in it. Open yourself to creation. Open your heart to yourself, to God, to life.

Life will become magical. And you'll think back and smile. You will wonder why it took you so long to open your heart.

Open your heart as
much as you choose, as
much as you can. Share
it with the world.

AUGUST 22

Heal Your Resentments

How fast resentments creep in during the course of an ordinary year. How much faster they can creep in during intense times, times of change, times of evolution—the kind of times we've been experiencing on our journey.

Things shift. Things change. We let go of the old and stumble toward the new. And resentments crop up along the way. People become angry with us for changing; we become angry with them because we believe their experiences have unjustly impacted us.

Resentments are tricky little things, devious little devils of energy that block and damage our souls and hearts. They tell us they're justified. They tell us we need them to protect ourselves. They tell us we should have adopted them a long time ago. They tell us we're not safe if we release them, if we send them packing.

Those are lies, illusions that keep us blocked, stuck, and often quite uncomfortable.

Go deeper into yourself. What do you feel underneath the resentment? Betrayed? Hurt? Ashamed? Embarrassed? Left out? Forgotten? Misunderstood? You're safe now. Go ahead and feel whatever you need to feel. Honor and recognize your gentler, softer side—those other feelings that make you feel vulnerable, those more tender feelings hiding behind, underneath, or to the side of the resentment.

Feel and release your resentment.
Feel the feelings underneath it, too.
You'll become clear. The resentment
will dissolve. And you'll return to love.

AUGUST 23

The Spiritual Experience Is You

"When I look at people now, I don't see issues," he said. "I see souls."

The man said he had a spiritual experience. Actually, he said he had four. He didn't go to the mountains, or the ocean, or the desert to have them. He had his four spiritual experiences in the same place—in the parking lot outside a Shell gas station in Portland, Oregon. "The car filled with light. I filled with light. My heart just opened up and I forgave everyone I was resenting," he continued. "Even my ex-wife."

We don't have to search for spiritual experiences. We are the spiritual experience—a spiritual being having a human life. Look at the people around you. Now look again and see souls. See them having many kinds of spiritual experiences in the form of human life.

When you look for holy ground,
look down. That's where your
spiritual experience takes place.
Right where you're standing,
wherever you are now.

AUGUST 24

Let the Lesson Reveal Itself to You

"What's the next lesson?" I asked.

"If you knew what it was, you wouldn't need to learn it," he said.

Often, in the midst of a lesson or experience, we tighten our minds into knots trying to figure out what we're learning, what's coming next, what the lesson is really about. But if we knew what the lesson was about, we wouldn't need to be learning it.

The learning we're doing on our spiritual path is often not possible from our heads or books. It's a process of discovery; it includes many twists, turns, surprises, and upsets, much confusion, wondering, and stumbling until we reach a moment of clarity. To learn the lesson, we need to go through the experience. And usually we learn best when we're a bit vulnerable and uncertain about what we're learning.

Trust that the lesson will reveal itself to you when it's time. Stay present for this moment. Let your experiences and guidance unfold. You're evolving and learning and growing right now. When the transformation is complete, you'll see what you've learned.

Other people may be there to help us,
teach us, guide us along our path. But
the lesson to be learned is always ours.

AUGUST 25

Where Do You Get Your Energy?

Think about your energy. Examine and learn what revitalizes you, refreshes you, renews you. Pumps you up. Makes you feel charged.

How do you recharge your battery? Do you wait until your battery is drained, almost dead, before you recharge? Are there people or things in your life that drain you, deplete you? Do you want to let them do that?

Where do you go to get recharged? Who are the people who enhance your life force, invigorate you? Who does it feel good to be around? What activities make you feel better? What forms of nature speak to your soul? What opens your heart, helps you feel alive, breathes life into your spirit?

Experiment. Spend some time watching, noticing the impact people, activities, and objects have on you. Know that as you change, the impact of your environment, what is around you, may change, too.

Tune into your energy field and the energy
of the world around you. Learn to be sensitive.
Open up to how things feel for you.

AUGUST 26

Open to Universal Love

Are you living with the belief that universal love isn't there for you?

When we look at what we've been through, sometimes we feel sad and abandoned. We see others dancing along their path, getting blessings, special help, gifts along the way. Then we turn to our own lives and see only those times we've been let down and left out, the times that life, people, and the world haven't been there for us. *Universal love may be real,* you say, *but it's just not real for me.*

Open your eyes. Open your heart. Open yourself to the universe. Begin to see and notice all the gifts you're given—the clues, the direction, the support. Stop looking to one person or source and let life's magic dance for you. See how you get what you need. See how naturally the guidance comes when you trust that it will be there. See the smiles, see the friendship, feel the inspiration. Feel the loving touch of a hand on your arm. Say what you need. Say it aloud. Direct your words to the universe. Treat it as if it were a loving friend, and it will treat you the same way.

Universal love is there for you. Learn to recognize its touch and rhythm, for it is the rhythm of life and love.

AUGUST 27

Let Your Storms Subside

Watch the pounding surf. Watch the waves lap against the shore, their beginnings somewhere far out to sea, their beginnings in a storm we might never see. Know your oneness with those waves, with the water of the seas.

Your emotions are like the surf. Sometimes they pound gently, sometimes fiercely. Sometimes the color is blue, sometimes gray. They may be the result of a storm, sometimes a squall far away. Let them pound. Let them pass through. Let them subside. Let them turn into the next wave. Each emotion is connected to a belief, a belief embedded in your soul. *I am abandoned. I am deserted. I am separated from God and love.* But you are not your emotions. Your emotions don't control your life, no matter how fierce, no matter how strong. No matter how relentless. No matter, at times, how overwhelming.

Let the emotions pass through. Feel all you need to feel. Say all you need to say to let the storm subside. Then pause. Wait. Rest. Let your body regroup and heal. You will have grown. You will have changed. And you'll be on your way to learning something new.

AUGUST 28

Make Yourself at Home

Once you accept yourself unconditionally, you'll be surprised at how comfortable you begin to feel, no matter where you are.

We may have tricked ourselves into thinking our security came from outside ourselves—that we needed certain other people or places, needed certain objects or items around us, or had to live our lives in a particular way to feel secure. But relying on things and people outside ourselves provides a false sense of security. False security will be shown for what it is.

There's a real security, a true safety, available to us all, no matter who we are, where we are, or what we're doing. That security comes from accepting ourselves. That security comes from trusting ourselves, trusting our hearts, our wisdom, our connection to the Divine and to the universe around us.

Once we accept ourselves unconditionally, no matter where we are, it will feel like home.

AUGUST 29

First Heal Your Heart

I checked into the lodge in Sedona, certain I was there to get my job done. I told the woman behind the desk, a delightful soul with brown hair, brown eyes, a warm smile, and an open heart, why I was there—to begin writing this book.

"Maybe you will," she said, "but that's not why you're really here. You came here to cleanse the past and heal your broken heart." I looked at her in surprise. I knew what she said was true.

Many of us show up at a place in our lives with a particular agenda. We think we are there to get the job done, build a relationship, accomplish a task. Then, life takes a twist, one we didn't quite expect or plan on.

We discover we're at a certain place for a reason different from what we thought. The real reason we're there is to cleanse the past and heal our broken heart. Healing our heart is a worthwhile mission, more purposeful perhaps than the one we intended. Healing our heart is worthwhile and crucial, something that often needs to be done first, so that we can accomplish what we intended.

The biggest block to service and love is a broken heart. To care about life again, to open our hearts, to dare to dream, to risk love again, we must first heal our heart. Decide on your mission. Be clear on your purpose. But remember, first things need to be done first.

Maybe you're where you are today
for a reason other than you thought.
Maybe the first thing to do is cleanse
the past and heal your heart.

What Would Feel Good to You?

What do you want? What would feel good to you? Ask yourself that question often as you go through your day, as you live your life.

When you don't know what to do next, when you're not sure how to find the path that's right for you, ask yourself what you want and what would feel good. That's how you'll discover what's right for you.

What energizes you? Which friends feel good to be around? What work excites you, infuses you with passion? Which hobbies interest you? How do you want to spend your time? We have endured *have to* long enough. We have pushed ourselves through *should* too many times. There is a better and different way.

Learn to recognize what lifts your spirits. Become conscious of not only what you need, but also what you want and like, what feels right to you. At first, doing what you want and what feels good to you may be uncomfortable, especially if you've spent much of your life doing what doesn't feel good to you. Learn to be comfortable with the new energy. Learn to become comfortable choosing what energizes you. By following your heart, by following your passion, you will find your path and you will find joy.

The possibilities for joy are limitless
if we can do what feels good to us—
in work, in life, in love, in play. Learn
to become comfortable with joy. You
have the power to create joy by choosing
what feels good to you. The time for
joy isn't later. The time for joy is now.

AUGUST 31

Serve Gently from Your Heart

Service. Gentle service that comes from the heart. That's the theme, the rhythm of life, work, love. See the trees, the grass, the flowers, the mountains, the ocean. Look and really see. See how effortlessly they serve. Their very life is service. Know that your life, too, is service. Let service arise naturally from your life.

Commit to your growth, to loving yourself and following your heart. Commit to joy, passion, gratitude for your life and all your lessons. Commit to honestly sharing and expressing who you are, what you feel, what you're going through.

Don't worry about what you will do to serve. Focus instead on loving yourself. Let your service arise from that, acts that spring from desire, joy, and inspiration. Cherish your life. It's a gift not just to yourself, but to others. To the entire universe.

Each star shines its light down from the heavens, making up the twinkling galaxy of the Milky Way. Each star is important and serves by playing its part—naturally, gently, by being what it is. You too have a part to play in the universe. Your part is to serve others by being yourself.

Service is your path. Let service spring
gently, naturally, from who you are.
Radiate your gifts to the world by
loving and sharing yourself.

September

SEPTEMBER 1

Make It a Labor of Love

The mirror was framed with a ceramic octopus. It had the sweetest, most peaceful energy. It made me smile when I saw it. "Do you like it?" my friend asked. "Arnold made it." That's when I knew why it was so delightful. Its energy—delightful, joyous, and sweet—was Arnold's energy.

The things we create have energy. A meal we cook. A task we perform, no matter how big or small. What we do contains our energy—the emotional energy and attitude we put into it. Have you ever cooked a meal when you felt angry and disrupted, hurried and harried? Have you noticed the difference when you cooked that meal in a loving frame of mind? Merely doing the job isn't always enough. We need to do the job with our best energy, our most positive emotional and mental attitude.

Take time before you begin a task to become conscious of the energy you want to put into it, the energy you want that task to have and reflect to yourself and others. Make conscious, deliberate choices. The larger the task, the more time you may want to spend developing your ideas about it. On particularly significant projects, you may want to spend time visualizing and writing down your ideas, so you can focus that energy into your work. Experiment with this idea. See how it comes to life as you do your daily tasks. See how much better the people around you feel when you do your tasks in love. See how much more joy and pleasure work brings to you.

There is honor in all work, in all tasks, but take it one step further. Make what you do a labor of love. Then your work will truly touch and change the world in the way you desire. The work you do, whatever your chosen field, will be work that heals.

SEPTEMBER 2

Listen to the Voice of the Soul

Listen to your soul. It speaks quietly, yet clearly, about what it wants, what it needs, what it's learning, what it yearns for. It speaks of its fears and dreams, its hopes and needs.

Learn to listen to the souls of others, too. Listen not only to the way people chatter and exchange ideas. Learn to listen to what they're really saying.

"My son is nineteen. He's moved away from home. He talks all the time about wanting to be grown up, wanting his independence. So my husband and I have really tried to give him his freedom," one woman said. "Yet recently, when he had a crisis, I heard for the first time what he was really saying. *Don't go too far away. Call me often. Be there for me. Let me know you're there. Let me know you still care.* Now I try to call him every day, just to tell him I love him and to let him know I'm close by. The crisis he had wasn't the issue. Not really. What he was really saying was he needed us."

Go beyond what you hear with your ears. Learn to hear what you're really saying, and what others are really saying to you.

Souls do talk. Listen quietly. Listen to
your own. Learn to hear the voice of others'.
A little soul talk goes a long way.

SEPTEMBER 3

Things Are Working Out

Right now, this moment, things are working out. We natter away, trying to control, shape, and form. Trying to figure things out. We back off, then come closer. We worry and wonder. But things are working out. Things are working out as beautifully and Divinely as possible. The dance of life is taking place in sync with the rhythm of the universe.

Everything is working out, moving forward, evolving. There is a rhythm, an energy, a life force that continues, that shapes, that grows. You do not have to fight, resist, control, or even understand it. All you need to do is be—be present for your life, your love, yourself.

Your soul will lead you on. Your inner voice, your heart, is leading you on. Quiet your mind and trust that where you are and where you're being led is perfect.

You don't have to try to get it all together. You don't have to strive to "have it all." You already do have all that you need.

How many times have you been through an experience, fretting and fearful about the shape things were taking, only later to exclaim, *Oh, I see now. Things were working out all along!* Learn to say and believe that now.

Let your mind see what your soul already knows: things are working out perfectly.

SEPTEMBER 4

Stay Connected to Yourself

The woman was describing her reaction to an area she had visited, a place poisoned by toxic chemicals, a piece of earth maimed and harmed by humankind. "It's not that I didn't feel connected there," she said thoughtfully. "I felt connected, but feeling connected meant feeling connected to pain."

The woman was describing more than a piece of land. She was describing a place many of us visit at times on our journey. We feel connected, but we're connected to pain and sadness. We may be reacting to an incident from our past or to something taking place right now.

We don't have to run anymore. We don't have to hide. We don't have to leave our bodies, or wonder what's wrong. We simply need to feel what's there, even if it hurts for a bit. Sometimes we're healing from toxic beliefs, feelings, and attitudes we've accumulated. Sometimes there's a message, a lesson to learn, an action to take. That will follow naturally if we're connected.

Open up to your connection. The price of being connected may mean that we occasionally feel pain, but the reward for staying connected will be consciousness, guided action, and an open heart.

SEPTEMBER 5

The Path Is One of Joy

I attended a church service at the Sanctuario de Chimayo in New Mexico. The church and its sacred healing ground had touched and healed me before. Today I came looking not for a miracle, but just a touch of its healing powers to help me on my way. Instead, I found another miracle. The miracle of joy.

When I entered the church, I noticed how glum and somber I became. I noticed how seriously, almost sadly, I approached much of my spiritual growth. I believed that spirituality asked—required—this of me. If I was doing it properly, I would be demonstrating what a grim affair it was.

After the service, I stopped at the church's gift shop and purchased some mementos to bring the energy of this holy place home with me—items to remind me of the spiritual powers available to us in everyday life, no matter where we are. I also visited another gift shop near the church. There I bought a string of chili peppers called holy chilis. Then I brought all my gifts back to the priest to bless: a wooden cross for the wall; a rosary for my daughter, one that glows in the dark so she'll know God's there; a small bag of sacred earth from the church grounds to remind me of the healing powers in this universe; a small jar of holy water to remind me that all of the journey is sacred; and a string of holy chilis to help me remember to smile.

The path does not have to be such
a grim affair. Let go of the heaviness
in your heart and soul. Sometimes
the best way to demonstrate your faith
is by learning to enjoy life.

SEPTEMBER 6

Imagine All the Possibilities

Think of all the possibilities for your life—for love, for work, for growth. Think of all the possibilities for adventure, for fun, and for service. This day, this week, this month, this year abounds with possibilities. Each task you have to do, each problem you encounter and need to solve abounds with possibilities. Your life abounds with possibilities.

For a long time, we only saw some of the possibilities life held. We'd look at a situation and see the possibilities for guilt, victimization, sadness, and despair. We'd tell ourselves there was only one choice, or no choice, or that something had to be done in a particular way—the hardest and dreariest way possible. We'd neglect to envision the other options—the choices for joy, for making any event more fun, more pleasant, more enjoyable.

You don't need to limit yourself anymore. You've opened your heart. Now open your mind. Look around. See all the possibilities. The universe is teaming with them. It will lead and guide you into this abundance if you ask it for help and then allow that to happen.

Open to life's abundance. Open to all its possibilities. The more open you become, the more creative you'll be—in work, in play, in love, in life. The more creative you are, the more possibilities you'll see.

SEPTEMBER 7

Let Your Creativity Blossom

Allow your creativity to blossom. For too long you have held back. For too long you have limited your natural creative leanings and talents. Maybe someone told you you couldn't create or being creative wasn't worthwhile. Maybe you started telling yourself that.

You are creative. You have a creative self within that wants to play, wants to be let loose, wants to create. Set that part of you free! Let yourself play—with life, with work, with projects.

Make a list of all the negative things you believe about your creative abilities—what you think, what you've been told, and what you tell yourself. Then burn it. Now make a new list of all the things that are true, or that you believe could be true, or that you want to be true. Let go of all the blocks. Write down that you *are* creative, that you *can* create, and that you're connected to the creative force of the universe.

When you find your connection to creativity, the entire universe will come alive for you. It will help you, guide you, inspire you. You will find yourself imagining something, then being lead right down a path that will help you create it. When you don't know what to do next, you can listen to your heart and let God and the universe guide you.

Creativity is the inherent nature of the world, the universe. The universe creates. And the universe needs your help in creating. Creating brings you into harmony with the universe, God, yourself, and the rhythm of life.

SEPTEMBER 8

Get Out from Under the Gun

How often in life, in the busy world around us, we begin to feel as though we're "under the gun." Daily pressures can mount until our body feels as though someone is actually pointing a gun at us saying, *Hurry. Finish. Do this or else.* That feeling is not conducive to joy, creativity, or doing our best. That attitude creates stress, sometimes unbearable stress.

Some of us have lived under the gun so long we're not even aware of it. But our bodies are. We feel tense, stressed, frightened, on edge. Many of us have felt that way so long we've gotten used to it. *That's just how it is,* we say with resignation.

But that's not how it needs to be. Gently take the gun away from whoever is pointing it at you. Lay it on the table. Tell that person the task will get done, the situation will come about much better, much more creatively, much more timely without the gun. Most importantly, tell yourself that, too.

Acknowledge commitments. Acknowledge the necessity of timely accomplishment of tasks. Then acknowledge the way and wisdom of the heart with joy. It will see you through to get everything done, and you won't have to be under the gun.

SEPTEMBER 9

Take Time to Be Pleased

Take time to be pleased with all the beauty in this world. Do more than drive by and casually notice a particularly beautiful stretch of scenery. Stop the car. Get out. Take it in. See it, smell it, touch it if possible. Absorb and feel the beauty you see. Then thank the universe for giving this moment to you.

Take time to be pleased with your creations too—your work, your life, yourself. Look around. Then look again. Take time to see the beauty in your own life. Take time to absorb and be pleased with the beauty you see.

Then take this gift to others, too. Take time to notice and really see all that is beautiful in the people you know. Then tell them aloud what they mean to you, and how beautiful you think they are.

Opening up to ourselves and the world means learning to recognize and absorb its beauty. Allow yourself to grow, to define and redefine what true beauty means and feels like to you. You may have deprived yourself of noticing beautiful sights too long. It's time to take those dark glasses off. Appreciate the beauty around you.

Our soul is nurtured and fed by taking pleasure in the beauty in this world.

SEPTEMBER 10

Laugh Often

"When I woke up the other morning, the blahs were back," a friend said. "I switched on the television. An old movie, a comedy, was on.

At first I thought it was a waste of time to get involved in it. Within half an hour, I was laughing out loud. By the time the movie was over, I felt good."

Remember to laugh. No matter what our circumstance, where we are, what's going on, laughter is important. It's essential. Laughter changes our face. It changes our outlook. Some even suggest it changes our biochemistry.

Lighten up. Joke a little. Laugh at yourself. Laugh at life. The truth need not always be a grim, serious business. Often, the truth we've been so serious about finding can only be found when we laugh.

Learn the power of humor. It will take you a long way. And it will help the road you travel be more fun.

SEPTEMBER 11

Heal Your Fear of Abandonment

Some say the fear of abandonment is a universal fear. It's common to most people in most places. It is that anguishing, heartbreaking moment when we believe someone is going to leave us. For many of us, the fear began when some important person did leave or abandon us—physically or emotionally. Now the very thought of it happening again terrifies us.

Although the fear may be universal, if we have it, it still belongs to us. It needs to be faced, felt, acknowledged, and released—it needs to be healed—or else it may control our lives and harm our relationships.

Sometimes we may fear being abandoned so much that we don't want anyone to leave us—even people we don't like—because it triggers that old familiar feeling. If we don't deal with it, however, people can use it against us. All they have to do is threaten to leave and we crumble, acquiesce at the mere thought of feeling that way again.

Underneath the fear of abandonment another fear may lurk too, a deeper fear, the fear that somehow we've made the people we love go away. Sometimes in our lives, certain people have had to go away, because that is where their path led them. But if they felt confused, guilty, or uncertain about the leaving, they may have lied to us. They may have told us we did something wrong, we caused the separation, it was our fault they were leaving. And their lie became embedded in us.

Did someone tell that lie to you? Tell yourself something different. Tell yourself the truth. You don't make people go away. You weren't the cause. If someone needed to leave you, that was his or her choice.

Heal your fear of abandonment.
Set yourself and others free.

SEPTEMBER 12

Energize Yourself

Don't tell yourself you have no energy. You are energy. Learn to energize yourself.

Get up. Move around. Play some invigorating music. Stretch your arms, stretch your legs. Move your body around. Get out and walk.

Watch children play. They seem to have an unlimited supply of energy. Remember what it was like to be a child. You had an unlimited supply of energy then. Most of us still do.

Yes, we do get tired from time to time, particularly with the schedules many of us have. And there are times in our life when less energy is available to us, such as during times of deep grief or during illness when our body is using its energy to heal a physical problem. And sometimes other people and their problems drain us. But sometimes we drain ourselves, too.

If you don't feel your energy, perhaps something is blocking it. You may be experiencing some resistance to what you're trying to do. Maybe an old emotion or belief is clogging your circuits. Maybe you've been sitting too long crunched up in your chair, blocking your own circuits. Maybe you're telling yourself you have no energy so loudly that you've begun to believe it.

Clear your circuits. Push through whatever's
blocking you. Then get up, move around,
connect to life. Learn to energize yourself.

SEPTEMBER 13

Surrender to Your Feelings

Sometimes we think being strong means not giving in to our emotions. But that's not strength; that's denial and resistance. Real power comes from being vulnerable enough to feel whatever we feel.

Keep going, we tell ourselves. *Don't give in. This will pass. . .* But the only way to pass through these times is by feeling what we feel. The longer we fight and resist our emotions, the longer the situation will continue that is triggering them.

We may not see the lesson until we feel the feeling. We may not see the issue, the next step, the way out or the way through until we give in, feel our emotions, then release them. It's not enough to talk about them, although that will help bring them into consciousness, into the light of day. But talking about our feelings is different from surrendering to and feeling the emotional energy.

Feel the feeling, then release it. Now your soul and the universe can move you forward into new circumstances, into growth. An issue to work on—such as freedom, forgiveness, acceptance, love, or valuing some part of ourselves or our lives—may naturally and automatically emerge. If we pay attention to the process by which we grow, we will clearly see that each step of the way—feeling our feeling, accepting it, and then releasing it—triggered the next step of growth. Soon we will see that we are learning a new lesson. We are on our way again.

There is magic in allowing our feelings to pass through us, magic in giving in. There is power, more than we think, in being vulnerable enough to feel what we feel.

SEPTEMBER 14

There Is Power in Powerlessness

Sometimes we can't help ourselves. No matter how hard we try, no matter how deeply we feel we should be doing things differently, no matter how committed we are to personal responsibility, free will, self-actualization, and self-determination, sometimes we simply cannot help ourselves.

We keep on doing the same old things. We can't seem to change, even though we wish we could. It doesn't mean we aren't responsible, doesn't mean we aren't accountable. It means simply that for the present moment, we can't change, can't help ourselves, can't do it differently.

Many of us have discovered a truth in these moments. There is power even in powerlessness. There is power in admitting powerlessness. By voicing the problem, by accepting the powerlessness, you are bringing—attracting—help. Ask for the help you need. Admit and accept your powerlessness.

Be gentle with yourself. You are not alone in your problem, your powerlessness, or your search for a solution. Let love lead the way to the answer you seek.

SEPTEMBER 15

Heal Your Broken Heart

I lay on the cot in the bathhouse at the mineral springs. I was wrapped from head to toe in a woolen blanket. As I lay there, the blanket covering my face, I could almost feel each break line in my heart. I could feel the fractures in a way I hadn't before. I knew then that healing my heart was one of the purposes of this journey.

Your heart may have been broken many times. Some breaks hurt more than others, but each break caused a fracture, a weakness in your ability and willingness, to love, trust, and heal.

Don't shut down. Don't go away. Don't tell yourself, *My pain is not important. I'm stronger than that. That's just the way life is.* Those are all lies we tell ourselves, lies to hide the pain of the break. The smallest betrayal unexpressed, at least to ourselves, can cause damage to our hearts. Willingness is the key—willingness to feel all we need to feel, willingness to heal, to love again.

As you go deeper into your journey, deeper into your joy, go deeper into your heart. Mend and heal all those tiny break lines, all the fractures, all the cracks. As you go deeper into joy, you will go deeper into your pain, your grief, your losses. Don't be afraid. That doesn't mean you'll return to despair or that you will live forever in grief and anguish.

Take the time now to mend the break lines. Go deep within your heart to help it heal. Bury the broken dreams. Release the hurts. Acknowledge the betrayals. And then lightly, gently, with love, rub a golden layer of forgiveness and love around your heart.

There comes a time in the journey to
the heart when it is time to let it heal.
The deeper we go into the healing,
the freer we will be, the more we will
know what we feel, and the more
we will feel joy.

SEPTEMBER 16

The Real Magic Is About to Begin

At some point in the journey, we may become tired, weary, and confused. Homesick. All the mountains, the scenery, the food, the people, the experiences just don't do it for us anymore. We want to go home. *What am I doing here?* we wonder. *Nothing worthwhile is happening.* Yet another part of us knows the truth and whispers, *Yes, something is happening, something worthwhile.*

Feeling homesick is part of the journey. It can mean we've reached a turning point. "When we get to that place," a friend once said, "it means the journey has really begun."

Stay present for yourself and all your emotions. You've worked through so much. Don't stop now. Getting through this place, this point, will turn your life around. You've learned and grown, you've worked so hard healing your heart and cleansing your soul. Your spiritual growth has been profound. But until now, all the work you've done has been to prepare you for where you're going.

You've seen only a little of what life has to offer. You're about to walk through a door. Now that your heart is open, you'll see, touch, and know even more of life's wonders. It's the reward for where you've been. Keep feeling your feelings and trusting your guidance.

Let the magic begin.

SEPTEMBER 17

Don't Hurry

Don't worry and fuss about what you're going to do tomorrow, or how tomorrow's answers will come. The way to get through a task, a day, a life is to stay in the present moment.

Racing, pushing, trying to force things forward doesn't work. Not anymore. Hurrying will not speed up the process, or the journey. In fact, if you race ahead of yourself, you may find you need to go back, return to the parts you skipped over, and go through it again fully present.

Yes, there are times we need to press on, times we need to push a bit more. But hurrying won't speed up the process. It will just keep us tense, out of step. To speed up the process, we need to fully immerse ourselves in the moment and then focus our energy, our presence, our emotions, our thoughts, and our heart.

Stay in the present moment. Listen to your heart right now. Be gentle and loving with yourself right now. Be open to the guidance around you right now, guidance that will make the present moment come alive.

If you stay in your heart, stay with
yourself, stay in the present, tomorrow's
answers will come just as today's did—
naturally, gently, and on time.

SEPTEMBER 18

Open Up to New Energy

As you change, what works for you may change, too.

The purpose of the journey is to open up. But with it comes the responsibility of watching how we feel, how our bodies feel in certain circumstances. With it comes the responsibility of knowing that certain things that used to work for us, certain things we used to be able to handle, may not work as well any longer.

As we change, we will want and need the energy around us to change, too. We'll want it to feel better, energize us, be good for us. At first we may say, *This never bothered me before. I don't know why I'm so sensitive now.* Then we may wait for our bodies and lives to return to normal, to return to how they used to be.

You are becoming more sensitive, more open than you've ever been. When you were closed, you didn't feel as much, didn't respond as much. Sometimes you weren't aware of what you were feeling or how your body reacted. Now that you are more open, your body, mind, spirit, and soul will be far more affected by what you take in—whether it is food, drink, or the energy of a person or situation. You will feel more intensely. You may want different foods, different people, different places, different clothing, different activities. As your energy changes, you will likely want different energy around you.

Listen to your body and emotions when they tell you something no longer works for you. Let the old fall away. Listen to your inner guidance as your heart leads you to someplace new.

SEPTEMBER 19

Weather the Storm

Storms come. The lightning flashes. Thunder rolls. Sometimes the hail pounds so loudly and incessantly it becomes frightening. Sometimes storms do damage. But storms are not forever.

Just as nature plays out her storms, sometimes with violence, sometimes with gray days, sometimes with a gentle cleansing rain, we have storms in our lives, storms in our soul. Storms are part of life, part of growth, part of the journey.

Light a candle. Wrap up warmly. Make yourself safe and secure. Then wait for the storm to pass, knowing it will.

Let peace return. Let security return. Let joy and meaning come back, the certain faith that you have purpose and your life is on track.

SEPTEMBER 20

Discover What Interests You

There are many magical things to learn in our world and many people happy to teach us how to do them.

Are there things or activities you've been interested in, but you've talked yourself out of? Is there something new you'd like to learn how to do or at least explore? What sounds like fun to you?

What interests you? You have a right to be creative. You deserve to learn and grow. Find activities that stimulate you, teach you, help you learn more about yourself and life. Do the things your heart leads you to do.

How easy it is to talk ourselves out of trying something new. Let yourself enjoy life. Let yourself do the things *you* want to do.

Begin a journey of discovery. Find out what interests you. Listen to yourself for a few days, for a few weeks. Discover what stimulates your creative juices. Then follow that idea through.

SEPTEMBER 21

Appreciate Your Sensuality

Learn to appreciate and enjoy your sensuality.

Caress the petals of a gentle magnolia blossom. Inhale its scent. Touch the stem of a rose and carefully feel its thorns. Put your finger on a cactus. Sit down and feel the grass. Touch a tree; put your hand on the craggy, rough bark and hold it there for a while. Cradle a rock in your hands; hold it close until you feel its temperature, its texture. Then place the rock next to your cheek and see what it feels like there. Feel the difference between a cotton sheet and a soft woolen blanket. Feel how water feels on your skin, or how the warm night air caresses your face. Touch a baby's foot.

Learn to appreciate your sensuality. It will open you up to the energy of the world around you. It will open you to the life, passion, creativity, and textures within yourself.

SEPTEMBER 22

Embrace Change

You don't have to fear change. What you need to fear, a friend once told me, is things remaining the same. When that happens, life has stopped.

Life is an evolution. Your life is constantly, quietly evolving each moment into something new, something different, something that adds gracefully, beautifully, and perfectly to what was. You can trust that process with all its insights, clarity, confusion, and emotions. You can trust that process with its peace, joy, laughter, and its side trips.

Learn to honor and love the process of continual evolution and transformation. It's how things grow. It's how you grow. It's how life is.

Learn to embrace change.

Listen to Your Body

The call to exercise doesn't come from gyms, health clubs, physical education directors, or diet books. The call to exercise comes from our bodies, from our souls.

I fought exercise for a long, long time. During the 1980s, when it became popular, I managed to resist. *It's boring, hard, and unpleasant,* I thought. *It won't work for me.*

When my daughter finally dragged me to the local health club, I felt like I was in a foreign country. I rode a bike for a few minutes, then wobbled to the water fountain looking like a penguin, legs numb, heart pounding, muscles aching, sweat pouring down my back. My daughter looked at me and firmly said, "You let yourself get in this shape. Now it's time to get out."

It took a while to understand that when I did some simple workouts, I felt better, not worse. The cycle happened naturally, over many months. But my body had said loudly, *It's time.*

The world is full of ways to move around, work our bodies, and exercise. Park the car in the space farthest from the store and walk. Carry groceries one bag at a time from the car to the house. Carry your own luggage. Go for a walk. Go for a run. Do sit-ups. Learn yoga. Take up line dancing.

Find some way to move your body that feels good for you. Start doing it, even if it doesn't feel good at first. Do it until you can hear your body, hear what it wants, hear what it needs, hear what feels good to it. Do it until you can hear your body tell you how and when it wants to move.

The better you can hear your body,
the more clearly you will hear your soul.

SEPTEMBER 24

Your Healers Will Come to You

The people, the ideas, the resources you need to heal will come. They'll appear on your path. Sometimes you'll think it's almost magical. Sometimes you'll resist, saying, *That can't be right. It's too easy.* But your healers will come when you need them, when you're ready.

You can trust the universe to send healers to you, but also trust yourself. Some of the healers and resources you encounter may not be right for you. Trust yourself to know what's right. And remember, healers aren't your source of power; they merely assist you in claiming your power. They come to help, to bring their gifts to you so that you can find yours.

Just as your healers will come to you, the people you are to bring healing to will appear on your path when it's time, when it's right. Trust yourself to make decisions regarding those with whom you share your gifts. Your heart will guide you if you listen.

Let yourself receive the healing you need. Let yourself share your healing gifts with others. Find the balance that's right for you. Trust yourself and the wisdom of your body, mind, and heart about what feels right, who feels right, and when it works for you.

SEPTEMBER 25

Discover Life's Rhythm

Step into the natural rhythm for your life.

You don't have to push through anymore. You don't have to push yourself, life, or the energy flow.

If you get tired, take a break. Take a walk. Take in the healing energy of the world around you. Listen to the birds sing. Hear the laughter of a child. Feel the warm smile of a friend, or smile at a stranger passing by. If you get stuck or tangled up, stop trying to force the solution. Back off, until the answer emerges naturally from that place of peace and natural instinct within you.

Step out of your tension, out of your fear. Laugh. Lighten up. Loosen up. Change your energy. Relax until you find the flow. Relax until you find your rhythm, until you feel life's rhythm again.

Step into the rhythm of love.

SEPTEMBER 26

Trust Even the Dark Moments

While on our journey, life can sometimes get bleak. Dark passages may envelop us.

Expect these moments. Often they come at the deepest period of working things out. It can be a time of despair, frustration, dead ends, anguish, and angst. Sometimes these moments are brief; sometimes they last a long time. But usually they are necessary.

Plan on these moments. They are not the end of the journey. They are the passageway through the tunnel and into the light. In just a little while, you will feel, see, and know the purpose of what you're going through. Soon it will become clear. You will move out of the darkness and into the light.

Trust even the bleak times.
When you reach the end of
the tunnel, then you will
know why this all had to be.

SEPTEMBER 27

Freeze Negative Energy

Police officers often say "Freeze!" when they want someone to stop, when they want to protect themselves. We can do the same thing. We can learn to freeze unwanted energy that comes to us from others.

Health professionals agree there are many causes of stress in our lives, from toxins in the air to problems related to love, money, self-esteem, or work. One subtle problem that can cause undesirable stress—an area we often overlook—is when people direct negative energy at us. We can learn to become aware of, and protect ourselves from, undesirable negative energy that others may unconsciously, or even consciously, be directing toward us—whether they're feeling angry, resentful, jealous, or downright hateful. We don't have to absorb the impact of that energy, and let it harm us.

We can freeze negative energy. We can mentally tell it to stop and refuse to take it in and make it ours. If something is really bothering us, try this trick one healer taught me. Draw a picture of the person or write a description of the problem, then stick it in the freezer underneath the bottom tray.

People are energy. Thoughts are energy.
Part of loving ourselves is not ingesting toxins.
Negative energy is toxic. Don't stress others

out by sending negative energy to them. Learn to tell when negative energy is stressing you, and then learn to tell it to freeze.

SEPTEMBER 28

Forgiveness Will Complete the Process

"Do visit Bryce Canyon," a man advised. "But do it later, after you've driven through the other parts of Utah. It's like the icing on the cake." So it is with forgiveness. It's the icing on the cake.

Forgiveness is a simple word, but a difficult, complicated process. Forgiveness is also essential if we want to find happiness and joy.

To forgive too soon, before we've felt all we needed to feel along the way, is incomplete. Forgiveness based on denial won't work. And not to forgive, after we've felt our emotions—our anger, rage, pain, and betrayal—will harden our hearts and keep us closed. We'll have loose ends to tie up, an unfinished connection to our past. We'll have unfinished business with others, even though we may not see them, speak to them, or consciously think abut them any longer. We won't be free, and neither will they.

Sometimes we need to seek forgiveness because we've tried everything else and nothing works to bring us back to peace. Sometimes forgiveness finds us, unexpectedly transforming our hearts, softening us, opening us, and renewing our hearts and our relationships.

Sometimes forgiveness surprises us because it's the last thing we thought we would need to feel whole again. Forgiveness is often the completion of the process. It's the icing on the cake.

SEPTEMBER 29

Do Something Nice for Someone Today

Why wait for Christmas? Do something nice for someone today. Give a gift, even when it isn't someone's birthday. Give a gift of love and joy.

Feeling down? Frustrated? Instead of depriving yourself when you already feel bad enough, do something nice for yourself. Love yourself. Be kind, gentle, and nurturing to yourself. Treat yourself to a new book, a bouquet of flowers, a sweater, or a hat—something that will bring you joy. Take yourself to a movie. Or give yourself a free gift of love—a walk, a bath, a relaxing afternoon in the sun. Send a card to yourself. Give yourself comforting, encouraging words. Tell yourself how well you've done and that you've done your best.

Give words of love and encouragement to others, too. Tell them you appreciate them. Tell them you think they're wonderful. Tell them they're perfect. When you give gifts of love to others, you give them to yourself.

Sometimes, the gift people need is words of love. "I pray for you every morning," my friend told me. "I ask God to bless you and help you. Then I talk to your angels. I tell them to take special care of you all day long and bring you lots of joy." That's one of the nicest gifts I've ever received.

You don't have to wait for Christmas to give gifts of love and joy. Give that love to others and yourself. Give it often. Give it freely. Give it all year round.

SEPTEMBER 30

You're a Healer

The healing you give to the world can happen as gracefully and naturally as the pine trees touch and heal with their life, their presence. Arousing your senses, they fill you with their fragrance. Their presence changes your energy, calms your fears, lets you know all is well.

Know you can stand tall, joyfully be who you are, and grow where you are. You have the ability to touch those around you in a way that heals them without hurting or draining you. One of your gifts to yourself and to the world is that of healer. You don't have to force it, strive to make it happen. It happens gently and naturally when you love and accept who you are.

Open to your healing powers, your ability to heal yourself and those around you. Receive this gift with joy; share it freely with all you meet. Open to your healing powers and you will cherish your past, all you have gone through and done.

Who you are is love. What love does is heal.

October

OCTOBER 1

Are You Ready, Willing, and Able?

Have you cleared the path you want to travel? Are you ready, willing, and able to do whatever it takes to have what you want?

Decide what you want. Be as clear as you can be. Say it. Write it. Share your idea with a friend. Then ask yourself if you are ready, willing, and able to do what it takes to have what you want. Ask yourself that question as often as you need to.

Watch how you feel when you say what you want. Look for objections, blocks from within, obstacles on your path. Look closely at yourself, your fears, your angers, your resistance. Let your feelings come up, acknowledge them, then let them go. One after another remove the blocks until the path you want to travel is clear. Remove the obstacles until you can clearly see your vision and your voice is strong and clear: I'm ready, willing, and able to have what I want and it's in my highest good.

The way to your dreams, the way to make your visions come alive is by taking a journey inside your soul. Are you ready, willing, and able to have what you want? Do you believe it when you hear yourself say it? When you do, the road will be clear, and you'll be ready to travel the path you desire.

OCTOBER 2

Trust the Unknown

Look! See how much you've changed. See the difference in your perspective.

Remember all those years you were so fearful, trying to peek ahead, trying to see what the future held. Remember how upset you got, how uncertain and abandoned you felt because you didn't know the plan.

Now life has taken you to a new place, a new place for you but a place that is ancient. All along, you were not supposed to be getting the answers about what the future held. You were supposed to be learning the magical way of trust and inner guidance, learning to feel your way through, trusting and committing to your vision, your energy, your purpose, your place, each day and moment along the way. You were supposed to be learning to allow the universe to magically unfold and trust that it would. You have been learning this lesson. You have been learning it well.

See how you delight in life's magic now, the surprises, the not knowing, the absolute trust in the universe to bring you your answers, manifest your visions, and help you when you can't quite see. See how much you cherish your relationship to the universe, a relationship so much broader and more encompassing, so much more vital than you could ever before imagine. See how joyfully you walk your path, enjoying all the sights, opening your heart to loved ones and strangers.

See how benevolent it really is when you are not able to see ahead. Not knowing has taught you about life's magic. It has connected you to yourself and to the universe. It has connected you to God.

Not knowing has taught you to know
more than you could ever imagine.

OCTOBER 3

Finish Unfinished Business

Finish your business with people. Unfinished business with others is the biggest block to an open heart, the biggest block to peace and joy.

The tangled cords that bind us to the past are easy to find. All we need do is become quiet and listen to the voice of our heart. Who do we resent? Who are we angry with? Hurt by? Who are the people we aren't at peace with? That's our unfinished business, the unfinished business of the heart.

Look deep inside. Find your secrets. Find your not-quite-finished pieces. Then discover what you need to finish. Often, the answer is only a breath away—a breath of fresh air, a breath of forgiveness, a breath of love. Take that breath. Let the past go. Let it go in peace, thankful for all you've learned along the way.

Tie up your loose ends. Heal your
connections to others and your heart by
finishing unfinished business. Then you'll

be free to move on. And you can go forward in peace.

OCTOBER 4

Let the Miracle of Acceptance Find You

I found this miracle in a small church in New Mexico. The Sanctuario do Chimayo is famous for its healing powers and miracles. The ground under the church, some say, is particularly holy and powerful. Crutches—evidence of the healing miracles people experienced there—line the walls of the church's back room.

Four years ago, a friend had sent me to the Sanctuario to find my miracle. It was three months after my son died. I didn't know what miracle could possibly fix my situation. Now, sitting in the back of the chapel, I knew. I didn't have any crutches to hang on the wall, but the miracle of acceptance had healed my heart and changed my life.

We may search for miracles that change our situation so we don't have to deal with the loss or feel the pain. Sometimes we get that miracle. Our circumstances change. But sometimes the miracle we get changes us. If the situation is too difficult, the loss too painful to accept in one leap, take smaller steps. Accept what you're feeling today. Accept who you are today. Accept what you think today.

Look for your miracles. Hope for the best. But when you can't change what you're going through, let the simple, quiet, daily miracle of acceptance find you.

OCTOBER 5

Spiritual Growth Can Be Easier Now

For so long, you thought that spiritual growth, healing, life had to be hard. And it was—for many reasons.

That's no longer the case. Do you see the rose struggling and straining to grow? Do you see a tree pushing and forcing its growth? Your growth can unfold as naturally, as inevitably, as beautifully as the tender shoots of a rose break through first with green, then a bud, then a fully opened flower. You have committed to life, you have committed to growth, you have committed to opening your heart and taking the journey. That is enough.

The rest will be revealed to you in time. The answers will become clear. The visions, the guidance, the leadings you are seeking will come. All you need to guide you through life will come—quiet spiritual awakenings, quiet revelations that profoundly change your life. Each awakening will take you to the next place. Each will lead you home.

Don't worry about what you have to do to achieve spiritual growth. Let yourself be. The growth will happen, and it will happen naturally and easily.

OCTOBER 6

What Are Your Priorities?

I was working away in my cabin, trying to print out the pages I had typed into my computer. It was taking half an hour to print each page;

I had one hundred pages to go. For the umpteenth time I checked my computer, checked the program, checked the printer, checked everything I knew to see why it was printing so slowly. It all seemed to be set up properly. Then I accidentally touched a control setting, one I hadn't noticed before. It was the priority control. It was set on low. I switched it to high priority. The pages now began to print at top speed.

Priorities are important. Learning how to focus our energy according to priorities—even though we're going with the flow—is an important part of our lives. It's one of the powers we're learning.

What are your priorities? Is living from your heart one of them? Are there tasks you'd like to accomplish? Skills you'd like to acquire? Is meditation, being centered, and living your life from a place of balance an area you've designated as critical?

Is loving yourself a priority? How important is your spiritual growth? What priority have you assigned to other areas like pleasure, having fun, feeling joy? Are your priorities set on high, medium, or low?

Look around and you'll see your answers. Your life as it is now reflects the priorities you have chosen so far. If something is happening too slowly, try switching your priority setting from low to high.

OCTOBER 7

Value the Power of Seeing

I have learned a valuable tool. It is one of the easiest and most powerful tools I've been given. I call it the power of seeing.

It is the simple act of observing myself: what I do, how I react, how I respond to others. It is particularly useful in situations that have gotten confused or sticky and I don't know what to do to become unstuck. When I feel overwhelmed or a situation gets too difficult and I can't see my way through, I watch myself. It helps.

Learn to observe yourself. Let yourself really see and be present in the moment in the situation you're in. Watch yourself as a neutral observer would, without judgment. Try to see the other person in the same way. Watch how the two of you interact, respond to each other. Watch yourself think and feel. See the actions you take. You don't have to talk about what you're doing; it's better if you don't. Just stay with yourself. Do it once. Do it twice. Then do it again.

Soon you'll begin to see something else: you'll begin to see the situation change, evolve, take a turn for the better. The power of seeing is one most of us can easily claim. It helps, heals, and sometimes produces miracles. Physicists have decided that the act of observing can impact the behavior, appearance, or energy of whatever is being observed. How we look at someone, including ourselves, can have an impact, cause a change.

There's power in seeing. There's even more power in seeing with the eyes of love.

OCTOBER 8

Leave When It's Time to Go

It's time to pick up, pack up, and leave.

You knew you wouldn't be in this situation in this place with these people forever. Trust the rhythms and cycles of life. Take responsibility for yourself within each cycle. Take responsibility for yourself as each cycle ends and a new one begins.

You don't have to hold onto messengers after they've delivered the message in your life, or escorts after they've taken you where you were trying to go. You don't have to stay in a classroom after you've learned the lessons and finished that course.

Open your heart. Thank the people, places, and things that have helped create your world, shape you, form your experiences. Then pick up, pack up, and leave. Say good-bye with love and gratitude in your heart.

And go on down the road.

OCTOBER 9

The Scattered Pieces Will Come Together

Scattered pieces. Sometimes we look around, and that's what we see. Scattered pieces of ourselves, our lives, a project, a season of our lives. Where is the connecting thread, we wonder? How can we ever pull this together into something that makes sense, something with purpose, something with meaning?

There are pieces to every whole; yet each piece is complete. Don't worry about how they will come together. Work joyfully on the piece that's before you, the piece that's in your life today.

There are many pieces of you, many beautiful parts. The universe will help you bring all those parts alive. It will bring mirrors to you, people who will reflect those beautiful pieces back to you. Look in the mirror of your life. What pieces do you see reflected? Know it's you you're seeing. Then let that part of you come alive.

Pull in the parts of yourself, the many beautiful parts that have come alive. Beckon your warrior, your healer, your playful child. Bring together your professional self, your adult, the passionate part of you, the nurturing part. Let all the parts come together. Don't send any of them away. You need them all. Each is a beautiful piece of the soul, the life, the person you are.

Trust. Trust the process. Joy is yours, available for the asking and the desiring—even in the developmental stages. Even before the puzzle has been put together. The scattered pieces will come together—the scattered pieces of yourself, your project, your life. The connecting thread is love.

The picture will be beautiful. Wait and see.

OCTOBER 10

We Are Transmitters and Receivers

We are a finely tuned instrument—body, mind, and soul. We receive messages, we receive guidance. And we transmit energy—the energy of love.

When we become off center, we become like two-way radios whose tuners aren't on the right frequency. We aren't receiving or transmitting clearly. We hear and feel the static. Often, instinctively, that's when we start broadcasting more loudly, sometimes screaming to be heard. Now is not the time to crank up the volume.

Take the time you need to get centered, to get peaceful. What do you need to do? What do you need to feel? What healing resources do you need to utilize? What's your voice, your quiet, trustworthy inner voice, the one that speaks through your heart, urging you to do?

Taking time to get centered and peaceful isn't selfish. It's not a waste of time. When we're receiving clearly, we transmit clearly.

And the frequency we use is love.

OCTOBER 11

Honor Your Connection to Your Body

Our bodies are matter, the physical form we have assumed. They are infused with our energy, our soul.

My awareness of the body-mind-soul connection came slowly, over many years. I had spent many years denying I had a body, denying its importance. I felt disconnected from it, as though it were something apart from me, a burden I had to carry around and live with. Then I began to see the connection between my emotions and the aches and pains—and sometimes illnesses—my body was experiencing. If I didn't feel the feeling, listen to myself, my body would pound out the pain until it was heard that way. Energy needs to be discharged somewhere. If it isn't discharged, the body will absorb and feel it as pain. I began to see the connection between changes in my life and changes in my body, the way the earth marks changing seasons and cycles.

I began to get massages, exercise, and slowly trust the wisdom of my body. I became connected to my body. Yes, I was a soul. Yes, I had a heart. Emotions. Thought. But to live on the physical plane of earth, we need a body. Our body is part of us. It is us. It holds the scars of our life to date, the stories of our life so far; it contains the wisdom and energy of what we need today and tomorrow.

Honor your connection to your body. Honor and value your body's wisdom. It can tell you may things about your life, your growth, your past, and your path. Learn to listen to your body, and it will speak openly and lovingly to you.

OCTOBER 12

Trust Yourself to Know What's Right

Sometimes we find ourselves with people or in places we can't adapt to. No matter how hard we try, no matter how much we want it to, it just doesn't feel right. Doesn't fit. We are trying to jam the proverbial square peg into the round hole. Only what we're trying to jam isn't a block of wood—it's us.

Sometimes in situations like these we revert to old ways of thinking, believing, and feeling. There must be something wrong with me if I don't like this, if this isn't working. If I try harder, control my emotions, jam a little harder, this square peg—me—will fit.

Those are the times we may begin to feel confused, weak, scattered, uncertain. We abandon ourselves. Our emotions disappear. Our passion wanes. We may begin sleeping, escaping, drifting further and further away. Our soul begins squirming in reaction to what we're trying to force ourselves to do. We may become physically ill. It's as though we're allergic to our surroundings. Sometimes, we may spend years in this process—depending on what we're afraid to face or what we're afraid to lose. Other times, this process may only last hours or days.

We can take as much time as we need to listen to and take care of ourselves. But if we love ourselves, we won't torture ourselves for long, because we know we don't have to. If a place or person or situation doesn't work for us, that's okay. We don't have to punish ourselves. We don't have to go away from ourselves. We can leave the situation.

Trust yourself—your body and your soul—to know what's right for you. Learn to feel the energy of a situation, place, or person. If something feels right, you feel in harmony mentally, emotionally, and spiritually. If it doesn't feel right, don't abandon yourself. Leave the situation. Try something else until you do feel right.

You may not always know at first when a thing, place, or person is wrong for you. But if you listen to your body and trust your heart, you can learn to tell when it's right.

OCTOBER 13

You Are on Time

Quit wondering, worrying, and blaming yourself for being late. Or worse yet, missing the boat.

"Nothing else in the universe frets about being late. Does the moon ask itself if it's where it should be? Does the sun say, 'I must hurry, else I'll be late?'" a friend asked one evening when I was worrying about not being on time.

Stare up into the sky on a beautiful moonlit night. Feel the quiet, timeless rhythm of the planets, the moon, the stars, the universe. Know that you're connected, tuned into a rhythm deeper and more secure than all your wondering could imagine. Breathe deeply. Relax. Let your pace spring from knowing that inside your heart.

Trust the rhythm of the universe. You are right where you need to be. You'll get where you need to go. You have all the time you need.

OCTOBER 14

Clear Out the Clutter

Have you ever noticed how easy it is to accumulate possessions and clutter in your home, things you pick up along the way? Have you ever noticed how easy it is to begin accommodating this clutter, getting used to it, thinking of it as just part of your environment?

It can be that way with our emotions, too. No matter how hard we strive to stay clear, we pick up bits of clutter along the way.

It's so easy to ignore deeply embedded emotions and their impact on our lives. Many of us have undercurrents of old emotional energy that have been with us for so long we don't see them. We don't see the anger, the fear, the sadness. We've lived with these feelings for so long they have become embedded in us, part of us. When one of these nudges us, we tuck it back in, pack it away, and go on about our lives. But the feeling stays with us until we consciously acknowledge and address it. It affects us and our lives until we heal it.

Find a way to heal those old feelings, perhaps journaling or writing your memoirs. Whatever technique you choose to begin this journey of deep healing, deep cleansing, take the time to become conscious of what you really feel. Observe yourself; listen closely to yourself. Is there an edge to your voice? Do you talk about a particular person or place with a high degree of emotional energy? Learn to become comfortable with the rhythm of allowing these emotions to surface. They aren't that hard to find. When it's time to heal them, they'll present themselves.

Release your fear of facing what's there. Tap into that deeper part of you. Acknowledge your emotional energy, and heal.

Start cleaning house. Each piece
of emotional clutter you clear out
will bring you closer to your soul.

OCTOBER 15

Discover the Power of Vulnerability

A new kind of power will emerge from vulnerability. The more honest we are with ourselves about how we feel and what we really think, the more power we will have.

We may have once thought that being powerful meant not giving in to what we felt, what we thought, or who we really were. But that attitude didn't garner power for us. It caused life, the universe, us to continue creating situations that would help open our hearts, help us to feel, help us learn the lesson of vulnerability.

The sooner we become honest with ourselves, the sooner we can be honest with others. The sooner we become honest with ourselves, the more quickly we'll grow and move on to a new place. Become vulnerable, at least with yourself. Be honest about what you think and how you feel. Write it. Speak it. Feel it. Release it. Then you will know where to go, when to go. What you are to do next will emerge naturally, quietly, and clearly.

Try being absolutely honest. Reveal your most private feelings to yourself. It's a new kind of power, a different kind of power. It is spiritual power, the power of opening the heart.

OCTOBER 16

Go for the Ride of Your Life

The roller coaster crawled slowly upward, inching toward the first and biggest hill. And suddenly we were screaming downhill at ninety-seven miles an hour. It is, they claim, the fastest roller coaster in the world. I laughed and yelled and clutched the handlebar. When the ride ended, the attendant turned to us as we were about to leave. "Would you like to go again?" he asked. "It's the last ride of the night." We all shouted yes and rode the course again, the wind whipping through our hair. When the ride ended, as all rides do, we sat in our seats and cheered.

Sometimes things happen. Things we didn't expect. Things we didn't plan on. An event occurs that changes our life dramatically. The event may be good or bad, desirable or undesirable, fortunate or unfortunate. No matter how we describe it, its impact is the same. We step off our usual path and go for a roller coaster ride.

You may have begun a time of deep transformation, a journey chosen by your soul. Feel all you need to feel. Allow your thoughts to flow. Let your body shift as you go through the curves. Let yourself be transformed. Enjoy the ride, the entire experience, with all its twists and curves. Scream in fear. Cry out in joy. Laugh aloud with glee.

If you find yourself on a roller coaster,
turn it into the ride of your life.

OCTOBER 17

Feeling Overwhelmed Is a Trap

Feeling overwhelmed is a trap, a tricky one at that. When we're overwhelmed, we see all that needs to be done and say, *That's too much. I can't do it. So instead, I shall do nothing.* Feeling overwhelmed occurs when we say, *I am already too busy so I can't do that and now all is pressing in on me and I can't do anything.* And the acts that are ours to do keep piling up and pulling on us. And we keep resisting. And stress and pressure build up.

Feeling overwhelmed leads to feeling stuck, and both are an illusion. How simple those things that overwhelm us actually become when we release the feeling and return to the rhythm of our lives. When we say, *Yes, I need to make that phone call, do that task.* How simple the task becomes, how simple life becomes.

What's bothering you that needs to be done? What's pulling on you? What's causing you to feel overwhelmed and maybe stuck, too? Make a list. Put your list aside, and begin by taking one simple action. Then watch as life unfolds. One act at a time, one thing at a time, all that needs to be done will get done. The stress will disappear, and you'll feel back on track.

You'll be given the ability, power, and guidance to do all that is on your path to do. Begin simply, quietly, by acknowledging feeling overwhelmed. Denying the pull of life and its tasks doesn't remove stress; it compounds it.

Surrendering to the simple truths,
even the simple truth of what we're
really feeling, will always set us free.

OCTOBER 18

Trust the Morning

I arrived in Sedona late at night, after ten o'clock. Motel offices were closed everywhere I went. The signs flashed "No Vacancy." I hung around the convenience store for a while, trying to figure out what to do, having second thoughts about spontaneity and trusting the universe. I regretted not having an itinerary. I was too tired to drive much longer. I no longer cared if my journey was magical; it was back to basics. I wanted to sleep in a bed that night.

I bought the daily paper and spotted an ad for a lodge. I called the number, but no luck. I got in my car, wondering what to do.

On the edge of town, I saw a motel with lights on in the office and a person behind the desk. I went inside and pestered the girl behind the desk for help. She finally relented, telling me of a little-known hotel about an hour away. She lived close by, she said. I could follow her there. An hour later, I gratefully checked into a room. I couldn't find the heat, but I did have a bed, pillow, and blanket.

The next morning, I discovered I was staying on the edge of a dry, dusty golf course. The area was surrounded by low, barren hills barely covered with shrubs. I headed the car toward Sedona, still tired, still wondering why I was there.

My car rounded a curve. Suddenly I was surrounded by spiraling red mesas shaped by nature into forms of bells, cathedrals, and carved towers reaching to the sky. The sunlight danced on the rusty red sculptures, lighting them with an orange-yellow glow. I smiled at the breathtaking view, grateful the experience had unfolded as it had.

Sometimes, the darkness and loneliness of night make the color and beauty of the sunrise and the new day all that much more beautiful. Contrast is an important part of creativity. Our Creator knows that. So does our heart.

Things look different in the morning.
Trust that the morning will come.

OCTOBER 19

Honor This Time of Change

I left Point Reyes, a seashore town close to San Francisco, heading for Sequoia National Park. I wanted to cross the Golden Gate Bridge, but I wasn't certain I could find it. City traffic was jarring after being in the woods, the mountains, and by the sea. Before long, however, I found myself at the foot of the Golden Gate. As I drove the span of the bridge, I felt the same electric charge surge through me as I had felt in Chimayo, in Ojo Caliente, and on the Flathead Reservation. It was the first time I realized that bridges are holy, sacred ground.

Times of change are holy. We may not know where we're going. It may not feel like our feet are on solid ground. They aren't. We're crossing a bridge to another part of our lives.

Sometimes we may find ourselves at this bridge unwittingly, not certain how we got there, not certain we want to cross. Other times, we may have sought, prayed for, hoped for, longed for this time of change.

Drive across the bridge. You don't have
to understand it all right now. Information
and understanding will come later. You'll get
to the other side. For now, trust and experience
what you're going through. Know that this
time of change is sacred, too.

OCTOBER 20

Fall into the Arms of Universal Love

Often in our lives we stand on a precipice. Something happens, a situation occurs, and in one moment our life changes dramatically in a way we hoped and prayed it wouldn't. We topple off. In that moment, we may feel as if we've been pushed off a cliff.

Other times when we stand poised and our life changes radically in one moment, it's a welcome change. We feel delightfully spontaneous, guided, powerful, centered. Ready to take risks. Ready to leap into the adventure.

Sometimes we're pushed; sometimes we
decide to make the leap on our own. Either

way, we're safe, we're protected. Either way we can trust that we'll land in the arms of universal love.

OCTOBER 21

Learn to Nurture and Be Nurtured

It was a quiet morning. I was holed up in a hotel room at the mouth of Bryce Canyon, working on this book. Working on my life. I stayed in bed for a while—thinking, pondering, wondering. Finally I got up, went to the restaurant for coffee and a roll, then went for a drive. *Soak up nature,* I told myself. *This journey is a living meditation.*

I drove into Bryce Canyon Park, letting the massive stones, the colors and spirals, the eternity of the canyon touch me, heal me, soothe my soul. An hour later, when I felt calmer and more energized, I got back in the car and headed for the park exit. Several cars were jammed up. I wondered if there had been an accident. Then I saw why the others had stopped. A mother deer was standing on the side of the road, gently nuzzling her fawn. She stood by her offspring's side, protecting and nurturing.

Many of us barely remember a mother's nurturing love; some of us do, with fondness and joy. Many of us have experienced the great gift of nurturing and loving our children, a joy that opens the heart in a way little else can. Some of us have learned to give and receive nurturing in other ways, to people outside our immediate families. But most of us, along the way, have learned the gift, the wonder, the awe, and the healing blessings of nurturing. Giving and receiving is a continuous cycle, a necessary part of the road to the heart.

Learn to nurture others. Nurture and love yourself. The whole universe will rally round and help. Others will applaud your efforts and learn from them, the way the passersby stopped to gaze on the deer and her fawn.

Celebrate the power of nurturing. Release its gentle love. It rests inside each of us, waiting to be seen, appreciated, and brought to life.

OCTOBER 22

Heal Your Past

Open your heart to the universe. Let it bring you love and comfort. Let it bring you healing. Let it take you back to your past long enough to heal, so you can move forward into joy.

Universal love can bring something other than straightforward movement. Sometimes it takes us backward into our past and leaves us there long enough to heal. An incident occurs, and we react strongly; our emotions are more intense than necessary for the present moment. We may not notice. We may think, *This is now; this is how I'm feeling about what's happening today.* But as we become more aware, some part of us says, *I'm feeling something from yesterday, too, something I wasn't safe enough to see and feel then.*

Let yourself feel your past. Then let yourself heal. Take responsibility for your behaviors. Let the emotions clear. Then you will see what the universe has done. It has just created a healing scenario for you—a gentle trigger to the past, a gentle step forward for your heart.

OCTOBER 23

Cherish Joy

Choose joy. Then cherish and savor it.

Joy is not a fleeting emotion based on outward circumstances, a transitory feeling of the moment, a reaction to the scenery around you. It comes from within your heart like the waterfall that rushes out the side of a mountain. Joy is a runoff from the wellspring within you. And sometimes it is a delightful, surprising contrast to the scenery around you.

Embrace joy. Relish it. Even if those around you don't have it right now, you can feel your joy. You don't have to be disrespectful of their feelings, nor do you have to let their lack of joy diminish yours.

You have done your work. You have chosen to open your heart. Now you have your reward.

Cherish joy. It's your treasure. You've found it. You've earned it. It's yours.

OCTOBER 24

Share Your Heart with the World

Share your heart with the world. Share willingly, openly, joyfully what you have seen, what you have learned.

Don't tell people how you think you should have handled things. That's shame. It teaches others to feel ashamed, too. Don't tell people how you wish you had handled things. That's needless regret that we pass on to others.

Share honestly and openly about yourself, the way you felt, the things you thought. Share how going through your experience changed you. Talk about your resistance, your pain, the imperfect way you did things, the way you handle things now.

Sharing honestly and openly teaches people around us the most helpful truth—that the imperfect way we live our lives is right for us at the time. When we love and accept ourselves enough to honestly share who we are, it helps those we touch to believe that they're good enough, too.

Share your heart with the world and you
will bring healing to those you touch.

OCTOBER 25

Replenish Yourself

Some of us don't know how tired we are until we try to relax. Then we realize we're exhausted.

We may have lived with exhaustion and stress so long it's become habitual. That doesn't mean we're bad or wrong, or even off track. Many of us are deeply involved in activities, work, projects, and relationships we enjoy. We like our lives and the things we're doing. But sometimes we've pushed too hard or too long. Sometimes we haven't given our bodies adequate time to relax, to rest, to really let go.

It's all right to take time out. Relax. Refresh. Regroup. It's all right to rest even if we're busy, rest often enough to keep ourselves replenished. Get in touch with your body, then stay in touch with yourself.

Find out how tired you are. Then let your body tell you what it needs to come back to life and love.

OCTOBER 26

Let the World Help You Open Up

The universe is gentle, loving, benevolent, full of gifts, full of life, full of love. Don't worry if you feel scared, or if you feel yourself closing down to life's magic. That feeling won't last long. It won't last forever.

Take a walk. Touch a tree; hug it until your fear subsides. Feel the earth under your feet. Watch a sunrise. Ask the universe and God to help you open up. Say it aloud. Then watch what happens. Go where your heart leads, where your inner voice directs you to go. You will find yourself in circumstances that bring you back to your heart.

The universe will help you open up. It will do all it can, lovingly, gently, and with care. It will teach you all you need to know, help you learn all you came here to learn. It will guide you and lead you, open doors and shut windows, until you reach your destination—an open heart and a soul aligned with love.

OCTOBER 27

Have You Been Working Too Hard?

Have you been working too hard at your job, at life, at your spiritual progress? Have you been working too hard on your relationships with people, on trying to gain insights, or on trying to figure out where to go or what to do next?

Many of us have had to work hard. To get from where we were to where we are, we had to push, force, put one foot in front of the other. At least we thought we did. But life doesn't have to be that hard. Not anymore. The biggest task, the smallest task, the task of living our lives doesn't have to be that difficult.

There's a natural rhythm for everything that happens along the way. There's a natural rhythm and order for all we're to do. Yes, there are times to begin. Yes, there are times to put one foot in front of the other and go forward. But the joy, the service, the way of life we're seeking doesn't come from force. It comes naturally, easily, much more easily than you think. Stop pushing so hard, and see how quickly that rhythm finds you.

You don't have to make life happen. In fact,
you can't. Relax. Let go. And let it happen.

OCTOBER 28

Let Yourself Take Side Trips

"You're on a journey," the Native American shaman from Sedona said, "but it's not what you think. Don't be like the deer, who looks straight ahead and sees only the destination. Let yourself take all the side trips you can. Travel the back roads, take your time. Talk to people and touch the trees. See all you've come here to see."

Sometimes we need to make side trips—side trips into experiences, emotions, situations that take us off center and somewhere new. Sometimes that's where our greatest learning and growth occur.

If a side trip is beckoning, perhaps there's a lesson there: an old feeling to be felt, healed, and cleared; a new attitude or belief to be acquired; a revelation, a surprise. Remember this: a side trip, with all it's emotions, isn't about another person. It's about you and your journey to healing, freedom, and joy. Ignoring a situation that can take you off center won't take you to the next place. Going more deeply into your own growth process, going more deeply into your soul is what will further your journey.

Everything that happens to you can be used, felt, shaped and transformed to further your journey. This process of growth, of side trips and healing, is your destiny, the magical journey of your soul.

To get to the next place, we need to
leave the comfortable main road we've
been traveling. Sometimes a side trip
is exactly what we need to make.

OCTOBER 29

The Best Is Yet to Come

Set yourself free from limitations, limitations you have placed on yourself. Sometimes in life we may begin thinking the best part is over. *I've done my best work, had my best times. What could be left?* That kind of thinking limits us. We don't have to limit ourselves, life or the universe.

You've had many great times, visited many interesting places, done excellent work, and had truly memorable experiences. You've experienced a lifetime of love—with friends, family members, loved ones. But the best isn't over. Whether you're at the end of a particular relationship, task, or part of your journey, the best is not over. It is still to come.

Memories of excellent times are to be cherished. Clinging to them in a way that limits our lives is a different issue. Often, it keeps us from cherishing the present moment and creatively participating in our future.

All endings are inexorably tied to new beginnings. That's the nature of the journey. It continues to unfold. It builds on itself. It can't help itself from doing that. Cherish the moments, all of them. You have seen and felt much in life so far. But still, the best is yet to come.

Open to all the journey holds. The universe is abundant. You are ready to be healed, calmed, empowered. You are ready to partake of the banquet of life, again and again. You are ready to take your place in new, creative experiences. There are many places still to see, soul mates yet to meet, lessons to be learned, joys to be experienced.

Transcend your limitations. Open your mind and heart to all that lies ahead. Call it to you often in the quietness of your heart by believing what is true.

The best is yet to come.

OCTOBER 30

Honor the Seasons of Your Soul

There are seasons and cycles in our lives, just as there are seasons and cycles to nature, to all of life. We move imperceptibly from one to the other—learning, growing, laughing, and crying along the way.

We accept with joy the seasons of nature. We honor them. We wouldn't think of pulling at the tiny blades of grass in early spring to force their growth. Neither would we chastise them for growing too slowly or wilting with the first frost of autumn.

We can learn to recognize and honor the seasons and cycles in ourselves. The answers will come—small glimpses at first, like the first tender shoots of grass. We get an idea, a clue, a hint, of what we're about to learn. Then come a series of experiences. Sometimes we immediately see the connection. Sometimes we don't. We go about the business of living our lives.

Then one day, we see. That tiny shoot has become a full-grown blade of grass, a rolling lawn covering the landscape. We see the connections, the lessons—and we'll honor all the feelings that we had along the way. We're different. We're changed. We're new. A new season has arrived.

And just when we think that the way it is now is the way it will be forever, another season begins. As naturally, as imperceptibly as the last. It, too, will build on what has already happened and create something new.

There are seasons and cycles in us,
just as there are in nature. Learn to
recognize and honor the seasons
and cycles of the soul.

OCTOBER 31

Something Important Is Happening Now

There's never a time when nothing is happening.

Something is always taking place. Growth is occurring. We're evolving, transforming, working things out, incorporating our last lesson, preparing for our next. Something is happening. We just don't always see it. And that's how it's meant to be.

When we see, when we know too much too soon, it's easy to let our heads get in the way. We think we have to control, have to force, have to make it happen, have to *do* something.

In a gentle but wise way, the universe takes into account our fears and our natures. It doesn't let us know too much too soon. It doesn't spoil the surprise. It doesn't want us to spoil it either.

Open your heart to the universe.
Trust that something is always
happening. And often, it's much
different and better than you think.

November

NOVEMBER 1

Open Up to Your Connections

Many religions teach about interconnectedness, the subtle effect each person and each movement in the universe has on all the others. I was profoundly reminded of this teaching at Chaco Canyon in New Mexico. In the remnants of the Anasazi culture can be found symbols for the connections the people believed in, taught, and lived. One dwelling was a structure in which over eight hundred rooms were built in a connected circle. Each room touched the next, and the structure contained all the areas the people needed to work, to live, to play, and to worship.

An exhibit in the visitor's center describes the spiritual philosophy of the descendants of the Anasazi: "The Pueblo people live at the center of their universe; all things are interconnected and form a part of the whole. Where the sky and the earth touch are the boundaries for all things to live. All things share in the essence of life through cycles of birth and death." Although the walls of the circular structure have crumbled and the Anasazi themselves have disappeared, the Pueblo philosophy still symbolizes the way we're connected to each other today.

Take time to remember how connected you are. You are connected not just to the people you've met and know, but to all who live, past and present, in this world. You are part of a dance, the magical dance of the universe taking place each moment in time.

Even if you live alone, you're part of a large family. Even if you work alone, you're really part of a team. Take time to honor your connections, and the impact of each person you've met. See how people have helped shape you; see how you've touched and shaped them. Each interaction creates a ripple affect; each encounter helps shape destiny.

You no longer have to be isolated or suffer from separateness. Take time to see and honor your connections and value your place in the whole.

NOVEMBER 2

See How Much Easier Life Can Be

The old way said do, do, do. Push, push, push. Only when the work was done could we allow ourselves time to rest. But when the work was finished, we often forgot to reward ourselves. The old way won't work anymore. We have learned too much, come too far. Our body won't let us. Our heart will object.

Let the work be more fun. Don't push yourself so hard. Let your actions be effortless—an easy result of learning to focus and learning to trust your inner timing. Learn to let your actions spring naturally and easily from there.

Let your inner voice and life guide you into breaks while you're working, while you're focusing on the task. Stop fearing it won't get done. Stop worrying if you're doing it well enough. Take breaks when you need to and really let go.

Take time at the end of the task, too. Take time to reward yourself, to feel pleasure in your accomplishment, to play at the end of the day.

See how balance occurs naturally when we trust our heart. See how much easier life can be when we live it from the heart.

NOVEMBER 3

You Haven't Lost Your Place

Sometimes when life shifts and changes, it can feel like we've lost our place.

During those times when our lives are changing, we may feel out of tune, out of rhythm, out of balance. Out of step. Maybe an old feeling is surfacing, clearing, so that we can learn something new and move forward to a new place. Maybe our attention is being diverted to a new focus so we can find and experience another lesson. Sometimes the form or shape of our life is changing dramatically. The old picture is being erased so a new one can be drawn. Familiar people are leaving; new people are entering. We may ache, feel irritable, and doubt the course of our entire journey. We may doubt whether the magical way we were living was even real and whether the magic will ever return.

Let the changes happen. Take extra loving care of yourself. Be attentive to what you need. The magic isn't gone; it hasn't disappeared. You're just going through a shift. That means things are moving, and movement is good.

For now it may feel like you can't
find your place, but that's because
your place is changing.

NOVEMBER 4

Move On to Joy

Are you willing to be here in constant, abject pain one minute longer? I'm not. Are you willing to be here suffering endlessly and needlessly through distressing situations—worrying, fussing, fretting about things you can do nothing about? I'm not. And we don't have to be.

We're here to feel joy and absorb all of life's beauty we can. If pain comes, let it pass quickly through. Then move on to joy.

It's a conscious choice.

NOVEMBER 5

Create Your Destiny from Your Heart

Be aware of life's energy moving, pushing, pulling, guiding you forward each moment of the day.

And know each moment is your destiny.

You're connected to and part of a mysterious, invisible life force. Let it guide you forward. Let it move you along. Clear yourself of all that blocks your connection to that life force—old emotions, old beliefs, remnants of the past.

Listen to your heart. It will take you, move you to where you need to go. No, you cannot see as far ahead as you would like, as far ahead as you used to think you could. That is because you have undertaken the journey to your heart. Seeing would prevent you from listening, trusting, opening to the magical guidance that comes from within. You would confuse things, think you had to control, manage, make things happen. You would confound yourself with the illusions of the past. You would become afraid.

Stay in the present moment. Listen to your inner guidance. Trust the wisdom of your heart. Feel the life force, guiding you, moving you forward. Go where it leads.

Embrace your destiny. Know you help create it by what you choose each step of the way.

Let your choices come from your heart.

NOVEMBER 6

Value Each Moment

How often we wait for those grand moments of revelation, those intense times that blast us into transformation, those turning points that forever change us and our lives. Those are the dramatic moments we write about, see in movies, and long for in our lives. Yes, they are wonderful. But turning points such as those happen only a couple of times in a movie and a few times in a lifetime.

Each moment of each day in our lives is a valuable turning point—an important part of our spiritual growth, an important scene in the movie of our lives. Each feeling is important: boredom, fear, hate, love, despair, excitement. Each action we take has value: an act of love, an act of healing. Each word we speak, each word we hear, each scene we allow ourselves to see, and each scenario we participate in changes us.

Trust and value each moment
of your life. Let it be important.
It is a turning point. It is a
spiritual experience.

NOVEMBER 7

You Are Being Led

You are being guided. You are being led. I say that a lot because I need to hear that a lot. The more I hear it, the more I believe it. The more I believe it, the more I see it.

There are times when life flows along, when it's easy and natural to believe we're being guided. But there comes a point in any journey, in even the most magical of trips, when we look around and say, *I don't know where I'm going.* We have no plan, we're short on ideas, and we're plumb out of vision. We've gone as far as we could see.

Now is the time to practice what you know. Trust. Let go. Stay as peaceful as you can. Stay right here in the present moment. Sharpen your tools—your intuition, your inner voice, your consciousness, and your awareness. Do the little things, the small actions that appear right, the things that are right before you. Feel your feelings. Move through the fear. Wrap up in self-love.

Then let the journey unfold. Trust that you are being guided and led.

NOVEMBER 8

Ease Up on Yourself

When you don't know what to do next, ease up on yourself. See how much more you accomplish, how much easier life is, how much more you enjoy life when you aren't forcing yourself. Forcing can turn into fear—fear that the job won't get done, fear that the natural way things would evolve won't be right, fear that you're not good enough.

Learn a different way, learn the way of love. Relax. Sit back. Let go for now. Do something different. Breathe deeply. Burn a candle. Read a poem. Light some sage. If fear is present, send it away. See it, feel it, then allow it to leave. Return to the task in love when it feels natural, right, and on time. Participate naturally, joyfully in creation, whether that's the creation of a relationship, a dinner, a garden, or a meeting.

Sometimes it's time to focus, to try hard. Sometimes it's time to ease up. See how much more you get done when you ease up. And see how much more playing and laughing and enjoying gets done too.

A Meditative Journey

Go deeper into the forest.

Walk among the trees, down the winding dirt path strewn with rocks and wood chips. See the salamander dart across your path. Listen to the birds chirp. Hear the rustling in the bushes. Walk down the path until you come to the quiet pond. Sit for a while and rest.

When you are ready, walk to the edge of the pond. Look down into the still waters. What do you see? At first, just water. Then gradually, a reflection emerges. It is you. It is your life. Gaze peacefully into the water, into the reflection of your life. See that it has been just as it should be, a lifetime of events causing ripples of love, peace, and healing in the universe.

See that it is now just as it should be. The people who are gathered around you are there for a reason. The places you have visited were not without purpose. The lessons you have learned are yours forever. You are right where you need to be. Gaze into your reflection in the quiet, deep mirror of the pond until you see that, know that, feel that. Gaze long enough to see truth, peace, contentment, Divine order.

Sit down and again, look around the forest. Take in its beauty, its wonder, its shimmering emerald leaves; the tiny white wildflowers cropping up everywhere, delicate surprises that bring joy. Inhale the smells, the fresh growth, the musk, the smell of cedar and pine. Inhale, breathe deeply, until the breath of life fills you with wonder. Let it flow throughout you; let it saturate every cell. Peace. Contentment. Divine order.

You are safe. The forest is your friend. It tells you that all is well. Look around. See the tallest tree. See that it has weathered every storm, and millimeter by millimeter, ring by ring, continued its growth over centuries. Know that you have grown that way, too.

Rise slowly when it's time. Find your path. Feel the earth beneath your feet, supporting you, giving you strength, filling you with grounded energy. Walk down the winding path through the glimmers of sunlight until you reach the edge of the forest.

> *Now you are in the light. Say good-bye to the woods; say good-bye to this time of deepest contemplation and reflection on all you have seen, all you have been, all you are. Go in peace. Go in contentment. Go now into the light of your life.*

NOVEMBER 10

Release Guilt

Do whatever you need to do to release guilt. Do it often. Make that technique a regular part of your life.

Guilt has gotten a bad name. Many of us insist that we won't feel guilt ever again, because we felt so much before, because it serves no purpose. Maybe we need to rethink guilt.

Guilt is a feeling. If it's there and you don't feel it, honor it, release it, it will block and stop you. It will control your energy and possibly control your life like anything else that's denied and repressed. Acknowledging guilt won't make it more real. Acknowledging guilt won't lead to condemnation. Acknowledging guilt will help you release it. Write it out. Talk it out. Use a ritual from your church. Let yourself know your secrets, even the ones you've kept hidden from yourself until now.

Choose a way to express your guilt. Then watch it loosen and leave. That's how we cleanse our souls.

NOVEMBER 11

You're Not a Victim Anymore

Sometimes people have problems that make it extremely draining to be around them, problems like alcoholism, other addictions, other issues. No matter where we go, who we are, how long we've been working on ourselves, a lot of people have these problems. That hasn't changed.

What has changed is us.

We've learned our lessons. We can't control the addictions, the problems of others. They may be the very problems they came here to solve. We've also learned, and learned well, that we don't have to stand and absorb the energy from these problems, energy that isn't ours, that no longer holds lessons or payoffs. We no longer need the payoffs of the past—that we're victims and can't take care of ourselves.

We're free to walk away with compassion and love.

But most of all, we're free.

NOVEMBER 12

Wash Old Pain Away

"I don't know what's going on," a woman told me, "but lately memories of the past have been coursing through me like a river. I see scenes from my life, then the feelings appear—old pains, old hurts, old wounds. Nothing is triggering this that I can tell. It's just happening spontaneously."

We walk around with old wounds, old hurts—remnants of other times, ancient times, in our lives. We may be aware of these old feelings, fully conscious they're there and why. Or we may only have partial awareness, a lingering sense that there's some hurt within, without a clue as to its source. We may get a glimpse of it when we open our eyes in the morning and notice something deep inside aches, but we don't know why. Or we may not be conscious of the pain or it's connection to a particular event. The pain is hidden away, deep within our soul.

It has become time to cleanse the past.

Let the feelings come to the surface and pass through your consciousness. Let memories emerge as they will. You aren't going back to your past. What's happening is normal. Your heart is finding a way to heal.

Clear away the past. Let the river of life wash old pains away. Feel the feelings until the river runs clear.

NOVEMBER 13

You're Almost Home

I only had a few hundred miles to go, but the stretch ahead seemed endless. I was tired and near the end of this adventure. I remembered the meditative words of a friend, words that had helped me several years ago, words that helped me again now.

"The life force is a force within you. You have the power to fire it, stoke it, expand its energy throughout your body. Don't clench up, tighten up. That limits the life force within you. Stop cramping your muscles and telling yourself you can't. If you say it long and loud enough, you'll begin to believe it. Relax. Relax your arms, your legs, your neck, your body. You've come so far. Look back at all the miles you've traveled. What lies ahead is a small portion, such a small portion of that.

"Breathe deeply. When you become afraid or tired, your breathing becomes shallow. That inhibits the fire. It keeps the life force from reaching your muscles, your vital organs, your brain. Breathe deeply. Stoke the fire within.

"Take a moment now to picture that core of light within you. See it in your solar plexus just inches below your navel. Picture it as a glowing coal, a candle, a flame. With each breath you take, picture the flame getting stronger, glowing more brightly, until you feel the vital life force begin to surge through you.

"Feel yourself being filled with healing, life-giving energy with each breath you take. Feel the flame burn more brightly within you. Inhale deeply. Exhale deeply. Feel your power spread through your body. Feel the power of the universe come in through your breath. Feel that power connect with and flame the burning coal of energy that is within you."

You've come so far. You've almost mastered that lesson, accomplished that task, unveiled that insight, the one you've been struggling with. Of course you're tired. You've been working hard. Take a moment now to light the fire within you. Let it give you the energy you need.

Don't stop now. You're almost home.

Find Your Center

"My life has changed so much," the man at Breitenbush told me. "I go with the flow now, try to be in the moment, be spontaneous. I'm a foreman, and even at work life goes much more smoothly. A year ago, I didn't know what it meant to be centered. Now I do and I work at staying that way." He looked around the camp, a nature retreat in the heart of the Willamette National Forest in Oregon. "And I know how to get there too."

For many years, I didn't understand what it meant to be centered either. If I was that way for a while, it was more accidental than deliberate. It takes time, practice, and mostly desire and commitment to make staying centered a way of life. But the time it takes is worth it.

Learn what it feels like to be centered, to be balanced. Learn what it feels like to be off center. Learn to tell the difference. Then, learn to come back to center as quickly as possible.

Quiet. Relaxed. Feeling right about what you're doing. On track. In harmony. At peace. In balance. No turbulent emotions racing through you. No disorganized thoughts clamoring through your head. Your body feels aligned, and you feel connected to it. What you do and say comes from your center. It feels right and honest. It feels like you, and you feel connected to your self, your deepest self, your soul. Your heart is open. And so is your mind.

That's the place from which we're seeking to live our lives. Find a way to get to that place, then go there often. Some helps include nature, listening to music, going for a walk, repeating a prayer, or forms of deep breathing or meditation.

It's hard to find a place we've never been to. Learn what it feels like to be centered. Know your center is in you. Then go there often.

NOVEMBER 15

The Light Will Illuminate Your Path

It was almost eleven o'clock at night. I was driving down a highway in Colorado on the west side of the mountains. I was exhausted, driving and driving, hoping I was going somewhere, hoping the road led to someplace where I could rest and replenish myself. Whenever I would become fearful, wondering if I had taken complete leave of my senses, I'd look up in the sky. A crescent moon was snuggled between two mountains. It seemed to urge me on, beckoning me to drive toward it.

Finally, I reached the place marked by the moon. It was a lodge not listed in any directory, in a town not even on my map. It had a mineral bath on the grounds and, yes, an available room.

Sometimes when I'm driving late at night on a strange road and I'm not sure which turn to take, I look for a light. The moon might be setting above a particular place, lighting it with its glow. The lights of a city might brighten one direction more than another. A certain road appears lighter, feels better, feels right.

Often that's what happens in our lives. When we get to a fork in the road and we're not certain which direction to go, there's usually one path that appears lighter than another. Sometimes the light is dim. Sometimes it can only be seen with the eyes of our soul, the eyes of our heart. But it's also a light that can be clouded and blocked by fear, tenseness, and lack of faith.

Relax. Tune into your body. Trust your heart. Look around. When you don't know which way to go next, wait. Soon a path will open up. It will appear lighter. It will feel right.

When in doubt, go toward the light.
When you get to a fork in the road,
choose the way that feels lightest. The
light will take you to the next place.
The light will lead you home.

NOVEMBER 16

It's Safe to Open Your Heart

You don't have to be so afraid to love. You don't have to fear losing your soul. You learned that lesson. It's in the past. That doesn't mean that people won't try to control or manipulate you. Doesn't mean that at times, you won't try to control or manipulate them. Doesn't mean that people with problems, agendas, addictions, and issues won't sometimes come into your life. They may.

But the lessons of the past are yours, yours to keep. It may take you a moment to remember, but you will. Be gentle with yourself. Open up slowly, carefully, as you're able.

It's not that life and people are different, although how we see life and view people probably has changed. We're different. We've learned about our powers. We've learned to take care of ourselves. We've learned how capable we really are.

Don't be so afraid to love. Now it's time
to learn about the powers of the heart.

Discover the Power of Loving Yourself

Sometimes it's hard to trust life with all its sudden twists, turns, and storms. When something unexpected or painful happens, when we become blocked or frustrated, when life takes a different course than we hoped it would, it's easy to stop trusting the flow of our lives. I didn't ask for this. It's not fair. I don't want this, we think. This road isn't leading anywhere, at least nowhere I want to go. Often, when we feel life has turned on us, we respond by turning on ourselves. But turning on ourselves doesn't help. In fact, it can compound the situation. It can prevent us from hearing and acting on the very guidance that will lead us through, get us through, and take us to the next place. It can prevent us from hearing our heart.

Keep loving yourself, and taking care of yourself, no matter what—through the storms, the twists, the turns, and the blocks. Take a moment, breathe deep, restore yourself to that sacred place of self-love and self-responsibility. Feel all your feelings. Then let them go. Love yourself until you can hear your heart and what it tells you to do. Love yourself until you find the courage to act on that guidance.

Loving yourself is a powerful tool, a powerful force for change. It can reconnect you to creativity, to universal love, to the best possible flow of events within your life. It can and will reconnect you to life's magic.

There is a trustworthy road through whatever life brings. Loving yourself will help you find it.

NOVEMBER 18

Live with Unsolved Problems

Sometimes we need to live for a while with a particular behavior, problem, or situation before we're ready to change it.

Sometimes we have to live with it so long—conscious that it's a problem but unable yet to solve or change it—that we can hardly bear it. We're fully aware that we want and need something different, but the situation still hasn't changed. The answer has not yet arrived. We worry that the situation will continue eternally and the problem will never be solved. During those times of living with a problem and the desire to solve it, we may long for the old days, those days when our denial system was intact and we didn't know what we were doing.

If you can't solve it yet, if you can't change it yet, it's okay to live with it, just as it is. Something is happening. The situation is changing. You're on your way to change.

Trust that the waiting part of change is necessary. Trust that your desire for change is the beginning of change. Trust that each moment you are moving closer to the change you desire.

NOVEMBER 19

Awaken to the Storyteller Within

Each of us has a story to tell, a story to share with the world.

Artists and writers are in the storytelling business. Others have different ways of telling and sharing their stories. The tackle shop owner sells bait, hooks, and sinkers and tells people where to fish and about the big one that got away. The master carpenter tells his story by carving and hanging a wooden door so well crafted that it swings shut gently on its own. The quilter tells her story by commemorating important moments from her life in quilts that are colorful works of art.

Each of us has a story to tell and our own way of sharing it with the world. It comes out through our words, through our work, and through the simple actions of our daily life. Listen to the stories of the people around you. Listen with your soul. Learn to value without judging and listen with an open heart to the beauty of each story and the importance of the storyteller. Learn to value and appreciate the story you are living now.

Awaken to the storyteller within and share your story with the world. Tell it with joy and flair. Commit to telling it with love and passion. Tell it through living your life fully, doing your work well, and creating the best life you can. Be who you are and love being that.

Live your life from your heart. Share from your heart. And your story will touch and heal people's souls.

NOVEMBER 20

Let Yourself Play

How long has it been since you played? How long has it been since you played at your life, had fun with it?

Our imaginations are so delightful when we're young. Watch a child sit in the middle of the floor and build castles with blocks.

Watch a child play—any object can be anything, and anything can be fun. Life can pound that out of us if we let it.

Breathe life back into your imagination. Come back to life. Let yourself see dragons in clouds and leprechauns in trees and velvet in a rose. Imagine what it would be like to grab a handful of cloud. Then touch the tree. And put the rose to your cheek.

Let your imagination come alive.
Play the game of "What If?" What
if anything could be anything? What
if life could be fun?

NOVEMBER 21

Cherish Moments of Solitude

The clerk at the lodge guided me to my cabin, a small secluded house a mile away from the main lodge on the northern California coast. "Will you be okay here?" he asked. "All by yourself?" I answered yes. And meant it.

My ability to be at peace with solitude has taken a lifetime of cultivation. Peaceful solitude is different from isolation, being forced to be alone. It's different from forced seclusion, where we grasp frantically for some kind of connection, something to make us feel not alone, then finally sink fearfully and unwillingly into isolation.

On our adventures, we are called to face many fears. The universe won't let us hide from our fears, at least not for long. One of the fears we may be called to face is the fear of being alone.

We may need to face it, feel it, heal from it—or we will be grasping, settling for, surrounding ourselves with anything or anybody so we don't have to be alone. If we don't face it, solitude will become, instead, solitary confinement.

Cultivate moments of solitude. Learn to cherish your privacy, your quiet time. Learn to be comfortable being alone with yourself.

The more content you can become in moments of solitude, the more joy and love you'll discover in times with others. Cultivate solitude. It will help you cultivate love.

NOVEMBER 22

Open Up to Who You Are

Stop criticizing yourself. Stop telling yourself everything you think, feel, want, and do is wrong. Or at least not quite right. You've been holding back, censoring yourself for too long. Your creativity, your intuition, the voice of your soul is the very voice you've been silencing.

For many reasons, we learn to criticize and censor ourselves. We may have grown up with people who stifled our inner voice, our wisdom, our knowledge of truth. Our sense of the truth may have caused them to feel uneasy. So they told us to hush. It met their needs to keep us quiet. So we learned to hush ourselves. It was how we survived.

No longer do we need to meet other people's needs, not that way. We don't have to be afraid of ourselves or what we will find if we look inside. We don't need to run from ourselves. We don't need to hide or hush ourselves. We are creative, loving, purposeful beings.

It's time to open up to yourself, to your grandest dreams and aspirations, your real inclinations and desires, your wisdom and knowledge about what is true and what is real. Open up to who you are. Listen to yourself. Express yourself. Enjoy who you are, and you will find others enjoying you, too.

NOVEMBER 23

Discover the Power of Your Heart

Much of the journey has held lessons about power. Many of us have experimented with different kinds of power. At times we may have used force, brute strength. Certainly most of us have experimented with power plays—only to find that they aren't the answer either. Along the way, some of us may have gotten hard, cold, rigid, even angry—thinking that was a way to own our power.

Often, these attempts don't signal power. They signal fear. True, for many of us, learning to experience, express, and release our anger has been an important milestone on our path to power. But the power we're seeking is different from force, coldness, hardness, or power plays. We aren't learning to flex our muscles that way.

Open to a new kind of power—the power of the heart. Clarity. Compassion. Gentleness. Love. Understanding. Comfort. Forgiveness. Faith. Security with acceptance of ourselves, and all our emotions. Trust. Commitment to loving ourselves, and to an open heart. That's the power we're seeking. That's true power, power that lasts, power that creates the life and love we want. In those situations that call for power, we can trust that brute strength, coldness, or rage won't get us what we want.

Relax. Stop flexing your muscles. Instead, open your heart. Let power come gently. Let a new strength flow through you. Defend yourself when necessary, but avoid any actions that take you away from peace and joy. Whatever your situation, relax your body, relax your mind, and trust your soul.

Your heart will lead the way, not just to love, but also to power. Let it come gently. Let it come freely. Then the power you receive will be true.

NOVEMBER 24

The Power of Gratitude Never Wanes

The haunting music of "Amazing Grace" followed me throughout my travels. I heard it first in the rustic cabin I rented in Arizona. The music from a distant flute wound through the air, filling it like incense, filling me with peace.

The next time I heard the music was at an old Montana hotel. The notes were clearer this time, as the soothing melody drifted across the courtyard.

Then, near the forest in Washington, I heard the hymn once more, again played on a flute. The notes rang out. The melody filled the air; gratitude flooded my soul.

"Amazing Grace" is following me, I thought. I thought again. No, grace wasn't following me; grace had found me.

The power of gratitude never wanes. Say it when you feel and believe it. Say it when you don't. Thank you. Thank you. Thank you.

Soon you will hear the music, too. This song of grace will touch you with its haunting melody.

Amazing, amazing grace.

NOVEMBER 25

Make Today a Healing Day

Take time for healing. Take time for what soothes your body, your mind, your soul.

Take a bath. Light a candle. Read a book. Take a walk. Get a massage. See your favorite healer if you desire. See a movie. Buy some flowers. Drink a cup of tea.

Sometimes we talk ourselves out of doing something healing for ourselves. We're too busy, too tired. But that is when we most need to take care of ourselves. Listen to your heart. What does it want? Listen to your body. What does it need? Trust what you hear.

Make today a healing day.
Then take some time and make
every day a healing day.

NOVEMBER 26

Take Time to Develop a Vision

As above, so below. First it happens in spirit. Then it manifests in the physical. Not the other way around.

First we see a vision. Our soul tells us through the words and eyes of our heart. Then the steps become clear and we see the order in which they should be taken. Then it is finished. By the time the vision has arrived, it is already, as some say, a done deal.

You waste so much time and effort when you try to accomplish something before you have envisioned it. Learn to let the vision come first. Take time to shape it in spirit before you try to shape it in physical form. If you can't see something clearly, the vision may not be complete. Take the time you need to think about it, to let it come into focus, to let the vision take shape in your mind.

Operating from vision will guide us onto our highest path. It will also make our life and work much easier.

Take time to develop a vision for all you want to do. Let your vision guide you. When it manifests itself first in spirit, the physical form will follow.

NOVEMBER 27

Forgiveness Isn't Too Much to Ask

Is your heart blocked? Are you experiencing a barricade you can't get around in a particular relationship? Forgiveness is a delicate, sometimes difficult subject, but once in a while that's what we need to ask for.

Part of being clear, and one of our powers, is the ability to identify and ask for what we need from others, from the universe, from God, even from ourselves. We may be extremely skilled at identifying when we need more time with someone, more money, more attention, or a different type of communication. But as proficient as we may have become at asking for some of what we need, we may still find it difficult to ask for forgiveness.

It is one thing to tell a person we're sorry. It is another to be intimate and bold enough to recognize the damage that comes when forgiveness hasn't occurred. Being unforgiven can block the kindest and warmest heart. It can destroy the most precious, beautiful, passionate, spiritual relationship. It can keep guilt lingering in the air. It can cause people to go away from each other.

Muster your forces. Prepare yourself if you must. Then take a risk, one of the greatest risks you'll be asked to take. Put your cards on the table. Say you're sorry, say it from the heart. Then don't get defensive, ruffle your feathers, or get mad. Ask for forgiveness.

Forgiveness is not too much to ask for,
if forgiveness is what you need.

NOVEMBER 28

Bask in Self-Love

The commitment to love ourselves may be a decision we only need to make once, but we may need to take frequent action to implement that choice. It's so easy to fall into that place of not loving and accepting ourselves. But it can become just as easy to decide to return to the place. We may need to do it daily, weekly, or whenever we begin a new part of our journey, especially a part that frightens or challenges us.

What would feel good? What would bring healing? What would energize or comfort you? And what purpose is to be fulfilled by depriving yourself of that?

However often we need to do it, we can return to that place of self-love. Each time we do it, it becomes easier. Each time we do it, we see the rewards of self-love: enhanced creativity, clearer decisions, a stronger connection to the Divine, and a more fulfilling connection to the world around us.

When we love ourselves, it becomes easier to correct our mistakes, admit our wrongs, share our deepest feelings, and love others. Our spirit dances, thrives. Self-love energizes us. It attracts more love. The universe responds directly and immediately to our choice to love ourselves.

Accept yourself. Love yourself just as you are. Your finest work, your best moments, your joy, peace, and healing come when you love yourself. You give a great gift to the world when you do that. You give others permission to do the same: to love themselves.

Revel in self-love. Roll in it.
Bask in it, as you would the sunshine.

NOVEMBER 29

Let Your Heart Open Gently

Let your heart open—gently, safely, surely, and certainly.

Do not let others decide when or even if you will open your heart, when or if you will embrace love. Those choices are too big, too important to let others make for you. Only you can decide when and how.

There was a time when it wasn't safe to open your heart. Pain was all around you. You were not equipped to be that open. That time is passed. You have learned. You have grown. You have learned that you are a loving being. You know now that your love comes from within you. It is safe to open your heart.

The universe awaits, ready, willing, delighted to be able to help you open, the same way it aids the opening of a flower with the sun, the rain, the earth. To deny your power and ability to love is to deny joy. To deny your loving essence is to deny yourself, your God, and the Divine in you.

Look around. It's not your location that makes you safe. It's where you are in your soul, your mind, and your heart. That place is good. That place is safe. Open your heart. Embrace life. Go joyfully on your way.

NOVEMBER 30

Trust Each Moment

Trust. Trust. Trust. Again and again, that's the issue. See how much of your pain, your anguish, your tension arises simply from not trusting the absolute perfection of the present moment. *I've lost my way. I'm off track. I'm somehow wrong—in the wrong place at the wrong time, doing the wrong thing. Where I'm going is a dead end. Oh, dear . . .*

You are not off track. You haven't lost your way. You're going somewhere worth going. Somewhere magnificent beyond the ability of your mind to comprehend. By trusting the perfection of each moment, you give yourself a gift: permission to enjoy the journey.

Don't just take the trip.
Let yourself enjoy the ride.

December

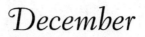

DECEMBER 1

Let Yourself Be Who You Are

It's difficult to be around people who are trying to be perfect—perfectly healthy, perfectly polite, perfectly poised, perfectly controlled.

Remember that being human means being imperfect, being flawed. Let yourself be. Let others be. Slouch in your chair. Eat with the wrong fork. Laugh out loud. Stand up and reveal who you are and know that you're good enough.

Stop worrying that people will find out who you really are. Instead, hope that they do. Help them by openly sharing yourself and being not who you think you should be, but who you really are.

Freedom is just a small step away—a step into self-love and acceptance. When you take it, others will follow. And they'll be grateful you led the way.

Learn to Visualize Your Path

Learn to visualize what you would like to see happen in your life. Use your mind and your imagination, in connection with your heart, to create a picture of the future.

Visions can help create our future and guide us down the path. If we have a picture of where we're going, it will help us know when we get there. It will help us know we're on track.

At times, we find ourselves easily using our imaginations to create a clear picture. We can see ourselves doing something a particular way, comfortably functioning in a particular situation. We can see how what we're working on is going to look. We can see ourselves living in a particular place, working at a particular job, or vacationing at that special spot. We know clearly what we want.

Other times, our vision may not be as clear. We may have only a few vague ideas about how a thing or place will look. We need to focus our attention and create as clear a picture as we can. Making a list of all we know about what we'd like it to be helps here.

Other times, we may be completely in the dark without a clue about where we're going. That doesn't mean we can't get there or that there is no place for us to go. It means that we need to ask God, the universe, to help us become clear on what would be good, clear enough so we can recognize the answer when it comes.

Learn to use your imagination to create the life you want. Take time at the beginning to develop a vision, an idea about what you want. Visualize how you would like things to be. Then let your visions guide you where you need to go.

DECEMBER 3

Let Go of Leftover Guilt

Why do you feel guilty when you're doing what you've been led to do?

That nagging, gnawing feeling of guilt is leftovers—leftovers from another period when we didn't love ourselves. It's left over from another time when we didn't trust ourselves. Left over from another place when we didn't know life could be fun, easy, natural, and joy could be ours.

Feeling guilty and anxious about that new thing you're doing, that new place you're going, that new adventure you're on is part of your resistance to the lesson. Part of your shying back from the idea that you can truly, absolutely, and fundamentally love yourself and enjoy all parts of your life.

Soon you will see that you've been led to the very place you're at right now. The very thing you are feeling guilty and anxious about is the very thing you've been led to do to take you on your next adventure.

Life is abundant. We can bask in self-love and the healing resources around us. Our movements, our activities, our days and hours and nights can flow easily. Naturally. And we can do the things we're led to do without feeling guilty.

Recognize the guilt and anxiety of resistance as just that: resistance. Then let yourself go on your journey of love without spoiling it with guilt.

You Decide

This is an old lesson, but it bears repeating and remembering. We don't have to let anyone control our lives, our choices, our joy.

No matter how well we thought we learned that lesson, it often reappears. Another person starts to pull our strings. We get involved, entangled, hooked in. We hear ourselves singing an old tune—*If only she would, if only he wouldn't, then I would be . . .* We realize that once again we have given up too much control. We have deferred our lives to the wishes, whims, and choices of another.

Yes, if we are living fully, we will have reactions to those around us. Our relationships will help shape us, teach us things. And yes, there are times we are so connected to others, love them so much, that their path does affect ours. But we don't have to let another person control our choices, our behaviors, or our lives.

Maybe she will. Maybe he won't. But what about you? What do you want? What course of action feels right for you, for your life? Do you want to assign responsibility for whether you take that course to another? Do you really?

Sometimes, no matter how much you love others, it's time to let go, time to let them walk their path. Time to realize that it is your responsibility to walk your own. Go in love. Go in peace. Go in gentle power. You are responsible for your life. You are responsible for your choices. It doesn't matter what the other person does. You are still responsible for you.

Take care of yourself, then take it one step further. Love, nurture, honor, and respect yourself.

Only you can decide what you're going to do.

DECEMBER 5

Life Can Be Fun

How careful and guarded we've been with fun, with playing, with sheer enjoyment—whether we're working, traveling, or wandering around town on a Saturday afternoon. Sometimes, we act as though there's a limited amount, a scarce supply, of fun available. We can't take too much, or it'll all be gone.

That's how I was for a long time.

One Saturday afternoon my son, Shane, asked if he could spend the night at a friend's house to play and have a sleepover.

"Why?" I asked.

"To have fun," he said.

"You just did something fun last night," I reminded him.

He thought for a moment. "Who said you can't have fun two days in a row?"

Have some fun—with life, with love, with work. Then go out and have some more.

DECEMBER 6

Discover True Power

Much of our journey involves learning about power. We learn about the powers we don't have—the power to control others, sometimes ourselves, and fate. We discover our true power—the power to take an endless journey into freedom and love.

We talk about, experience, and experiment with many kinds of power along the way. The power of authority. The power of money. The power of prestige. The power of control. The power of rage, anger, intimidation. We see many kinds of negative powers—manipulation, deceit, fraud. We see people trying to steal power from others. We see people letting others take their power away, crawling into shells, hiding, and being dragged along by others.

We see that many forms of power are illusions. Money goes just so far. Prestige is fleeting. Popularity holds no immunity from life's experiences. Control is only momentary: we turn our backs and the situation reverts.

We trudge the road searching for power, learning about our own. Somewhere on the journey, we begin to see the truth. It awakens quietly within us, shaking our soul, transforming our vision, teaching us what we knew all along. The power that lasts, the power that stays is the power of the heart.

Stillness. Faith. Gentleness. Kindness. Compassion. Joy. Forgiveness. Comfort. Vulnerability. Honesty. Courage. And love. Now we're talking about power.

DECEMBER 7

Let Go of Feeling Overwhelmed

So often the simple tasks of life can seem overwhelming. But feeling overwhelmed is only a reaction to them.

Many things need to be done—laundry, housekeeping, car maintenance, bills, taxes, appointments, work—the everyday responsibilities of our lives. The task of quietly beginning, doing the first step of the first task can help us find our way through. Once we begin, we see that things aren't overwhelming. The simple act of setting to the task simplifies it. Our sense of peace reappears in the magic of the present moment.

Magic and power don't come from contemplating all that lies ahead, how much needs to be done, all that might go wrong, whether we'll get through. That's fear. We don't find the magic and power by denying, escaping, or ignoring our feelings, even feelings of being overwhelmed. Feel what you need to feel. Release it. Go forward in love, one moment at a time.

We will be given the power to do all we need to do. Take the simple steps that lie before you. Take one step at a time. You'll find the way again.

DECEMBER 8

Don't Pick Up Energy That's Not Yours

I walked into the small-town diner and sat down at the counter. I was the only customer, but the waitress ignored me. I waited while she sat in a booth, reading the paper. Finally, she lowered the paper. "Is there something you want?" she barked from across the room.

By the time I left the restaurant, I felt as crabby as the waitress appeared. It took a while to figure out what happened, what had changed my mood. Then I realized I had picked up her negative energy—feelings that had nothing to do with me. It was like someone had splashed my windshield with mud.

Most of us have crabby days and an abundance of our own feelings to deal with. We don't need to let others splash their negative energy on us. We don't need to pick it up and carry it around. If someone splashes your windshield with mud while you're driving down the road, what do you do? You wash it off and go on your way.

Learn to tell when what you're feeling is your emotions, and your business. Learn to tell when someone has splashed on you. You don't have to take responsibility for what's not yours. Be done with it as quickly as possible.

Thoughts are energy. Crabby thoughts and crabby emotions can be like mud. If someone splashes you, wash off your windshield, send them a blessing, and go on down the road.

DECEMBER 9

Claim Your Own Life

Claiming our own lives creates fulfillment and joy. We don't need to be controlled. We don't deserve to be repressed or stifled. We don't have to let anyone convince us that we do. We can trust ourselves. We know what we need, we know what we yearn for—we long to be set free.

What once seemed so overwhelming—creating and taking responsibility for our lives—wasn't really so. It was our belief that we couldn't do it, couldn't handle it, couldn't be trusted that made it so. We created our own prison by believing we were trapped, stuck. We became controlled by believing others knew better than we did what was best for us. We were afraid to take responsibility for our choices, so we gave up our power.

Now it's time to step out, leave our prison of fear. We can take responsibility for our lives. We can take responsibility for what we create. We don't have to be afraid of making a mistake or doing something wrong. If we create a situation we don't like, we can create something different. We're free to create the life we want.

We're free now to claim our own lives and
create fulfillment and joy. We always have been.

DECEMBER 10

Heal from Past Betrayals

Healing from betrayal is connected to healing and opening the heart.

Many of us have become quite skillful at denying feelings of betrayal, ignoring those situations when we not only feel betrayed, we truly have been betrayed.

Life happens. Sometimes people do things that hurt us. People may have let us down, not protected us. People may have deceived us. We live in a world with people who have a lot of issues. We live in a world that moves fast and isn't always kind, just, or fair.

We may be moving so fast that we gloss over situations where we have been betrayed. Things just weren't right. The numbers don't add up.

If we haven't dealt with past betrayals, if we haven't cleansed and healed those break lines on the heart, we won't be able to deal with the betrayals going on right now. The part of our hearts that's sensitive to betrayal has been numbed, sometimes damaged, because it hasn't been allowed to heal. We may stay in situations much longer than is good for us to do. We may not speak up when we need to. We may quietly stand there saying, *That's just how people are.* And so our hearts break a little more and we go a little more numb. And that beautiful, precious part of ourselves, our heart, closes—not just to the person betraying us, but to all the beauty in life.

Yes, sometimes, that's just the way life is. But we don't need to stand there and keep letting life do that. We can open our hearts by healing those break lines. We can keep it open by being vulnerable and safe enough to feel, express, and take whatever actions our heart leads us to when betrayal occurs.

The head is connected to the heart. This connection is important. Healing betrayal will help keep that connection clear.

DECEMBER 11

Make Time to Play

Go play. Yes, take a break and go play. When your head starts to pound and your back starts to ache, stop. Do something you want to do. Do something that feels good, feels fun. Leave your worries behind. Put them in a box, then close it and go play.

We make sure that our children take time for recess every day. But we forget that we need recess, too. The lingering threads of work and worry can tie us to tasks done and undone. They can block our connection to joy, creativity, and the vital life-giving force that courses through us all.

We no longer need to slump with tension and fatigue. It isn't necessary and it doesn't help a thing. Most often, it hurts. Your fatigue may be from lack of play as much as lack of sleep. You might begin to see that you don't need a rest, a nap, or more vitamin C. You need to play.

Play as much as you can. Find time—take time—
to play. It may give you the energy you need.

DECEMBER 12

Protect Your Energy

Just as we strive to protect and conserve earth's energy resources, we can strive to protect and conserve our own. Become more aware of the impact of things, people, and activities on you and your energy. What feeds you, charges you? What drains and depletes you?

As you grow and become more sensitive to how things feel to you, you'll naturally grow to dislike and be uncomfortable with whatever drains or negatively impacts your energy. Yes, some difficult, draining situations are inevitable. But we can learn to protect ourselves in those situations. Sometimes we need to let go of people, places, and behaviors that don't work for us anymore, that drain, exhaust, and deplete us.

Pay attention to the impact of certain people, places, behaviors, and events on your energy. Pay attention to how you feel when you eat certain foods, drink certain beverages, go certain places. Learn to listen to your body, your emotions, and your heart. Be prepared to let go of some things and people along the way. Be gentle with yourself while you do.

Learn to conserve your energy.
It is a precious, valuable resource.

DECEMBER 13

Learn to Live with Ambiguity

Sometimes, the picture isn't finished yet. Ideas, possibilities, hopes, dreams float around, circling us like asteroids around a planet. We may think events in our lives are happening aimlessly, without purpose. All we see are disconnected, floating blobs. We reach for them, try to grab them in our hands so we can connect them, force them into a whole, force them into a picture we can see, something that makes sense.

Let the pieces be. Let yourself be. Let life be. Sometimes, chaos needs to precede order. The pieces will come together in a picture that makes sense, in a beautiful work of art that pleases.

You don't have to force the pieces to fit together if it's not time. You don't have to know. There is power sometimes in not knowing. There is power in letting go. Power in waiting. Power in stillness. Power in trust. There is power in letting the disconnected pieces be until they settle into a whole. The action you are to take will appear. Timely. Clearly. What you're to do will become clear.

Let the pieces be, and they'll take shape. Soon you'll see the picture.

DECEMBER 14

Open Your Heart to Universal Love

We live in a magical, living, vital, and personal universe, a world where universal love is real.

We don't just live in it, we're part of it, visibly and tangibly connected to it. The phone call that comes at the right time. A book that teaches us what we needed to know. A movie that has the message we need to guide us and open our hearts. An opportunity that arises, at just the right moment. An idea triggered by something someone says or an object we didn't notice before.

The more we open to universal love, the more it will be there for us, embracing, loving, holding, guiding us. The more we learn to see it, the more it will be there—until we wonder why we never saw it before.

Open your heart to universal love.
It's more than merely there. It's
there for you. Jump into the arms
of a living, magical world and you
leap into the arms of universal love.
See how real it can be.

DECEMBER 15

Awaken Your Life Force

The Chinese call it *chi*. The Japanese, *ki*. It refers to energy, the life force, the Divine spirit of life that permeates all that is. That permeates you.

Awaken your life force. Do things that stimulate it, bring it alive. Walk on the ground with your bare feet and let the earth's energy surge through you. Reach your hands toward the heavens and let Divine energy come down to you. Move around. Release the blocks. Feel. Love. Sing. Shout.

Come alive. Discover what it means to become vital and fully alive. Feel the life force surge through you, up through your legs, your spine, your head. Feel it wash down upon you through your arms, your torso, down through your toes and into the ground, rooting you to this planet like a tree. Know you have roots. Know you have branches.

Fill yourself with chi. *Fill yourself until you*
feel vital, alive. Feel it until you become happy
and joyful, grateful to be alive on this planet.
Feel it until you know you are one with God,
one with life, one with love. Feel it until you
see how connected you are with all that lives.

DECEMBER 16

Be an Angel

I often imagine that we keep the angels very busy. They tell us to turn here or there, warn us of dangers, say *Listen!* and *Look!* They tell us things will be okay, and they're sorry we hurt. Angels in our lives encourage us to hope, dream, dare, and trust. They point out beautiful sights. They shine a light on our path, so we know where to step next.

Most of us are not as sure of ourselves as we'd like others to think. We need guidance, faith, and hope. We need to know we're on track and that someone cares. We need the angels to help us.

The angels in our lives give us a kind word, share a kind thought, offer a helping hand and a warm smile. Their words empower and comfort us. Their touch heals, their loving looks warm our hearts. They radiate love and faith.

"I've learned it's easy to be loving," one man said. "What takes work is to be kind."

Make it easier for the angels, and easier for others.
Practice being loving and kind. Be an angel, too.

DECEMBER 17

Don't Complicate Things

The simple, clear answer for life's situations can be easily found in the heart. Don't limit its wisdom to just one or two areas; let it guide you through all of your life.

Are you struggling with finances? Feeling overwhelmed by taxes? Not certain what to do to help someone you love? Do you have a problem with a friend? Has a business relationship gotten sticky, maybe hopelessly adversarial? Are you at war with the person you love? Problems with children? Problems with parents? A landlord who just won't get the job done? All of these areas, and more, can be brought to your heart.

Do you need to find a new hobby? Are you stuck on a project? Do you need an idea, some creative inspiration? Do you need a new place to live, or a way to fix your current home? Take it all back to your heart.

Calm your mind. Let go. Get quiet. You don't have to know the plan. Just put out the question, then listen to your inner voice. It will guide you through any maze you've been lost in.

Don't complicate things or try to figure it all
out. The answer is simple: look in your heart.

DECEMBER 18

Celebrate Holidays but Honor Your Holy Days

Holidays help us remember important national and religious events. Holidays are marked by the calendar.

Holy days are something else. Holy days are the days we remember not because they are marked on any calendar, but because they are important spiritual events to us. These are the days our souls remember. A birthday. The day a loved one left this earth. The anniversary of a relationship. The anniversary of a significant change in our lives—the day we started something, the day we stopped doing something, the day we accomplished something important to us, a new beginning.

Celebrate the holidays marked by the calendar in whatever way you choose. Some of these may be holy days for you as well. But remember to honor your own holy days, the ones that are special to you.

Celebrate holidays, but honor your holy days, too.
Choose your own rituals. Honor what is sacred to you.

DECEMBER 19

Look for the Deeper Picture

The two men were sitting in a restaurant booth, staring intently at the Magic Eye pictures on the wall. "I've tried for years to see the picture hidden inside, but I can't," said one. "Everyone says it's there though, so I'll just have to trust that it is."

Magic Eye pictures have been popular for some time. At first, the picture looks like a print; it's often a repetitive pattern of the sort you see on wallpaper or a tablecloth. It's pretty to look at, but it's not really a picture. But another picture, a 3-D picture, is hidden within the print or pattern—one you can see only if you relax your vision and look in a special way. Then the real picture, the deeper picture, appears.

I have always thought these pictures contain a lesson. They remind us to look past the daily superficial events of our lives and trust that there is meaning, that there is a deeper picture, one that can be seen only with the eyes of our soul.

As we go through our days, weeks, and months, what we're experiencing doesn't always make a lot of sense. Sometimes it causes downright distress. We're uncomfortable. We feel out of place. We wonder if what we see is all there is. Those are the times to stop staring so hard, relax our vision, and let the deeper picture, the real picture, come to us.

Life goes on, with all its troubles, stresses, changes, and disappointments. But it isn't a disconnected series of random events. It's not punishment. And it's not without meaning. Something important is being worked out in your life and in your soul.

Learn to relax. Look for the reflection of something else in the picture of your life. Learn to look more deeply. Learn to look and see with the eyes of the soul.

And sometimes, like the man in the restaurant, if we can't see the picture or the real meaning, we just have to relax and trust that it's there.

Discover Common Bonds

"So many people have lost their families," the man said to me. "I have. But I'm beginning to discover that I'm part of a larger family, too. I'm beginning to see my connections to people all over the world."

We all have people we love deeply and dearly, those people we call our family. We have blood ties, genetic ties, long-term relationships with the people in our life. But as we open our hearts, we'll discover a larger family, too.

We have a kinship with those we've never met, even if they live in other cultures. We share many of the same emotional responses to the experiences in our lives, even though our journeys may be taking place on different parts of the planet. If we study history we will see our connection to those who have lived before. The hardships they experienced, the lessons they had to face, were similar in many ways to those we face today. Lessons repeat themselves. The ones that are true seem to last. That's why they're called universal truths.

What are you going through in your life right now? Don't feel you're the only one. Open your eyes. Open your heart to your connections with your larger family. Let them share their stories with you. Let them share their strengths, hopes, fears, and joys. Stop looking for what's different and what makes you separate and apart. Go on an adventure of discovering your common bonds.

You're not alone. We're in this together.
That's why it's called universal love.

DECEMBER 21

Reduce Your Stress

"Stress can be caused by many things," a man, a healing professional, said. "It can be caused by toxins in the air, by food, work, money, or love. And sometimes tension and stress are caused by reacting to old beliefs—the messages in your mind."

We can't always eliminate the situations that produce stress. Some stress in life is inevitable; it is part of being alive. Stress is often the impetus that moves us forward into growth, into emotional release and healing, into awareness and change.

While we can't and don't want to eliminate all the stress in our lives, we can reduce its impact. We can eat foods we respond well to. We can monitor the quality of the air we breathe in many situations. We can leave a work or love situation that has become too stressful, or we can take better care of ourselves in those situations we choose to stay in.

And we can work on changing stress-producing beliefs within ourselves. *I can't measure up. I can't get the job done. I won't be liked. I can't trust myself.* Many of these beliefs are outdated reactions to other times in our lives, and now we know we have the power to change them.

What's causing stress in your life?
Do the things you can to reduce
stress in your life. Reduce as much
toxicity in your environment and
in yourself as you can.

DECEMBER 22

Practice the Power of Respect

It is a quiet power, one that caught me by surprise on my journey. I had heard about it before, but somehow, in the shuffle of life, I had forgotten it: respect.

Respect is a spiritual power, a power of the heart, one that's closely connected to gratitude, yet somehow different. It is an attitude toward people, toward life, toward ourselves that only takes a moment to convey, yet somehow has far-reaching effects. It does more than free people to be themselves; it encourages them to be their best. It honors people, life, and the mysterious connection we each have to the Divine.

Have a series of life experiences caused you to forget respect? In your anger, did you decide that certain persons or groups of people were undeserving of respect? Has familiarity with yourself or another caused you to forget to practice respect? Let go of the past; it's over. But your power to transform the future has just begun.

Respect and honor yourself. Respect the needs of your body, the needs of your heart, and the dictates of your soul. Respect the lives of others. Respect the gift of life. Bow in spirit to all you meet. Bow to the gifts of the universe—the sun, moon, earth, sea, and stars. Honor all that lives, the trees, the wildflowers, the eagle soaring high. The deer in the woods, the squirrel scurrying up the tree, the june bug that lights on your shoulder. Each has its place in this world. So do you.

Discover the power of respect. Then practice it often. Let it change your world.

DECEMBER 23

Bring Your Healing Gifts to Others

Let your healing gifts to the world spring naturally from who you really are.

You want to be a healer. You want to be a force for good in this world. Many of us believe deeply in healing, service, and love. But until you know what heals and helps you, what the truth is for you, you won't know what heals and helps others.

True service, healing that touches the hearts and souls of men and women, doesn't happen when we ignore who we are. It doesn't happen when we try to be who we think we should be or when we pretend, out of fear, that we're someone we're not. The ability to bring healing to others can only come when we genuinely accept and love ourselves, past and present, and are vulnerable enough to be honest about what heals and helps us.

When we love and accept ourselves, we will love and accept others. And only from that place of acceptance can true healing spring.

Love yourself. Accept yourself. Be honest about what heals and helps you. Then you'll bring your healing gifts to others. Your life will be a gift to the world.

DECEMBER 24

What Does Service Mean to You?

For a long time, service meant drudgery, something grim and tiresome to me. Having to say yes all the time, even when I wanted to say no. Doing a lot of things I didn't want to do because someone asked me to. Doing an act of service even if I wasn't asked. Solving any problem, filling any need I saw any time, anywhere.

But much of the time, what I did didn't help others or me. Usually I felt angry, resentful, tired, and unappreciated. After years of living this way, I started avoiding people so I could avoid the responsibility of having to solve their problems. I shied away from people. I shied away from service.

Before I was able to return to service, I needed to change my definition of it. Service isn't something we do; it's a way of life. Service is what our lives are when we're loving ourselves.

Now, to me service means that we take our place in the universe naturally and easily. We listen to our hearts, trusting the guidance about what we want to do, what feels right for us. We listen when our hearts say no, too.

We love ourselves. We do what we're led to do. We do what we enjoy and have a passion for doing. That's service. We enjoy life. We open our hearts to the people around us. We laugh openly, we cry openly, we let ourselves be who we are. That's service. When a task or job arises that it's our job to do, one that feels right and appropriate for us, we do it—in joy and love. That's service. We allow ourselves to be in the present moment, realizing the value of work and of giving. Then we take it one step further. We allow ourselves to have fun and enjoy what we're doing while we're doing it. That's service.

If a task seems too grim to bear, if we can't find the reserves or resolve to accomplish it, if no way to do it opens up, we quietly say no. We have not failed. We have succeeded at listening to our hearts. We have succeeded at true service.

We give of ourselves, our resources, our love. We give of our time and our smiles and our joy in those places and with those people that feel right to us. We don't worry about what we're going to get back while we're giving. We focus on the giving, because we're doing something we want to do.

> *If service has become drudgery, redefine it until it becomes joy. True service won't make you back away from people and life. It will bring you closer to God, to yourself. True service helps you become a part of the magical dance of universal love.*

DECEMBER 25

Remember Faith

There is a church in New Mexico where the ground is said to be holy, sacred, healing. As I sat in a pew in that church, I was amazed at the numbers that flock there. I watched one man carry in his sick wife, a woman so ill she couldn't walk or stand by herself. They came to pray, to touch the holy ground. They came for a miracle. I sat, watching and listening, in awe of the tremendous power of faith.

Many things in life test us, strain us, deplete us, and sometimes leave us without hope. Yet, there is a place in us where the ground is sacred and holy. That place in us is called faith.

Remember faith. It's important. Without it, life is dull, useless, and joyless. We may have moments when we say, *What's the use? Nothing will help.* We may go through times when we're angry at God and don't want to believe anymore. But faith has the power to transform us. Faith can instill joy, bring peace, and restore a sense of acceptance and fulfillment in our lives.

Faith is a simple place, but it is also a place of profound power. Faith can turn our lives around. Faith may not bring us the miracle we want, but it will always bring us the miracle we need. Cultivate faith, touch it, hold it in your hand.

In the back room of the Sanctuario de Chimayo is the ground that's said to be holy and healing. Visitors are invited to take some with them. I scooped up a portion, just a tiny bit, placed it in a small plastic bag, and put it in my Jeep.

Faith. You don't need much.
A little bit goes a long, long way.

DECEMBER 26

Take Time to Be with People You Love

I left Colorado driving toward the canyons of southern Utah. I had a lot of places left to visit on my journey, a lot of work left to do. But something, rather someone, was pulling on me. My daughter, Nichole.

She was in college in Arizona. When she finished exams, she planned to head to Minnesota to spend the summer there. We had talked about meeting somewhere midway. Now it didn't look like that would work out. It might be months before we saw each other again. From where I was in Colorado, she was a hard day's drive away. Besides, I had already been through Arizona, and it would take another day to get back to where I was now. I continued on my way.

The pull from Nichole continued, too. Finally, I turned the car around and headed toward my daughter. When I arrived at her dorm about ten that night, I called her room. She asked where I was now on my journey. I told her I was downstairs in the lobby of her dorm. She flew down the steps. We hugged and kissed. And we spent the next three days at a nearby hotel. She studied and wrote her term paper. We visited. Watched movies. Ate food. Laughed. Cried. And shared memories. It was one of the nicest times we'd had together in years.

When it came time to leave, Nichole packed her car and headed for Minnesota. I headed back toward Utah, stopping to enjoy the scenery of the Grand Canyon, scenery I had missed along my way. I felt renewed and refreshed. I hadn't lost any time. I had gained the gifts of the heart.

We search for sacred spaces, spiritual experiences, and truths. But the holiest places are often found when we spend time with people we love.

DECEMBER 27

Embrace Your Destiny

Her words were simple but profound: "Fall in love with your destiny."

How often we search outside of ourselves for some elusive moment, for an experience like someone else is having, for an emotion we'd like to feel but aren't, at least not right now. How often we long to be somewhere other than where we are, or someone other than who we are. How easy it can be to complain about and regret our past, thinking it's somehow wrong.

The answer is to fall in love—fall in love with our own life. Our destiny isn't some far-off moment or something that happens to someone else. Our destiny is taking place right now. It's been happening all along.

Destiny is that mysterious force or energy that magically intertwines with choice, free will, and fate. Let all those elements weave together and create your life. But know you can help to create it too, by falling in love with your own life. Love all the places you have gone and all the places you will go. Love the lessons you have learned and the way you have learned them.

Most of all, love where you are right now.
Because that's where your destiny lies.

DECEMBER 28

Heal Yourself

Infuse healing energy into yourself, into your being. For too long, we've been attracted to things that drain us, exhausting our body, depleting our soul. That time has passed.

The world is a spa, a nature retreat, a wealth of healing resources. Pour Epsom salts and essential oils into your bath. Sit quietly by a tree or in a garden. Walk around the block in your neighborhood. Spend an afternoon in a nearby park or a day at the lake or beach. Throw stones into the river while you sit on the bank contemplating the eternal stream of life. Allow beautiful music to quietly imbue the stillness with healing instead of the pounding of your mind. Light a fire and awaken that darkened hearth to glowing flames and soothing warmth.

Rise from your bed early in the morning. Open the curtains. Watch the sunrise. *Feel* the sunrise. Let it infuse you with its message. Let it energize you, invigorate you, fill you with life. At day's end return to the window. Or step outside. Watch the sun set. Absorb its changing colors spreading out beyond the horizon. Feel how it changes the earth and all it touches.

Pet a puppy, stroke a piece of velvet, listen to a symphony. If you can't slow down long enough to absorb the energy the first time, do it a second and a third. Absorb revitalizing energy until you can hear your voice, hear your heart tell you what would feel good, what would bring peace, what would bring stillness and joy. Before long, doing what brings healing and joy will become as natural as it used to be to do what drains, tires, depletes, and exhausts.

It isn't enough to draw near to the light. Absorb it into you. Let it charge you and change you with its energy and its power. Healing is all around you. Wherever you are, whatever your resources, healing, energy, and joy are there.

DECEMBER 29

Experience the Thrill of the Climb

Don't stop now. You're almost there.

You've worked so hard to climb this mountain. In the beginning, you were excited. Exhilarated at the prospect of the mountain you were about to climb. Now, you are almost to the top. You've struggled, gotten weary, and kept going. Now, your goal is in sight.

Keep going. Guidance is still there to help you. The life force, the one that keeps you going, keeps you moving forward, is still there too, burning brightly within you, charging all that you do with its energy. It is more difficult for you to feel it, but that is only because you're tired.

See the mountain climber as he climbs the mountain. There are dangers and precipices and challenges along the way. But the higher he climbs, the steeper it gets. The more tired he is, the more energy he has to put into the climb. Don't tell yourself that the way you feel is an indication you should stop. The way you feel now is the way anyone would feel who was so deeply committed to life. It's the way anyone would feel who had committed to climbing that mountain.

> *Don't stop now. Relax as much as you can. Know that the rhythm of life is still there, moving you forward. Don't look back. Focus intently on each step. Soon you will reach the top. Soon you will reach your goal. Soon you will experience the victory. Keep your eyes focused on the path; look straight ahead. Embrace the thrill of the climb.*

DECEMBER 30

Joy Is Your Next Lesson

Learning compassion, understanding love, and experiencing joy. That's our purpose, our reason for being here. That's our true mission on this planet.

Learning compassion may have been difficult, because in order to feel compassion for others without judging, we had to go through difficult times ourselves. Times when despite our best efforts we couldn't help ourselves, times when despite our searching we couldn't find the answers. As many say, it is usually our own pain and problems that makes us compassionate.

Understanding love may have taken many years, many heartbreaks, and much searching and grasping until we discovered that the key to love was our own heart. Until we discovered that love wasn't exactly what we thought or hoped it would be. Now it's different. And better.

Don't give up. Don't stop now. Don't let the residue, the pain from the early parts of your journey, stop you from going forward. We first had to learn about compassion and love in order to learn joy.

The hard work is done. Now you have reached your reward. Now it is time to learn joy.

DECEMBER 31

Honor the Ending

"How was your trip?" a friend asked, as my trip drew to a close.

I thought for a moment, then the answer came easily. "It had its ups and downs," I said. "There were times I felt exhilarated and sure I was on track. Other days I felt lost. Confused. I'd fall into bed at night certain that this whole trip was a mistake and a waste. But I'd wake up in the morning, something would happen, and I'd see how I'd been guided all along."

The journey of a year is drawing to a close. Cherish the moments, all of them, even the ups and downs. Cherish the places you've visited, the people you've seen. Say good-bye to those whose journeys have called them someplace else. Know you can always call them back by thinking loving thoughts. Know all those you love will be there for you when you need them most. Honor the lessons you've learned, and the people who helped you learn them. Honor the journey your soul mapped out for you. Trust all the places you've been. Make a scrapbook in your heart to help you remember.

Look back for a moment. Reflect in peace. Then let this year draw to a close. All parts of the journey are sacred and holy. You've learned that by now. Take time to honor this ending—though it's never really the end. Go to sleep tonight. When you wake up tomorrow a new adventure will begin.

Remember the words you were told
when this last adventure began, the
words whispered quietly to your heart:
Let the journey unfold. Let it be
magical. The way has been prepared.
People will be expecting you.
Yes, you are being led.